PRAISE FOR *ETHEL ROSENBERG*

"Brilliant . . . could not be bettered." —Claire Tomalin, critically acclaimed editor and author of *A Life of My Own: A Memoir*

"Timely, superbly written, and ultimately devastating." —Anthony Horowitz, *New York Times* bestselling author of *Moonflower Murders*

"A shocking tale of betrayal, naivety, misogyny, and judicial failure." —Sonia Purnell, bestselling author of *A Woman of No Importance*

"Beautifully written and superbly researched." —Simon Sebag Montefiore, bestselling author of *The Romanovs*

"A wrenching story of the corruption of justice by influence, ambition, and fear." —Nancy Thorndike Greenspan, author of *Atomic Spy: The Dark Lives of Klaus Fuchs*

"Magnificent." —Carmen Callil, bestselling author of *Bad Faith* and founder of Virago Press

"A tragic and gripping tale." —Caroline Moorehead, bestselling author of *A Train in Winter*

"Enthralling and deeply moving." —Ariana Neumann, bestselling author of *When Time Stopped*

"Riveting . . . with a message that will strike contemporary nerves." —Nicholas Shakespeare, prize-winning biographer and author of *Priscilla*

"Masterful, original, and painfully gripping." —Philippe Sands, author of *The Ratline* and *East West Street*

"Peels away the layers of historical and sometimes deliberate misinformation to reveal the extraordinary truth." —Anita Anand, journalist and author of *The Patient Assassin*

ALSO BY ANNE SEBBA

Les Parisiennes

That Woman

Ethel Rosenberg
AN AMERICAN TRAGEDY

ANNE SEBBA

ST. MARTIN'S PRESS
NEW YORK

First published in the United States by St. Martin's Press, an imprint of St. Martin's Publishing Group

ETHEL ROSENBERG. Copyright © 2021 by Anne Sebba. All rights reserved. Printed in the United States of America. For information, address St. Martin's Publishing Group, 120 Broadway, New York, NY 10271.

www.stmartins.com

Endpaper photo: Mike Rogers

Designed by Omar Chapa

The Library of Congress Cataloging-in-Publication Data is available upon request.

ISBN 978-1-250-19863-1 (hardcover)
ISBN 978-1-250-19865-5 (ebook)

Our books may be purchased in bulk for promotional, educational, or business use. Please contact your local bookseller or the Macmillan Corporate and Premium Sales Department at 1-800-221-7945, extension 5442, or by email at MacmillanSpecialMarkets@macmillan.com.

Originally published in Great Britain by Weidenfeld & Nicolson, an imprint of The Orion Publishing Group Ltd, a Hachette UK company

First U.S. Edition: 2021

10 9 8 7 6 5 4 3 2 1

In memory of Mark Jonathan Sebba, 1948–2018,
whose encouragement to write this book has sustained me.

For Sam and Evelyn Sebba,
whose future has also sustained me.

Contents

This country is so heated up about communism at the present moment that the public temper identifies as a friend of the United States any person who is a foe of Stalin.

—*Robert Jackson, US Supreme Court Justice, 1941–54*

Personal relations are despised today. They are regarded as bourgeois luxuries, as products of a time of fair weather which is now past, and we are urged to get rid of them, and to dedicate ourselves to some movement or cause instead. I hate the idea of causes, and if I had to choose between betraying my country and betraying my friend I hope I should have the guts to betray my country.

—*E. M. Forster*

Loyalty means nothing unless it has at its heart the absolute principle of self-sacrifice.

—*Woodrow Wilson, twenty-eighth US president*

Introduction

Friday, June 19, 1953, dawned typically hot and humid in New York, the sort of day later memorably described by the poet Sylvia Plath as sultry. Occasional bursts of sunshine seemed to promise something better, but it was a promise stubbornly unfulfilled. In Washington there was even light rain.

But the weather made little difference to one young couple, who spent the day inside, behind bars, in the condemned cells of the women's wing at New York's high-security Sing Sing Prison, at least allowed to communicate with each other from noon until 7:20 p.m. through a wire mesh. It was the day after their fourteenth wedding anniversary, when together they had composed a last will and testament and final instructions to lawyers. "Words fail me when I attempt to tell of the nobility and grandeur of my life's companion, my sweet and devoted wife," he told his lawyer in shaky handwriting with frequent crossings-out. "Ours is a great love and a wonderful relationship. It has made my life rich and full."[1]

That Friday, their last day of life, they wrote heartbreaking farewell letters to their two sons, Michael, aged ten, and Robby, six, "our pride and most precious fortune."[2] This "sweet and devoted wife" tried to offer her sons advice to guide them through the rest of their lives without parents. "At first, of course, you will grieve bitterly for us, but you will not grieve alone. That is our consolation and it must eventually be yours."[3] She concluded: "Always remember that we were innocent and could not wrong our conscience."[4] Ethel Rosenberg, thirty-seven, believed deeply that she was not only innocent; she wanted to be morally correct, on the right side of history.

She then left her boys with some carefully chosen literary quotes, penciled on a scrap of prison paper, for them to ponder, including the following: "Geo Eliot said, 'This is a world worth abiding in while one man can thus venerate and love another;'" and "Honor means that you are too proud to do wrong—but pride means that you will not own that you have done wrong at all."[5]

Julius's personal effects had been boxed up into three cartons and left with the warden. Ethel owned little more, and the inventory of her meager possessions at the time of her death included deodorant, stockings, and a shoebox of letters from her children. At the time of their arrest the FBI had confiscated most of the couple's possessions, including all family photographs. She asked their lawyer, Emanuel Hirsch Bloch, to ensure that her children received her Ten Commandments religious medal—a gift from a friend she had made in her first prison—and her wedding ring.

Once the final requests for clemency had been denied, the establishment was in a rush to get on with the executions after almost three years of imprisonment for the couple. The executions had been set for 11 p.m., the usual time at Sing Sing. But Bloch appealed to the trial judge, Irving Kaufman, not to execute the Rosenbergs that evening as it was the beginning of the Jewish Sabbath. Both he and Rabbi Koslowe, the seventy-five-year-old Orthodox Jewish chaplain at Sing Sing who had grown close to the Rosenbergs over the last two years, were now fighting for extra hours. Koslowe had spent Friday helping the young couple prepare to die in the electric chair, but nonetheless never gave up hope that he could prolong their lives. "The priority is life, even one minute of life," he said. "If I can prolong a life by one minute I am duty-bound by Jewish law to do so."[6]

But he failed. Judicial officials, insisting they were showing their respect for the Jewish Sabbath, decided to execute them three hours earlier than the schedule called for. This accelerated timetable forced the prison to dispense with the traditional "last meal." Julius was instead offered an extra pack of cigarettes. Ethel did not smoke.

As the hour approached, heavy details of police and state troopers were brought in to protect Ossining, the town bought in 1685 from the Sint Sinck tribe. Sing Sing prison still stands there today, located on a steep hill of white marble overlooking the Hudson, thirty miles north of New York City. In other circumstances, a most beautiful spot. Two telephone lines were opened between the office of prison warden Wilfred Louis Denno and the White House in Washington. A party of five legal witnesses and three reporters arrived and were told to sit on four rows of benches resembling church pews. There had been a panic to locate the executioner, Joseph Francel, who had thought he would not be needed until 9 p.m. But even that minor crisis proved in the end not too difficult to overcome. Francel arrived well before sundown and was stationed in an alcove to the left of the room.

Having been assured that all the necessary signatures for the rental of the wooden chair with leather straps from the State of New York had been obtained and that voltage tests had just been carried out to his satisfaction, there was one further check required. This was to ensure that, should either of the condemned prisoners decide to make a last-minute confession or name names, the line-of-sight arrangements between FBI agents and the warden were active so that the execution could be immediately stopped. But Ethel and Julius refused to the end to trade secrets or name other names to save their own lives.

The authorities had debated which of the pair to execute first. The warden was in favor of Ethel, believing that Julius would, at the eleventh hour, break down and deliver the longed-for confession. But J. Edgar Hoover, the long-standing FBI director with one eye on public opinion, had all along been against the death penalty for Ethel, and was now especially alive to the criticism that would attach to the FBI if, after she were killed, Julius, the husband and father, repented and his life had to be spared. "Nothing would embarrass the Bureau more than to have the wife and mother of two children die and husband survive. It would . . . be a public relations nightmare."[7] Anyone with any knowledge of Ethel knew the impossibility of her either repenting or recanting if her husband had been killed; she could never have lived with herself under those circumstances.

And so at 8 p.m. Rabbi Koslowe, in his long black robes and white prayer shawl—intoning the words of the 23rd Psalm, "The Lord is my Shepherd, I shall not want"—led the thirty-five-year-old Julius Rosenberg from his holding cell, in an area of the prison incongruously referred to as "the dance hall," into the execution chamber. Julius's mustache had been shaved off, his glasses removed, and he turned without guidance to sit in the electric chair. A black helmet was placed on his head, black straps fixed around his chest, and electrodes placed on his right leg. The warden signaled to his aides to flick the switch that would send three massive charges of electricity through the man's body. Minutes later two doctors with stethoscopes declared Julius Rosenberg was dead.

As soon as his body was laid out on a white table, covered with a sheet, and wheeled out, it was Koslowe's grisly duty to lead Ethel, wearing a state-supplied, sleeveless green-and-white-patterned dress, down the same cement path from her cell. This time Koslowe was reading both the 15th Psalm, "Lord, who shall sojourn in thy tabernacle?" and the 31st, "In thee, O Lord, do I put my trust." Had she looked down Ethel would have noticed the pawprints of a frightened rat, who had evidently encountered the wet cement decades earlier, firmly facing the opposite direction. But instead, knowing that her beloved husband had been killed minutes previously, she entered the execution room with her head high. Although, as she had admitted earlier in private to her lawyer, "she shivered from head to foot"[8] when she thought of getting into the electric chair and having an electric current run through her, she had made up her mind, as she promised him, "to die with honor and with dignity."[9]

Ethel stopped in front of the chair, started to move toward it, but suddenly turned instead toward the two women who had entered the room with her: the prison matron, Mrs. Helen Evans, a companion of sorts for the last two years, and telephone operator Mrs. Lucy Many. Ethel extended her outstretched arm to the short, white-haired matron, pulling her toward her for a brief embrace. The women quickly kissed before Mrs. Evans, visibly moved, left with Mrs. Many. Mrs. Evans had been appointed an official witness but, after the embrace, she bent her head and rushed from the room, unable to watch.

Ethel then took her place in the chair, allowed the helmet to be put on, the straps and leg contacts to be attached. She closed her eyes as the electrodes were fitted to her head, declining one last look at the sky through the skylight window above. She was ready for the first charge. After three charges went through her body she was lifted down and examined by the doctors, who told the expectant officials that, unimaginably, Ethel's heart was still beating. She was returned to the chair, the straps reattached, and given a further two jolts, five in all, taking a gruesome four and a half minutes to die. This was evidence, according to some commentators, that she really was the stronger of the pair. More likely she was too small for the equipment or the contacts had been insufficiently moistened.

So closed the story of Julius and Ethel Rosenberg, most reporters wrote in their accounts of the day. But they could not have been more wrong. Ethel Rosenberg was not, I believe, a spy. Nor was she a saint. She was obstinate, determined, prone to self-doubt, and did not make friends easily. She was also a committed Communist, highly intelligent, and fiercely loyal to her beloved husband, who undoubtedly was a Communist spy, passing military secrets to the Soviet Union during World War Two. Ethel's downfall inevitably raises questions about the extent of her complicity as well as the fallibility of the law. But it is also a tale of betrayal, both of a country and by a family. Ethel was betrayed by her own flesh and flood—by her brother David Greenglass, also at one time a fervent believer in Communist ideals, who worked as a technician at the Los Alamos atomic bomb development site in New Mexico, and by his wife, Ethel's sister-in-law, Ruth. Unlike Ethel and Julius, Ruth and David, both of whom had been actively involved in espionage, escaped the electric chair. Ruth avoided all punishment. Ethel was also betrayed by her own mother.

This is the first time that Ethel's ambiguous story has been told in the light of the final piece of testimony from the grand jury—the institution in America that ascertains if there is a case to answer—eventually released after David Greenglass's death in 2014 at the age of ninety-two.

This evidence reinforces the sense of a deeply personal, Shakespearean tragedy. Yet Ethel's tragedy was also America's tragedy, illuminating how US culture and politics had been shaped by the country's rapid descent after World War Two from military euphoria to Cold War paranoia. These are epic themes, as many in that terrible execution chamber understood. But perhaps the darkest and most disturbing of all was the willingness of a government to orphan two children when it knew that the trial at which their mother was convicted was riddled with miscarriages of justice. Conspiracy was almost impossible to disprove—of course she had had conversations with her husband and brother. The jury, however, was instructed to consider that Ethel did more than this, that she was a traitor, a quite different charge with horrific consequences. Yet right up until hours before the execution, the government, which in public appeared so certain of Ethel's guilt, was so unsure that it privately instructed officials to ask Julius: "Was your wife cognizant of your activities?"

·   ·   ·

Julius and Ethel Rosenberg remain the only Americans ever put to death in peacetime for conspiracy to commit espionage, the only two American civilians executed for espionage-related crimes committed during the Cold War that roughly lasted from 1946 to 1991, and Ethel is the only American woman killed for a crime other than murder. Today there is widespread recognition that Julius did pass *military* information to the Soviet Union, yet skepticism that the couple had, according to the phrase used at the time, stolen "the secrets" of the atomic bomb. Much was known about the basic physics involved in making a bomb; the main difficulty was devising practical weapons and the aircraft and missiles to deliver them. There is equally widespread recognition that the three-week trial at which both Rosenbergs were convicted and sentenced to death contained multiple miscarriages of justice and that the only "evidence" against Ethel was the perjury of her own brother David. But over and above this, Ethel was also the victim of a government terrified of showing weakness in the face of an unyielding fear of Communism at the height of the Cold War and which knowingly allowed this perjury.

Why is it important today to understand the motivation of a woman who believed in the values of a now largely discredited Communist system in the second half of the 1940s and early 1950s? What drove a child born of immigrant parents from Eastern Europe both to embrace the American Dream that enabled so many immigrants like her to flourish and at the same time seek to improve it? In the 1930s, a belief that the new philosophy of Communism, with all its inherent contradictions, was the route to create a world without poverty, inequality, and racism was common among many intellectuals on New York's Upper West Side as well as poor workers on the Lower East Side. It was an especially attractive philosophy to Jews who believed that the Bolshevik revolution offered the prospect of a life freed from cruel bondage. In 1933 America had finally recognized the Soviet Union and established diplomatic relations with the new state. Just three years later, in 1936, the year Ethel met Julius, many of the same people believed it was morally imperative to support Spain's democratically elected Popular Front government, which included Communists, against the right-wing military uprising led by General Francisco Franco. The Spanish Civil War became a cause espoused by internationally minded New York liberals who believed strongly that Fascism had to be stopped; some even volunteered to fight in Spain and gave their lives.

During the 1930s, many of the same New Yorkers were informed about Communism in the Soviet Union by reading the naive reports of the Pulitzer Prize–winning journalist Walter Duranty, Moscow correspondent for *The New York Times,* who denied the widespread famine of 1932–33 and later sugarcoated Stalin's purges. Briefly the idea of a Popular Front in government at home in America was even something that many who had once been fervent Communists now believed offered the best route to defeat the rise of Fascism, not only in Spain but also in Italy and Germany. From 1933 until his death in 1945, President Franklin D. Roosevelt, a Democrat and author of the New Deal, which was intended to steer America out of the Depression and restore prosperity to all Americans, held on to power and in 1941 forged an alliance with Communist Russia. For the remaining years of World War Two the Soviet Union was not only an ally but a critical bulwark in defeating Hitler.

Yet attitudes changed dramatically in 1945, almost before the war was over. Republicans were desperate to stop what they saw as a partly dynastic Democratic dominance following the death of Roosevelt shortly after the Yalta Conference in February, when Roosevelt, Stalin, and Churchill had begun dividing up the postwar world. Roosevelt's vice president, Harry S. Truman, had taken over, and was to remain in office until 1953. Shrewd and well advised, Truman was an unpretentious, plainspoken senator from Missouri who regarded Stalin with great suspicion when they met at the Potsdam Conference in the summer of 1945. Almost immediately there was a marked change of tone in rhetoric, not simply in America but in Britain too, where the newly elected Labour Prime Minister, Clement Attlee, was also alarmed by Stalin's postwar intentions.

In March 1946, Britain's Conservative wartime leader, Winston Churchill, made a speech at Truman's invitation in Fulton, Missouri, declaring that an "Iron Curtain" had fallen across Europe. This imaginary boundary divided the continent into two separate areas of influence, the one Communist and the other democratic. Churchill argued in his speech that strong US-British relations were essential in stopping the spread of Communism and maintaining peace in Europe. A year later, in a dramatic address to a joint session of Congress, Truman declared that the whole world faced a choice: a way of life "based upon the will of the majority" or one "based upon the will of a minority forcibly imposed upon the majority." This latter regime, he suggested, relied upon "terror and oppression."

The Truman Doctrine, as it became known, was seized on by the Republican Party, which was desperate to regain power from the Democrats. Truman's case that the Soviet Union posed an existential threat to the West, and particularly to the United States, seemed unarguable in the late 1940s, as Eastern Europe and then China fell into Moscow's orbit. Yet in the hands of unscrupulous Republican politicians such as the young Californian congressman Richard Nixon and Senator Joseph McCarthy from Wisconsin, the same threat became the pretext for anti-Communist hysteria at home, centered on alleged conspiracies by "Reds" and "un-American" fellow-travelers. McCarthyism, as it became known, fed on the suspicions of many Americans that they had been dragged into an unwanted war and were now in danger of losing the peace.

Ironically, many former US Communists had shed their illusions about the Soviet Union by the late 1940s, confronted by the hard evidence of Stalinism's brutality in Eastern Europe.

Should Ethel and Julius also have renounced Communism? Even in a "free" society, surely defined by the ideal that anyone is entitled to hold whatever political beliefs they want, while it is hard to argue sympathetically for anyone engaged in subversion, who betrays their country by giving information to another state, it is at the same time not only possible but, I believe, imperative to project empathy for any individual who finds him- or herself at the mercy of a well-prepared and rehearsed government charge sheet without necessarily agreeing with their political ideals. And this is especially true for Ethel, whose precise motivation and involvement in Julius's crimes requires deeper exploration than she has been granted during her long post-execution afterlife. Even in death, Ethel has been framed by some merely as an appendage to Julius, the junior partner in "the Rosenbergs," by others as "the master" who drove her apparently weaker, younger husband—positions taken often according to preexisting political views. In the absence of proof as to exactly what, if indeed anything, Ethel knew, or what she and Julius said to each other in the privacy of their bedroom, and the reliance of their trial on circumstantial evidence at best, it seems to me important to try to understand who was this woman, barely known to the point of obscurity at the moment of her arrest in 1950 yet an international icon some years later? How did that transformation happen? Having left school and all formal education behind when she graduated at fifteen, how did she discover the strength to survive three years in prison, two of them isolated in solitary confinement, to reach a point of unassailable dignity and belief that the cause for which she was prepared to give her life was indeed a worthy one?

．　　．　　．

I first encountered Ethel Rosenberg as a young mother myself living in 1970s New York, discovering American literature in general and one novel in particular that immediately gripped my sense of "what if." My grandparents too had left Eastern Europe as impoverished Jews but ended up in England, not America. E. L. (Edgar) Doctorow's *The Book of Daniel* was, at the time I lived in the city, a pocket-sized paperback of a few years' standing but still current, small enough to sneak into my handbag on the subway from Brooklyn to Manhattan and devour in the dark if one of my two small babies woke in the night. I still have the book, its pages now yellowing and unglued, and can transport myself back to that room where I first learned about Ethel through a highly fictionalized but desperately dramatic version of events.

The reason why I believe Ethel's story is as important today as ever is to realize what can happen when fear, a forceful and blunt weapon in the hands of authority, turns to hysteria and justice is willfully ignored. In the past it has suited those who wanted to prove Julius's guilt to refer always to "the Rosenbergs"; Ethel was used as a pawn in the hope that the threat to her would elicit a confession from him. But even in 1950 it should have been impossible to argue that Ethel, merely by agreeing with Julius's political ideals and refusing to abandon him, was legally complicit. She was not. So when people say to me, "Ah yes, the Rosenbergs, spies weren't they?" I now shudder at the ease with which such lazy thinking has taken hold. Part of my task in the pages that follow is to extrapolate Ethel, to see her as an individual, perhaps a victim of her times as much as of an implacable government that found itself inert, like a cumbersome juggernaut caught at an intersection, seeing the oncoming traffic but unable to turn itself around.

•   •   •

A good place to start trying to understand Ethel is with her appearance. She was unexceptional to look at, with short, wavy brown hair, and a round, rather sweet face that made her appear chubbier than she was. When she smiled she became pretty, but she had neither the money for nor any interest in fashionable clothes. She preferred to use what little cash she had on self-improvement, such as taking a course in mothering, or guitar lessons—hoping she could then teach her sons. She loved music and looked forward to singing and playing with her children, wanting them to be enriched by the lessons she had not been allowed as a child by a mother who was scathing about the value of the arts, an indulgence.

Ethel's relationship with her mother, Tessie, is excruciatingly painful. Tessie always favored the boys in the family, of whom there were three, doting especially on her last-born, David. In Tessie's eyes girls were expected to have no ambition beyond finding a Jewish husband (perhaps because her own life had been so unrewarding), so she never praised Ethel, the clever child, for doing well at school. Although Ethel's father, Barney, was a gentler soul to whom Ethel was closer, he had no authority in the household. So Ethel learned from an early age to manage her life without praise, to decide for herself what was right. When she met Julius, a man who admired her talents and appreciated her intellectual qualities, she fell deeply in love. He also offered her an escape. And when Ethel became a young mother, first in 1943 and then again in 1947, she determined to do things differently from her own mother in whatever way she could. But at the same time she craved her mother's love and approval almost to the end, remaining for as long as she could a dutiful daughter, within the bosom of family. When after the war Julius tried to get a small business going, initially selling army surplus and offering some machine repairs, it seemed obvious to involve two of her brothers, Bernie and David. But the business never flourished.

It was this seemingly unassuming woman, a diminutive Lower East Side housewife, whose fate became catastrophically entangled in some of the greatest political, social, and cultural issues of the twentieth century: the development and subsequent use of atomic power, fear of Communism, anti-Semitism, misogyny, and the definition of what it meant and still means to be an American.

But at its heart, Ethel's story is about a woman; a mother, sister, wife, and daughter, the roles she was called upon to play in her short life before it suddenly disintegrated in the spring of 1950.

One

Becoming Ethel

"Little David, a Russian spy!" one of Ethel's first cousins reacted when she learned that David Greenglass had been charged. "It seemed too ridiculous to believe,"[1] commented Florence Dubner, daughter of Harry Greenglass, Ethel's uncle from Minsk. In Florence's view David was perfectly pleasant but not intelligent enough to be a spy.

Little David, born in 1922, was the youngest child of Barney Greenglass and his second wife, Tessie. Barney had also been born in Minsk, now in Belarus, then part of the Pale of Settlement—an area comprising the western part of the Russian Empire including Moldova, Lithuania, and Ukraine, in which Russian Jews were permitted to live from 1835 and where many remained even once enforcement came to an end in 1917 with the fall of the Russian Empire. He arrived in New York at the age of twenty-five in 1903, five years after his younger and more enterprising brother Harry (born Herschel). Like millions of other Eastern European Jews, the brothers had left behind grinding poverty and persecution, which in Minsk—half of whose population was Jewish—was spearheaded by regular attacks from Cossacks, often with the complicity of the Russian government. In the case of Harry Greenglass, a teenager, government cruelty was compounded by familial: he was also apparently escaping a stepfather whom he loathed so much that he had already run away once and slept in the factory where he worked. The brothers were close, so Harry, once settled, urged Barney to join him. America offered "a flash of hope,"[2] literally a New World, a chance for human dignity to flourish and for money to be made. Few had exalted spiritual motives or aspirations for great riches.

Given the harshness of life in Minsk, the city was, perhaps not surprisingly, also a major center of radical politics and activity organized by the Bund, a progressive political and secular organization formed in 1897 that defended Jewish cultural and civic rights and played a key role in shaping the relationship of East European Jews to socialism. According to a recent historian of Minsk, Barbara Epstein, it was the Bund that led to the flowering of Jewish radicalism, especially on New York's Lower East Side, and provided the impetus for many to join the Communist Party. "One of the things that strikes me about this tradition is the numbers of Jewish women who became activists and also the fact that within the Jewish left, women's activism was taken for granted, it wasn't remarkable in the way that it was in the non-Jewish left."[3] While there is no evidence that Ethel's father, uncle, or aunts were politically involved in any way, some of this radicalism would have been in the impoverished immigrant air that Ethel breathed.

Harry escaped in 1898, aged eighteen, by riding a bicycle from Minsk to Hamburg, sleeping rough in ditches along the way, then organizing a passage in steerage from Hamburg to New York. Hamburg was the port of choice for most would-be emigrant Jews from Ukraine and Southern Russia as, once they had crossed the Austro-Hungarian border, probably illegally, they were less likely to be asked for a Russian passport, which was not only expensive but came with the risk for young men of draft age that they might be sent back and conscripted.

Once in America Harry soon made his way doing odd jobs, and within a year of his arrival had applied for citizenship and signed the required document as Harry Greenglass.* There is no account of Barney's

---

* The anglicization of his surname also occurred at this point; there are a number of Gringlaz and Gringlauz names listed in Belarus databases from the late 1880s to 1912.

escape route, but he was shortly followed by three sisters as well as an elderly uncle and aunt.

At first, the two Greenglass brothers set up shop together at 91 Columbia Street, in the heart of the Lower East Side. Their business was fixing sewing machines, a vital skill in those busy streets teeming with recently arrived Jewish immigrants, many of whom brought tailoring expertise and little else. Having their own repair shop was hardly a route to riches, but it was better than working in a factory or sweatshop, where dozens of people would be squashed into a few dark, damp rooms in a dilapidated tenement building, all of them engaged in different tasks to make a single garment for an often unscrupulous boss.

Barney soon found a wife, Beckie, and in 1909 the couple celebrated the birth of their son, Samuel Louis Greenglass. But when Sam was two, Beckie died of kidney failure at the age of thirty-five. Despite his bereavement—young death was not uncommon and had to be faced—Barney wasted no time in finding another wife and stepmother for Sam. In August 1912, ten months after Beckie's death, he married a twenty-nine-year-old Austrian immigrant from Galicia (modern-day Ukraine) called Theresa Feit. Nobody believed that romance had anything to do with the match.

Tessie, as she was known, was a buxom woman with long, wavy hair who had grown up close by Columbia Street on Willett Street. She remained illiterate throughout her life and never learned to speak English fluently, conversing with Barney in Yiddish. In Minsk this was the principal language for Jews, and signs throughout the Lower East Side were often in Yiddish. Soon after they married, the new Greenglass family moved around the corner to 64 Sheriff Street, a five-story tenement block where the two men set up their repair shop at the front, with a big window overlooking the street on which their name was painted and the main door to the entire building to its right. The family lived in the rooms behind the shop.

It was here, three years after marrying Barney, on September 28, 1915, that Tessie gave birth to their first child together, a girl whom they decided to call Esther Ethel, always known as Ethel, or sometimes "Ettie" as a young child. From the start of her life she was not universally loved within the Greenglass family. Sam was almost seven when Ethel was born and had been accustomed to being the sole focus of attention. He never warmed to his little half sister, nor Ethel to him.

And Ethel's birth seemed to signal other changes in the wider Greenglass family. The more ambitious Harry, determined to speak English and become an American, married in 1916, aged thirty-five. Soon afterward he moved away with his pregnant wife, Esther (née Bernstein), a cousin, to Crown Heights, Brooklyn. Here, with their two daughters, Della and Florence, they lived above a store that Harry turned into a cigarette and sweet shop. It was a largely Catholic neighborhood where many public-service workers such as police and garbage collectors lived. Their fixed salaries ensured they did not suffer from the Depression that hit so many on the Lower East Side, thus helping the Greenglass Candy Store to flourish.

The two families remained reasonably close for a while, continuing to meet regularly at religious festivals such as Passover, which is where Della and Florence got to know (and formed opinions about) their cousins, Sam, Ethel, and later two more brothers.

Two years after Ethel was born, Tessie had a son, Bernard Abraham, known as Bernie. She then suffered four miscarriages in quick succession until at last, after a distressing and debilitating few years, her youngest and final child was born on March 2, 1922, a boy named simply David. From the moment of his birth Tessie, now thirty-eight, was thrilled by this longed-for child. The entire family doted on David, or "little Doovey" as he was called when he was a chubby-cheeked, curly-haired toddler. Ethel, almost seven, adored her baby brother and willingly became something of a surrogate mother, a role nonetheless expected of her by Tessie. Ethel was "crazy over Doovey,"[4] a friend recalled later, remembering how she always loved reading David stories, especially when he was older and she could share with him melodramatic novels by the popular author Booth Tarkington,* a favorite of hers, or else tried to teach him French, at which

---

* Best known for his novels *Alice Adams* and *The Magnificent Ambersons,* Tarkington was a prolific novelist who appeared on the cover of *Time* magazine in 1925.

she excelled. Sometimes Ethel took David for a fun outing to Uncle Harry's candy store in Brooklyn.

Growing up at 64 Sheriff Street, Ethel, like her brothers, became accustomed to the surrounding stench. Opposite their cold-water tenement house an old stable housed the horses that pulled delivery carts around the cobbled streets of the neighborhood. The street reeked of filth and excrement, especially on summer nights when the pungent odors of rotting fruits and food that the vendors had failed to sell wafted out of a storage space for the pushcarts a few doors down from the stables. But nonetheless children played outside in the street, sometimes tag or occasionally rougher games, the sort of "stupid games children play," according to a neighbor who was exactly Ethel's age.[5]

Inside the tenement, the six Greenglasses lived in the same cold, cramped conditions as everyone else. Barney's shop at the front of the building advertised itself through a glass window revealing dozens of broken machines and tools all over the room, as well as indicating a place of refuge, or sanctuary almost, for a man who was happy here, a man not fired by ambition. The Greenglass Machine Shop was an identifier in the area. Immediately behind the messy shop was Tessie and Barney's bedroom, and behind that the kitchen, where most of the family's life took place. Children, clothes, and dishes were all washed in the same large kitchen tub, requiring Tessie to heat a wood fire and boil several pots of water. The rest of the airless apartment was damp and cold, except in the fetid summer months when it was still damp but stiflingly hot. Residents of tenements such as these had to go to one of the many public bathhouses on the Lower East Side if they wanted shower or bath facilities. There was a male and a female bathhouse a few doors down at 62 Sheriff Street. "The name of the bathhouse was Gang's. It was owned by a man whose surname was Gang . . . You took a bath and you slept over . . . they had cots."[6]

There were no windows in any of the rooms other than at the front and rear of the building, while the narrow staircase running through the center of the structure was permanently dark, meaning the family had to use a candle or grope their way through the gloom when they needed to use one of the shared toilets on each floor. Sam, the eldest child, had a bedroom at the end of the apartment with a window overlooking a yard. By the time David was born, Barney and Tessie rented three additional rooms upstairs so that Ethel, Bernie, and David could sleep separately; as Ethel's was the front room, she had a window overlooking the street.

Why did so many of the newly arrived penniless immigrants congregate around this area? There are stories, perhaps apocryphal, that, not knowing where to go and speaking little English, they were simply directed to the already densely settled Jewish districts by policemen pointing truncheons who said, "Just keep walking until you see a lot of Jewish people," or else by representatives of one of the various immigrant aid societies. According to Edward Steiner, an older Austrian immigrant who was one of the first to make any kind of study of immigrant life at this time, they brought their European world with them and tried to live in the same way. "To them, Rivington Street is only a suburb of Minsk," wrote Steiner.[7]

Unlike Harry and Esther, Barney and Tessie did not seem to aspire to escape from this ghetto, or perhaps they could see no way out. The traditional Jewish respect for learning, books, and self-improvement appears to have been absent from their hearts. Yet Tessie, in spite of her linguistic handicaps, was nonetheless competent enough to become superintendent of the entire tenement block where they lived, collecting rents and organizing household repairs, a job that helped to supplement the family's meager income. According to some estimates, there could be as many as eighty people in a building as occasional boarders swelled numbers and increased the risks and dangers from overcrowding. She was also a more assertive character than Barney, and, although they were not an observant Jewish family, rarely attending synagogue, she found time to bake her own challah bread on Fridays like many Orthodox Jewish wives as well as plunging into her other duties as a homemaker. Meanwhile, Barney minded his little repair shop at the front of the building. In the recollections of friends and neighbors Barney comes across as fundamentally contented with his lot: "an adorable little man with high red cheeks . . . Ethel was wild about him. The kids ran in and out of his shop, asking for a penny or a nickel, and, although he was always working, he seemed to like the chatter."[8]

Where Barney appears warm and easygoing, the impression gleaned of Tessie from the same recollections is of a cold and domineering person: "a bitter woman whose affection such as it was all went to the boys in the family."[9] The children of Harry and Esther believed that Tessie was a lot like their own mother; both women, Tessie and Esther, constantly expected more of their husbands and were not afraid to say so. "No matter how well the store was doing, Esther let Harry know it wasn't good enough . . . [Harry] decided he would be best off keeping quiet," commented a grandson. Barney adopted the same tactic. Both wives were "always worrying that something terrible was going to happen to their children."[10] Favoring sons was common in Jewish families, but Tessie took it to extremes. She was, according to one of Ethel's childhood friends, "more bigoted than religious. The God she pictured to her daughter was always on the mother's side and the side of practicality. If God had meant for Ethel to have music lessons he would have provided them. As he hadn't there was something sinful about music lessons."[11]

Ethel's capacity to displease her mother increased painfully once she started at Seward Park High School (SPHS) in 1926 at the age of eleven. By this time Ethel had been at elementary school for at least four years, learning the basics of reading, spelling, writing, English grammar, and arithmetic, and had already proved to herself what she could achieve if she dedicated herself to hard work. According to a childhood friend, "she adhered to a rigid schedule of study that was so effective she was considered to be one of the two best students in her grade school and junior high."[12] As a result, when she first entered SPHS—still on the old Hester Street site—she was placed in a "rapid advancement" class, a relatively new experiment at the school that enabled exceptionally bright students to complete three years of junior high school in two.

And then, in 1929, SPHS opened on a new campus bounded by Essex, Broome, Grand, and Ludlow Streets, where it still stands today. Now, as Ethel and her friend Laura made the short walk every morning along the narrow back streets of the Lower East Side, they left behind the squalor of their tenement block. The two girls entered through the school's splendid triple-arched entranceway on 350 Grand Street into an inspiring building full of fine decorative artwork where they were transformed into proper little American schoolgirls.

Miraculously—at least to Jewish immigrants from the most deprived corners of Eastern Europe—education at Seward Park was free, funded by the New York City government. And the school was filled almost entirely with Jewish pupils, plus just a handful of Italians. Thanks to free education, even the poorest local children had a chance at the school to escape their background and live the American Dream of prosperity and personal fulfillment. Ethel was determined not to waste that chance, and Seward Park offered an especially thrilling route to freedom. Its majestic assembly hall doubled as a theater, fitted out with plush seats and state-of-the-art stage lighting. Upstairs there was a spacious, well-stocked library and in the basement an Olympic-sized swimming pool. No pupil was allowed to graduate until they had completed a basic swimming test. All the performing arts, but especially acting, were encouraged and SPHS alumni would include Ethel's contemporary Sammy (later Zero) Mostel, Tony Curtis (born Bernard Schwartz), and Walter Matthau. It was here that Ethel not only learned to sing but had a real grounding in classical music: she and two friends, Dora Stahl and Anna Silverman, formed a trio that regularly performed German *lieder,* especially Brahms, at school concerts.[13]

According to Laura, all Ethel wanted to do in those days to realize her own dream was sing and act. "Her work was dramatics and there was no limit to her ambitions, although at the same time she had her self-doubts."[14] Laura recalled how, while the two girls walked to and from school in the shadow of the Williamsburg Bridge as the trains roared by, or past the live chicken markets on Delancey where the squawking fowl were being unloaded, Ethel would often hum little tunes she had made up with words satirizing the smells they met on the way, or else she was immersed in the part she was learning for a school play, or maybe she would talk about a novel she was reading at the time.

At other times Ethel would confide in her friend that her greatest ambition was "never having to live like her mother, forever going about the streets with a big shopping bag searching for bargains trading with the pushcart men."[15] Her disdain for her mother's way of life was becoming corrosive.

Ethel's love of drama was nurtured initially by Barney, who had occasionally taken her as a little girl to performances of Yiddish theater. This lingering East European tradition had once thrived on the Lower East Side but was now past its heyday. This may have been where her passion for performing first took root. Or it may have been from the discovery that, on stage, Ethel could become a different person; she could not only escape the dismal life of Sheriff Street but also what some of her classmates described as shyness in lessons. When she trod the boards she banished any sign of that. According to one school friend, Ethel was less interested in boys than in books. "Ethel kept aloof," recalled the friend who spotted early her single-mindedness. "She was cute and alive and quick and could be witty. But to most of our gang of girlfriends, who used to tell each other everything, and talk endlessly about our boyfriends, Ethel seemed to think she was too good for the boys we dated."[16] More likely, she did not think she was good enough.

Yet away from the stage, where she blossomed, her life was still constrained by poverty and worries about her health. According to one story, Ethel stuffed old shoes with newspaper when they developed holes because her family could not afford to buy her a new pair and, during New York's freezing winters, she would often visit a friend's apartment to do her homework, because her own unheated tenement was too cold to concentrate. When she was about thirteen she was diagnosed with scoliosis, or sideways curvature of the spine, and had to wear an uncomfortable brace for about a year to prevent the problem from getting worse. Every once in a while the pain flared up and gave her a severe backache and sometimes a headache, forcing her to go to bed.[17] One school friend remembers her sitting self-consciously in class, trying to raise one shoulder to equalize with the other.

On June 24, 1931, Ethel was one of 144 girls and 200 boys who graduated from SPHS. After the graduates sang Mendelssohn's hymn "In

Heavenly Love Abiding," the school orchestra played a selection of classical music by Grieg and Cherubini and Rimsky-Korsakov's *Scheherazade*. In between there was a salutatory address, a violin solo by a child prodigy, and dozens of awards, diplomas, and prizes. Ethel was not among the prize winners, although her friend Dora Stahl received an award from the East Side Chamber of Commerce. The rabbi from Temple Emanu-El gave an address and benediction and then, after the whole school sang "The Star-Spangled Banner," the orchestra finished with Saint-Saëns's "Marche militaire française," all in all a perfect blend of Old World culture, immigrant aspiration, and Jewish wisdom.

Ethel's 1931 yearbook photograph shows her as a pretty fifteen-year-old girl with a round, very sweet face and dark, wavy hair; the comment alongside says "Can she act? And how."[18] On page twenty, under the heading "Celebrities of the Classroom," Ethel Greenglass is named as the class actress.

Yet when Ethel left SPHS she entered a world full of foreboding. Two years earlier—and only a short walk from the school—the Wall Street crash had tipped America's overheated economy into a slump that reached its nadir in the early 1930s. On the Lower East Side, unemployed dockworkers formed long lines around the block for the few badly paid jobs on offer. Furniture was often seen strewn along the sidewalk as whole families were driven out of their lodgings because they could no longer pay the rent. Ethel had to find work urgently to help her family and that meant taking shorthand and typing lessons with some bookkeeping, a practical course that she had resisted at school in the hope that she could attend college instead, something that was just becoming available for women.* Any acting or performing would have to be fitted around this routine. In putting her own ambitions on hold Ethel was being a dutiful and responsible daughter, and indeed sister. She was needed to help around the home as David was just nine when Ethel left school. David did not follow Ethel by attending the aspirational SPHS. It is not clear why, but perhaps it was already evident that, being less academic than his sister, he would

---

* Women were first admitted to the free City College in 1930.

be better off at a more vocational school or perhaps, because of the uncertain economy, it was recognized he would have to earn a living as soon
as possible. In any event he was sent to Haaren High School in midtown
Manhattan, where he took some engineering classes.

Ethel studied hard for six months and, as soon as she qualified from
the secretarial course, started looking for a clerical job, which was at least
better than unskilled factory labor. In February 1932 she was hired as a
shipping clerk for the National New York Packing and Shipping Company,
based in midtown Manhattan near the Pennsylvania railway station.

But Ethel was equally determined not to abandon her theatrical ambitions. At around this time she won a scholarship to join the Clark Players,
a local amateur dramatic group attached to the Clark Settlement House
based in "a friendly old brick building on Rivington Street."[19] This became
a place of refuge where Ethel could escape to enjoy culture and education
most evenings, continue her quest for self-improvement, and make friends
with a group of fifteen or so like-minded young men and women. She began leading two quite separate lives from now on: one involved drudgery,
helping at home in her overcrowded tenement block, the other lifted her
spirits through art.

The East Side settlement houses, "where the social fervor of immigrant Jews rubbed against the moral earnestness of young Americans re-
sponsive to the idea of service,"[20] played a vital role in educating many
first-generation immigrants. "Here socialism and puritanism came to
gether in a compound of practical selflessness; here men who later might
compromise, hedge, and retreat were fired by sentiments of social com-
passion."[21] The young Eleanor Roosevelt worked at a settlement house on
Rivington Street in 1903 when she was nineteen and remained a lifelong
supporter of the settlement house movement as a force for good. According to Rhina, a teenage friend interviewed after Ethel's death, Ethel did
not simply want to flee the poverty of the slums or achieve fame; "it was
just that she was in love with art, as I was."[22] As Rhina pointed out, "most
of the plays they put on were a hodge podge of mediocrity and the training
wasn't very good." Ethel and Rhina often walked home together and discussed their hopes for the future or the plays—some largely forgettable,

including a British comedy called *Green Stockings,* which made fun of a spinster, and an American farce called *A Pair of Sixes.* Yet Ethel also appeared in some Shakespeare plays around this time, including *Romeo and Juliet,* and a one-act drama called *The Valiant* by H. E. Porter and Robert Middlemass, about a man facing execution in spite of serious doubts as to his guilt. He goes bravely to his death reciting the lines from *Julius Caesar*: "Cowards die many times before their deaths; / The valiant never taste of death but once." Ethel played the man's sister.

Ethel was gaining a small reputation among her thespian friends as a passionate performer. As she and Rhina gained in confidence, they went out together to the nearby Paramount Cafeteria on Delancey Street and chatted about their acting. All the "Players Gang" went regularly to the Paramount, but initially Rhina and Ethel were scared to join them. "We were afraid we wouldn't know whether to use a fork or spoon. Here it was, just a cafeteria, but to us it was like going to the Astor Roof."[23]

Meanwhile, Ethel was nursing another ambition. Every week she handed over most of her average wage of $7.00 for basic clerical work to her mother, keeping just enough back for lunch and subway fares. Yet, somehow, Ethel also managed to save enough to buy a secondhand piano, possibly from someone down on their luck in those Depression-era days who had to sell a family heirloom cheaply to pay the rent or to fit more children into a single room.

Ethel put the piano in her sparsely furnished bedroom on Sheriff Street and set herself a tough practice schedule. She also started to enter local singing competitions, and one Thursday night at Loew's Delancey Theater she won second prize of $2 in a weekly talent competition. This modest success encouraged her to undertake a tour of various New Jersey towns holding similar contests and she came home with several $2 prizes. Tessie was unimpressed, according to Rhina: "One Saturday I went over to her house and when I asked where she was her mother lamented bitterly: 'Where is she? Where do you suppose she is? Out singing somewhere in New Jersey. I don't understand why she don't go out and get a job,'"[24] ignoring the fact that she already had one.

Ethel, however, believed her high soprano voice was good enough to audition in 1934 for the prestigious amateur Schola Cantorum chorus, based at Carnegie Hall, whose chief conductor was the British-born Hugh C. Ross. There were a number of successful choirs and choruses in New York City but the Schola Cantorum was at the pinnacle, performing regularly at Carnegie Hall and occasionally at the Metropolitan Opera with some of the greatest musicians of the day, including Otto Klemperer, who had fled Germany in 1933, and Arturo Toscanini, an outspoken anti-Fascist and opponent of Hitler, as guest conductors.

Ethel had to audition at Carnegie Hall before a panel of judges—a far cry from the talent contests she had been entering so far. She was initially rejected because she could not sight-read music, a key requirement for Schola Cantorum singers. Undaunted, Ethel went home, with remarkable dedication slowly taught herself sight-singing, and reapplied a year later. On the following occasion she triumphantly passed the audition. She was still only nineteen, one of their youngest members, and while names of choristers were not included in concert programs it is likely that Ethel sang in performances of Brahms's German Requiem, conducted by Toscanini, and Mahler's choral Resurrection Symphony under Klemperer, and would have discussed world affairs with her fellow singers.

There is no evidence that any of Ethel's family went to watch her perform. Certainly, Tessie never bothered, while Esther, mother of Florence, considered in hindsight that "Ethel was a snob, worrying over Italian arias and Russian peasants instead of her own family."[25] But Florence, who was to be so dismissive of David, was making a similar break, almost a mirror image of Ethel's. Florence was studying to be a ballet dancer, not a traditional Jewish pursuit. But it was, said her son, "a way to continue being European and to forget about troubles. My mom embraced having a pursuit that was sophisticated and historic and involved costume and language that was more interesting than life in Brooklyn. I think it was aspirational . . . and it is noteworthy that the aspirations of these two women [Florence and Ethel] went way beyond the history of their families [the Greenglasses]."[26]

Throughout this period, Ethel had continued to work as a shipping clerk for the National New York Packing and Shipping Company, her other life. The company made its money by receiving packages from merchants in New York City and beyond, which were consolidated into larger packages and shipped under cheaper bulk rates around the world. Its workforce of around 150 men and women dealt with approximately 10,000 packages per day and speed was of the essence. Mostly the men handled the boxes, which came around fast on conveyor belts, while women like Ethel wrote the receipts as swiftly as they could. Ethel was a member of a small Shipping Clerks' Union, which was seeking to affiliate with the much bigger International Ladies' Garment Workers' Union and in the summer of 1935 formed a committee to press management about serious concerns regarding wages and working conditions. The president of the company, Andrew Loebel, refused to meet the committee, and demanded instead a smaller and more easily controllable negotiating body. The workers rejected his demand and a strike was called. "Ethel was the most active of all the women in our plant in the strike," recalled a fellow worker. "I would say that next to two men who were the leaders there, she was the most active striker."[27] One of the employees, Helen Yelen, remembered that up to this point Ethel had struck her as "a timid little girl." But she seemed to gain strength from the strike. She spoke individually to many of her fellow female employees, explaining why strike action was necessary and urging them to fight for their rights. Ethel was one of the workers who lay down on her raincoat on the street outside the main entrance to stop trucks from entering the premises with deliveries and "dared the drivers to move," *The New York Times* reported on August 31. Another female worker remembered Ethel on the picket lines as "small, very slim, rather round-faced, her hair piled high on top of her head—a lot of hair—and big eyes . . . A youngster and quite excitable."[27]

The record is not entirely clear as to how the strike was ended. Some concessions were offered, but Loebel was still unhappy about recognizing a union. And then, on October 12, after the strikers returned to work, nine members of the union were fired for no reason, including Ethel. Five who were employees, all men apart from Ethel, appealed to the newly formed National Labor Relations Board. The NLRB had been created in

July 1935 specifically to supervise union elections and prevent businesses from treating their workers unfairly.

It took the board seven months to conclude on June 29, 1936, that Ethel, like her four male colleagues, had been unfairly fired "because of union membership and activities." The board added in its ruling that Loebel's "antagonism to Ethel Greenglass undoubtedly arose by virtue of the fact that she was active in organizing the union, was a member of the first and second committees and had urged employees who were working after Goldblatt's [another employee's] dismissal to cease working and protest against it." Under the ruling, the company had to grant the five workers "immediate and full reinstatement in their former positions without prejudice to rights and privileges previously enjoyed," as well as compensating them for lost wages since they were fired, minus any sum they had earned elsewhere during this time. In Ethel's case this was a pittance: she had made just $20 from singing engagements in a theater and, as she told the NLRB, an additional $4 from "canvassing," presumably for the union, but she did not specify for whom.

Ethel never forgot the heady words of the judgment. She was later to tell a friend in prison that her strike action and subsequent vindication was the most formative experience of her young life.[28] According to her fellow worker Helen Yelen, Ethel was starting to move in Communist circles; Helen remembered going with Ethel to have lunch in places where union members with Communist sympathies liked to gather. But, like so much else that was said about Ethel by former acquaintances after her execution, Helen's testimony too must be treated with caution.

During the strike Ethel had of necessity started looking for a new job. Early in 1936, she was hired as a stenographer on a higher weekly wage by the Bell Textile Company. Meanwhile she attended regular rehearsals of the Schola Cantorum and probably performed that winter in two performances of Beethoven's Ninth Symphony at Carnegie Hall with the Boston Symphony Orchestra.

Ethel's exposure to the highest level of European musical culture must have been exhilarating and it inspired her to aim higher—perhaps even with a view to becoming a soloist. She hired a singing teacher, whom she never identified to friends beyond calling her "Madame," to give her voice and piano lessons at Carnegie Hall Studios. And then, just as she began ascending to the next stage of her musical career, she left Schola Cantorum after only one year, possibly because the choir went on tour and she needed the money from a regular job. Ethel ended her lessons with "Madame" and now limited her singing to performances of light operettas and well-known Italian concert arias that were popular at rallies she attended. Most of these were organized by the socialist Workers Alliance, which Ethel soon joined and which was linked to Communist-affiliated councils for unemployed workers.

It was not just Italian immigrants who loved hearing Ethel singing their favorite Puccini songs at these rallies. Her Lower East Side audiences also included Jewish sweatshop workers whose families had recently arrived, like her own parents, from all corners of central and Eastern Europe, from Germany to Russia. Many still had relatives in the "old country" at a time when almost all the news from Europe was deeply disturbing, seeming to confirm their wisdom in escaping poverty and persecution. In Italy, Benito Mussolini had destroyed the last vestiges of parliamentary democracy in 1925 when he declared himself "Il Duce" and established a Fascist dictatorship. In Germany, Hitler had seized power in 1933 and within months had exploited the burning of the Reichstag to outlaw all opposition and launch anti-Semitic campaigns to restrict the political and civil rights of Jews. In Spain, the outbreak of civil war in 1936 saw the emergence of a third potential right-wing dictator, the Nationalist general Francisco Franco, whose uprising against the left-wing Republican government was backed by Hitler and Mussolini. Only Stalin's Russia—Ethel's ancestral homeland—seemed to offer any real hope for the Lower East Side militants who packed the Workers Alliance rallies.

But closer to home, times were tough for many of these people as the Great Depression dragged on and the American economy failed to take off in the way that President Roosevelt had hoped when he presented his first New Deal in March 1933. In the spring of 1935 he launched a second, more aggressive series of federal initiatives, sometimes called the second

New Deal, which included the creation of the Works Progress Administration (WPA) to provide jobs for unemployed people in public works
projects such as the construction of buildings, bridges, highways, parks,
and schools; Seward Park benefited from WPA programs. The WPA also
tried to find work for artists, writers, theater directors, and musicians, and
some of Ethel's closest friends around this time were unemployed musicians from WPA organizations in whose apartments she liked to spend
cold winter evenings at the beginning of 1936—especially if they had
steam-powered heating—making music and discussing politics.

And there was much to discuss—above all Soviet Communism,
which still seemed miraculous to many self-styled "progressives" in the
West because of the totalitarian efficiency of Stalin's propaganda machine
and the naivete and wishful thinking of a gallery of dupes, from the playwright George Bernard Shaw to Walter Duranty of *The New York Times.*
"The wholeness of the C[ommunist] P[arty] world was so complete, so
deeply felt, that it was impossible not to believe it capable of making the
revolution not in some unforeseeable future but right now, today, tomor-
row, certainly within one's own lifetime,"[29] wrote Vivian Gornick, the
daughter of Louis and Bess Gornick, two ardent New York Jewish socialist
parents who had emigrated from Ukraine.

Steadily, Ethel was becoming a believer in the same miracle. Everything she had witnessed or directly experienced in her young life, culminating in the strike, was drawing her and many like her on the Lower
East Side into the small but growing Communist world. By the mid-1930s
the area where the Greenglasses lived had approximately 250,000 inhabitants, of whom 3,000 were Communists, readers of the *Daily Worker* or
the Yiddish newspaper *Der Freiheit.** *The Forward,* launched in 1897 as the
voice of the immigrant, still had a Yiddish-language radio station and the
future Nobel laureate Isaac Bashevis Singer on its staff. For these people
a belief in Communism was also a version of the American Dream or a
passion, "a hook on the soul that made of Communism the metaphoric

---

* In 1936 total membership of the Communist Party of America was estimated
at about 40,000; it rose to its peak of 83,000 in 1943.

experience that it was . . . it was passion that converted them, passion that held them, passion that lifted them up and then twisted them down," recalled Gornick.[30]

> The Communist Party was a condition. Being a Communist was a condition. Your life as a Communist was everywhere: in the shop, at home, at meetings, in the neighborhood. You were always being a Communist. There was never a time when you weren't a Communist. You were a Communist when you went to the store to buy a bottle of milk, when you went to a movie, attended a party or a meeting, voted in the shop, sewed up the last two dresses of the day for the woman at the next machine whose kid was sick, returned a dollar to a clerk who had short-changed himself, sent an ignorant neighbor to a tenants' council when the landlord wanted to evict her . . . it was all one. The life was of a piece. There was nowhere in my life that I turned that I didn't know who and what I was . . . Ah yes! *That* was a life.[31]

But there were other forces at work that did not see how Communism could possibly play a role in the American Dream. Most Americans, equating Communists with Jews, were profoundly concerned about accepting large numbers of Jewish refugees from Nazism in Europe. A Gallup poll in January 1939 asked if Americans would support bringing even ten thousand German refugee children into the country; the result was two to one against. Among those troubled by the negative effects of such an influx were established Jews, worried that it could destabilize the privileged position they had won for themselves.[*]

Still there were articulate voices reminding all Americans that

---

[*] US immigration laws set strict quotas that limited immigration, especially from southern and Eastern Europe. From 1933 to 1938, about thirty thousand German Jews emigrated to the United States—but the government only gave out 30 percent of the visas it had available for Germans.

fulfillment of the American Dream depended on "the cross-fertilization of the many peoples, races, religions, cultures that live within it. The moment a nation determines upon a policy that shuts her from the currents of new ideas that nation is doomed." In a speech to the Institute of Contemporary Jewish Affairs in Washington in December 1939, Dr. Baruch Braunstein, the Philadelphia-based historian and lecturer, told his audience:

> When any Jew is attacked all Jews are attacked . . . in Germany some Jews believed anti-Semitism was directed not against them but against other Jews they called "East European Jews." But when Hitler came to power he refused to discriminate between Jews and persecuted them all regardless of how well they spoke German or dressed or deported themselves. It is a snare and a delusion to believe, as some Jews do, that they will be immune when the hour comes. Anti-Semitism brooks no distinctions. It encompasses all Jews.[32]

•   •   •

Throughout 1936, Ethel was delighted whenever she was asked to use her singing talents around New York City at Workers Alliance rallies, at fundraising events for American volunteers fighting General Franco in Spain, and on Saturdays by entertaining striking employees outside Ohrbach's, the department store on 14th Street in Lower Manhattan, who had been demanding better pay and conditions for the past eight years.

On New Year's Eve, when the International Seamen's Union held a benefit, her local reputation made her the obvious choice as lead performer. But for some reason she had an attack of nerves that night.

According to a later version of events, she overcame her nerves thanks to the intervention of an eighteen-year-old engineering student, Julius Rosenberg, who had come along to the event for political reasons. Julius had already noticed twenty-one-year-old Ethel walking in the neighborhood without knowing her name, as his own family lived nearby. Now he spotted her in the hall, awaiting her turn to sing, and asked a friend to introduce them. When she admitted her nervousness to him he suggested they find an anteroom and that she rehearse just to him before it was her turn to perform publicly. Thanks to the warm-up, when her turn came Ethel soon found her voice and sang her heart out for the good of the cause with a selection from her usual romantic repertoire, ending with the popular classic Italian waltz aria "Ciribiribin" by Alberto Pestalozza. Julius was tall, good-looking, polite and, most of all, full of admiration for Ethel and her beautiful voice. Flattered, Ethel accepted his suggestion that they leave together, and he walked her home. From then on they became inseparable.

"I have loved her ever since that night, and always when I hear her sing it is like the first time and I know that they can never part us—nothing will,"[33] Julius insisted later.

TWO

Wartime Mothering

Meeting Julius Rosenberg that night in December 1936 transformed Ethel's life. He fit into a new pattern Ethel was establishing: keenly educating herself about workers' rights and world politics but still finding time for her first love, theatrical activities. Julius would draw her further away from her own family, where none of the men went to college nor looked far beyond their own economic survival.

Julius, always called Julie by his close friends and family, was the youngest of five children born to Harry and Sophie Rosenberg, both immigrants from Bialystok, Poland, who had met and married in New York when they were still teenagers. Sophie at first started work in a textile factory, sewing on buttons and putting tags on shirts. Harry had been in the tailoring trade in Poland and at the time of Julius's birth in 1918 was trying his luck running a cleaning establishment in Harlem. When this venture did not prosper the family moved to the Lower East Side, where they initially lived in great poverty, with Julius and his brother David having to share a narrow single bed. In these unhealthy conditions, Julius was a sickly child who suffered from various ailments, including measles and later asthma, as well as having poor eyesight.

Gradually, life improved for the Rosenbergs. Harry returned to the garment industry, becoming a highly skilled sample maker, sometimes

earning as much as $125 per dress. He was always an active union sup-
porter and, although he had no formal education, had taught himself Yiddish, which enabled him to read a newspaper. Shortly before 1936 the
family had moved to an apartment in Lavanburg Homes, 124–142 Baruch
Place, a model affordable housing cooperative around the corner from the
Greenglasses. Their new home was vastly superior in terms of sanitary
conditions and possibilities for self-improvement. These 113 apartments
had been constructed in 1927 as an experiment funded by the Jewish
philanthropist Fred L. Lavanburg, who believed that "most inhabitants of
the slums of New York had the capacity to raise their children in a manner
conducive to the wellbeing of the nation, if society were . . . to make it
possible for them to live in decent, comfortable, dignified living quarters."[1] The development boasted a roof terrace, which offered a safe environment for children to play, and a basement intended as an area for adult
amateur dramatics and other social activities, including a mothers' club.
Inside the apartments, tenants enjoyed the great luxury of both steam-
powered heating and electric lighting.

As a young boy, Julius had studied Hebrew with an intensity and
seriousness that led his teacher to think he would become a rabbi. But by
his midteens he had come to value political action over religious learning.
Julius was moved by cases such as that of Tom Mooney, the labor activist
who he was convinced had been wrongfully convicted and imprisoned in
1916 for alleged involvement in a left-wing terrorist bombing attack in
San Francisco. In 1934, at the age of sixteen, Julius abandoned any idea
of a career as a rabbi and decided to follow a secular path through life. He
was accepted to study electrical engineering at New York's City College
(CCNY), the university in the heart of Harlem sometimes dubbed the
poor man's Harvard. Founded in 1847, CCNY was the first free, publicly
funded higher education institution in the United States, with a mission to
educate the children of poor immigrants and the working class generally.
Once mandatory chapel attendance was abolished, the college attracted
many brilliant Jewish students who otherwise could not have considered
a university education. One of them, the sociologist Nathan Glazer, who

attended CCNY from 1940 to 1944, was dazzled by its magnificent mock-Gothic buildings, built using black Manhattan schist for the stone facing, accentuated by white stucco trim around the doors and windows for gargoyles and other features. "One could not imagine anything so grand being built today for a free college,"[2] Glazer commented.

Like Julius, Glazer grew up in a tenement, the son of a Polish Jewish immigrant father who worked in the textile industry. Glazer had a vivid recollection of CCNY's central building, "a half circle on Hamilton Heights, with a large spike coming out of the center. In the basement of that spike was the cafeteria, with alcoves along both sides." These alcoves were places of noisy debate for all the antagonistic leftist student factions—Stalinist, anti-Stalinist, Trotskyist, or socialist. The anti-Stalinist alcove (where students ranging from Trotskyists to Social Democrats met and debated) was right next to the Stalinist one, but the two sides rarely argued directly with each other, according to Glazer.[3]

City College was already a maelstrom of political activity when Julius enrolled six years before Glazer. Throughout the 1930s the college witnessed student strikes and regular political meetings of various left-leaning groups. For Morton Sobell, a fellow student and close friend of Julius from then on, joining the Young Communist League (YCL) was an easy choice. "When I joined the YCL at City College it was set up on a schoolwide basis but wasn't a very formal organization. We had our meetings Friday nights. Discussion centered on Fascism in Germany and Italy and the fight going on in Spain. There wasn't much talk about school issues."[4]

Julius made many close friends at City College, mostly Jewish and all left-wing, and appeared at times to allow his political activism to take precedence over his studies. He was a leader in a protest group called the Steinmetz Society, which Sobell insisted "was never an affiliate of the Young Communist League,"[5] although it was loosely connected with it. In 1935 Julius and a group of Steinmetz Society friends staged a dramatic raid on a German liner, the *Bremen,* ripping off the Nazi flag when it docked in New York harbor. Julius later became a member of FAECT, the Federation of Architects, Engineers, Chemists, and Technicians, a radical union for professionals that, from its establishment in 1934, was often accused of having Communist sympathies.*

Sobell believed that Julius chose electrical engineering because it offered a better chance of employment, although "he might more suitably have become a Greek scholar."[6] Engineering was certainly no soft option, requiring long hours of study for students who wanted to do well. Even then, successful City College engineering graduates were aware that they faced prejudice from large corporations, which often regarded them as either too radical, too Jewish, or both.

By the time Ethel met Julius, the Rosenberg parents had survived their years of greatest poverty and were proud of having two college sons. They did not object to their son marrying Ethel, but believed the couple should not get married quite yet. Sophie Rosenberg later recalled: "They wanted to be married before. Ethel said: 'I like him. I want to marry. I will work all my life.' My husband, who never would have let a wife work, said: 'And how can you? No there will be babies, you cannot work you must wait. Wait until Julie is through school.'"[7]

The attraction between Ethel and Julius seems to have been powerful and immediate. According to friends, from the moment they met Julius practically never left her side. Julius, slim, well presented, and a good talker with a ready smile, was Ethel's first regular boyfriend, although she had had other male friends and had "walked out" a few times with a man she met on the strike committee who had worked at National New York Packing and Shipping. The appeal of Julius for Ethel was partly the heady feeling of having a man who was clever and stimulating, a college student, who not only admired her but had fallen completely in love with her.† But there was also a physical attraction, evident to everyone who knew them. Ethel, neither conventionally pretty nor glamorous, must have held an appeal for Julius perhaps initially through her voice and stage presence,

---

*   The scientist Robert Oppenheimer and his brother Frank were both members.

†   Five years on, Julius made it clear to Alexander Feklisov, his Soviet handler, how much he adored Ethel by closing his gray-green eyes and blowing a kiss into his hand when he spoke about her.

which can be transformative, but later because of her passionate commitment to left-wing causes, intellectual curiosity, and determination. Whether or not they had a physical relationship before they were married can only be a matter for speculation, but, in the cultural milieu in which they moved, it would not have been unusual if they had.

Although Ethel was committed to her job at the Bell Textile Company she was still singing, which fed her love of performing. She had also joined another amateur dramatic group, the Lavanburg Players, which until 1938 met in the basement of the Rosenbergs' building before moving to the 400-seat Henry Street Settlement Playhouse on nearby Grand Street. This group was well known for its Friday night lectures by actors and directors, including such illustrious guest speakers as the left-wing playwright Clifford Odets and his friend the film director Elia Kazan, both briefly members of the Communist Party USA (CPUSA) in the mid-1930s. The Lavanburg Players regularly staged plays that dealt with issues of social significance, such as *Kingdom of 137,* about a tenement fire at 137 Suffolk Street on March 4, 1937, in which at least 148 people died, including several firefighters. Meanwhile, Ethel continued to sing for pleasure some evenings at the homes of fellow workers and friends wherever there was a piano, steam-powered heating, and the chance to talk about progressive politics.

Ethel was determined to ensure that Julius graduated so they could marry with his parents' approval. She encouraged him to spend more time studying and less time fighting Fascism by inviting him to her family home at Sheriff Street. Sometimes they talked and worked in the kitchen or sometimes in her bedroom, which had a window, her treasured piano, and, most importantly, some privacy. Here, on nights when she was not at Lavanburg lectures, Ethel helped Julius prepare for exams by typing out his notes on a secondhand portable Remington typewriter, which she had bought from an acting friend for thirty dollars. It was more than she had paid for the piano.

Nobody in her family seems to have raised any eyebrows at the arrangement. Years later, Ethel's elder half brother Sam claimed that her mother and father were underwhelmed by their daughter's new boyfriend's table manners. "He spoke before he swallowed his food," commented Sam. "Sometimes he even appropriated Barnet's regular chair, oblivious to one of the few prerogatives that his future father-in-law was afforded," he reportedly remarked later.[8] The one member of the family who was thrilled by Julius was David, fourteen at the time he first met Ethel's boyfriend. From the very beginning David looked up to Julius, who gave him secondhand engineering books and a slide rule, on which David scratched out "Rosenberg" and put his own name. Julius educated David about engineering and, more significantly, gave him various books and pamphlets about Communism. He and Ethel also took David to some jolly propaganda films about the Soviet Union and encouraged him to read left-wing classics such as the eighteenth-century English-born radical Tom Paine's *Common Sense,* "which left a big impression."[9] David claimed later that his political induction into the Communist web had been Ethel's work more than Julius's, since "I was already in it before I met him."[10] The known facts do not unambiguously support David's version of events because he joined the YCL at the age of sixteen, a year or so after he was first introduced to Julius.

In 1939, Julius Rosenberg eventually graduated from City College with a bachelor of science degree in electrical engineering. He had to stay on for an extra semester in order to pass—at the second attempt and with Ethel's active encouragement—a course in Spanish. Then came the long hunt for a job at a time when more than one in five Americans of working age could not find employment. But even without a salary, Julius and Ethel were married on June 18, 1939, a sunny Sunday, warm but not stifling. The celebration was low-key and small, in an old Lower East Side Orthodox synagogue that may have been selected simply for convenience. There were dozens to choose from, with at least five synagogues in Sheriff Street alone. Some were built specifically for congregations from particular villages in Eastern Europe to worship among their own townspeople and a few had ritual baths in the basement, an Orthodox tradition that Ethel would have eschewed.

Ethel's brother Bernard was best man, and a rabbi whom they barely knew officiated. But no photographs of Ethel on her wedding day have survived. When she was asked at her trial for details about her wedding she responded in an offhand, possibly even slightly embarrassed way: "I believe it was Rabbi Zin." This lack of ceremony in a marriage was not unusual for Communists at the time, and in any case she and Julius had very little money and were not interested in the religious or ceremonial side of Judaism. Ethel had been brought up in a culturally Jewish but not observant family. Being Jewish was simply a given, while regular attendance at synagogue, other than on high holy days, was for those with a deep religious bent. The Greenglasses were not intellectually interested in studying the Torah and were too busy earning a living. Getting married in a synagogue, having a religious blessing on their union, may have been to please both sets of parents, but it was also part of their identity as Jews even if, like many of their Communist friends, they might have described their beliefs as atheist at this time. According to Abe Oshcroff, their longtime friend and comrade who had fought in the Spanish Civil War, the wedding was so Jewish that "you could smell the pickled herring."[11] Jewish food, however, was the cultural norm on the Lower East Side at the time for both Jews and non-Jews: 1,500 kosher delicatessens offered traditional Jewish food including kneidlach, gefilte fish, and schnitzel, and scarcely reflected religious feeling.

Immediately after the wedding, Julius moved in with his new wife at Sheriff Street, but this arrangement lasted only a week or so. They went next to stay briefly with Julius's parents at Lavanburg Homes, where Ethel enjoyed the luxury of the Rosenbergs' gas range and private, tiled bathroom with a medicine cupboard and fitted basins. Julius's sister Ethel, married to an older man, Oscar Goldberg, a prosperous grocer, soon invited the newlyweds to escape the city heat and stay with them at a rented summer cottage in Spring Glen, a beautiful rural setting about ninety miles north of Manhattan in upstate New York. At the end of the summer they went to live with Julius's friends from City College, Marcus and Stella Pogarsky, fellow Communists who suggested the two couples share a four-room apartment in the Williamsburg section of Brooklyn. This plan also did not last long, and so Ethel and Julius moved back into the city.

•   •   •

Now, Ethel and Julius faced the same wholly unexpected dilemma that confronted all of their young Communist friends. On August 23, 1939, the Soviet Union and Germany astounded the world by signing the Molotov-Ribbentrop nonaggression pact, named after their respective foreign ministers. Under a secret protocol in the treaty, Germany agreed not to attack the Soviet Union and promised Stalin a sphere of influence that covered eastern Poland and the Baltic states of Lithuania, Latvia, and Estonia. In return, Stalin undertook not to intervene militarily if Hitler invaded western Poland, which happened one week later, forcing Britain and France to declare war on Germany.

Some American Communists immediately left the party, stunned by this new alignment of the Soviet Union with its ideological archenemy, Nazi Germany. A larger number accepted Stalin's volte-face blindly. Ethel and Julius seem to have fallen into this second category of the true Soviet faithful, despite their hatred of Nazism. There is no evidence that they ever commented publicly on the Nazi-Soviet pact. Whatever their private feelings, they appear simply to have accepted the CPUSA's absurd line that the treaty was an act of self-protection by Stalin against the supposed threat that the West would use the crisis over Poland as the pretext for a counterrevolutionary invasion of the Soviet Union.

Julius and Ethel's main preoccupation during the first year of their married life was much more immediate. Like millions of other young men, Julius struggled to find work, accepting a number of freelance engineering assignments and enrolling in various technical courses to increase his skills. He was aware that several of his college classmates, including his friend Morton Sobell, had found work with the Navy Ordnance Department in Washington, DC, where the federal government did not have the same qualms as private employers about hiring CCNY graduates and paying them good salaries. In 1940 Julius decided to go down this route as well and take the civil service exams.

While he was applying, Ethel remained the couple's sole breadwinner, thanks to her $700 annual salary from the Bell Textile Company. She decided that she too should seek work with the federal government and took the civil service exams, which she immediately passed. In May 1940 she was offered a job as a temporary clerk with the Census Bureau in the US Department of Commerce in Washington at an annual salary of $1,440, more than double what she was currently earning. In June she and Julius set off for Washington, where they found a single room in a boardinghouse recommended by a friend of Julius.

It took Julius—who had also passed the exams—three more frustrating months to secure a civilian job as a junior engineer with the US Army Signal Corps, based at Fort Monmouth, New Jersey, just south of New York City. The pay was good, at $40 a week plus $5 per day for travel, so Julius decided to return home immediately and live with his parents. Ethel agreed to give up her job and come home to New York as soon as she had worked out her one month's notice, in line with how a dutiful wife of the era was expected to behave: the man would go out to work and when he returned a meal would be on the table, ready for him. Yet for Ethel, who had been the main or sole breadwinner since she and Julius were married, this must have hurt, especially as her government job had been prestigious and the return to New York necessitated that they moved in, once again, with her Rosenberg in-laws at Lavanburg Homes until they could find a small place of their own. Presumably it had been an understanding between them that, once Julius secured a job, he with his college education was likely to earn more than she could. Even if they were doing the same job, she would have earned less than him. And although Communism theoretically championed the equality of the sexes, it was not theory that interested Ethel. From now on she gave up her dreams of being an actress or a singer and turned instead, in her single-minded way, to political activism and Julius. She had hitched her star increasingly to this man and the children they were planning to raise between them. That was the prism through which she viewed her life.

Yet neither Julius nor Ethel at this point in their lives appears to have hidden their passion for Communism. Several friends recall them as outspoken or active in promoting Communist beliefs and even, in Julius's case, openly selling the CPUSA's *Daily Worker*.[12] But were Ethel and Julius card-carrying members of the party? Only in 1954 did it actually become illegal to be a member of the Communist Party when Congress passed the Communist Control Act, a law that was never enforced. However, four years previously the Internal Security Act, while specifically noting that mere membership in the Communist Party was not illegal, nonetheless established penalties for anyone belonging to a group "calling for the violent overthrow of the American government," as some Communists were accused of wanting. Previously, in 1940, the Alien Registration Act (sometimes known as the Smith Act) had performed a similar function. The House Un-American Activities Committee had been created in 1938 to investigate alleged disloyalty on the part of Fascists as much as Communists. But by the 1940s it was the committee's anti-Communist investigations—especially the nine-day hearing in 1947 into alleged Communist propaganda in Hollywood and its resonating question, "Are you now or have you ever been a member of the Communist Party of the United States of America?"—for which it was best known. Membership itself may not have been illegal, but an admission was easily turned into something that was. Some historians, such as Ronald Radosh, maintain that both Rosenbergs had "graduated to full membership of the Communist Party and Julius, always a dedicated activist, had become Chairman of Branch 16B of the party's Industrial Division. The group regularly held its meetings in his and Ethel's new apartment."[13]

Yet there is no evidence that Ethel ever joined this small group, which had a mere handful of members and functioned mostly as a discussion forum. There is also no proof that she ever officially became a CPUSA member, however strong her Communist beliefs. At the time of the 1935 packing company strike, her friend and colleague Helen Yelen said that Ethel was a member of the small but highly effective militant group Local 65, which did not actually become a union until 1936 when it was called District 65. Ethel admitted her membership in this group during her trial when she said she was "active in the union."[14] Helen Yelen remembered her friend's openness in espousing views put forward by Local 65, such as the importance of organizing among the lowest-paid workers and creating a working-class culture that went beyond normal union issues of better pay. Ethel later joined the Women's Auxiliary of FAECT, Julius's union, helping to raise funds for children made homeless by the Spanish Civil War. Important though those ideals were to Ethel, she also looked to broader concerns that would transform American society.

Max Elitcher, college friend, later neighbor, and best man at the wedding of Morton Sobell, in his grand jury testimony described how he became a member of the party at a meeting in 1939 almost without knowing, "Just by saying that I would be a member." There was no ritual and no oath-taking, and after the meeting, to which he had been taken by Sobell, he found himself in a six- or seven-man cell.[15] Asked about the necessity for "Commie cards," he replied: "No cards were ever issued."*

Yet according to Radosh, the FBI had a photostatic copy of Julius's membership card dated December 12, 1939, and another dated 1944, based on material they had confiscated from his home. The authors Emily and David Alman have always argued that there is still some uncertainty surrounding the couple's membership in the party and, since the alleged membership cards belonging to Julius were never shown or produced as evidence at the trial, question their authenticity.[16]

For her 1988 book the psychotherapist Ilene Philipson interviewed Ethel's own psychotherapist, Saul Miller, whom she quoted as saying that the CP "offered [Ethel] a window to the world . . . where she could begin to see something different from the Jewish Ghetto where she grew up, where girls were not educated and boys were."[17] No doubt; but that was only part of the attraction, and Ethel's attempts at ongoing education were similarly inspired by this desire to break free from the restraints of her birth. She put enormous faith in the discoverability of all things through books and the written word.

In the decades since the collapse of Communism many writers and intellectuals have tried to explain the extraordinary attraction of the movement to non-Russians in the 1930s. Why did even regular revelations of the shocking brutality of the regime—including the Great Purge trials in 1936 of "old" Bolsheviks like Nikolai Bukharin, or the execution in 1943 of two former socialists (and Jews) Victor Alter and Henryk Ehrlich—not compel otherwise empathetic individuals to leave the party

---

* Elitcher, having agreed to testify for the prosecution at his friend's trial, then admitted at the trial that he had falsely stated in a loyalty oath he had never been a Communist. He was never indicted.

and denounce their former commitment? It's what the British writer Da-vid Aaronovitch, the son of two Communists, describes as the "defiant senti-ment" that he saw in his own mother and was certainly applicable to Ethel. The strength of the party was "that it was about belief and faith as much as about intellect. No—more than it was about intellect. Because if it had been in any way 'scientific,' if it had involved a cold appraisal of the truth, then how could party members have been so obtuse as not to see what was so apparent to others?" he asks.[18] Morton Sobell, explaining his motives for joining the party, commented that he was "well aware that the Commu-nist Party USA was following the lead of the Russian Communist Party, often subordinating the needs of American workers to the interests of the Soviet Union. I also believed that the security of the Soviet Union was of paramount concern at this time since, if the USSR were overthrown, the Parties of all the other countries would be immeasurably weakened . . . in my heart I felt that the Party was the way. It was, I suppose, a matter of faith."[19]

Perhaps part of the attraction of Communism was that "it offered nothing and demanded everything, including the surrender of spiritual freedom," Richard Crossman, the British Labour Party politician, wrote in disillusionment in 1950.[20] "Once the renunciation has been made, the mind, instead of operating freely, becomes the servant of a higher and unquestioned purpose." But was it evident at the time that totalitarianism was an inevitable consequence of Communism?

Although Ethel continued to believe fervently in Communism after the war, an FBI report in August 1950 (after Julius had been arrested) stated that "we have no information that she is a member of the Commu-nist Party, although she definitely adheres to this philosophy."[21] Whether or not Ethel was a card-carrying member of the CP is almost irrelevant. She clearly believed in its ideals but was prepared to jettison them when it suited her, in getting married in a synagogue, giving up her job to help her husband, and seeing a psychotherapist.

The earliest official concern about the Rosenbergs' Communist activ-ities seems to date from January 1941. That month, shortly after starting work at the US Army Signal Corps base in Fort Monmouth, Julius was called in for a loyalty hearing, much to his apparent surprise. A neighbor of Julius and Ethel in the summer of 1939, when they had shared an apartment in Brooklyn with the Pogarskys, reported that Ethel had signed a Communist Party nominating petition for a would-be member called Peter Cacchione. Confronted with this evidence, Julius said that Ethel's actions should not be held against him, and that "even if [Ethel] did sign a petition, I don't see how that would affect me. After all she is a different person and has rights."[22] Julius added that his wife was "no Communist . . . We never discuss politics, but I am quite sure her views are similar to my own."[23]

The matter did not end there. At a further hearing on March 8, 1941, Julius told a slightly different, more conciliatory story, admitting that Ethel had signed the petition:

> Her memory on the matter is not entirely clear, but she told me that a man who she did not know, came to the door one day. He said he lived in the neighborhood and gave her a long rigmarole, all to the effect as to whether she wanted all sides of a question represented. She said that she guessed she did. He said, then sign this. She asked what it was and he said it would put the Communist Party on the ballot. She asked, "Will this make me a Communist if I sign?" He said, "No," so she signed. I guess it was carelessness on her part, or maybe she just lacked sales resistance. However, I know that she is no Communist.[24]

For Julius, the realization that the FBI had a file on Ethel for such a trivial matter must have been unnerving. He was now making $2,000 a year in the Signal Corps, while Ethel was not in paid employment. It was enough for them to live on but Ethel needed something useful to fill her days.

Julius further explained at his second hearing why he had recently rejected a better job offer as a junior aeronautical engineer working for the National Advisory Committee for Aeronautics at Langley Field, Virginia. "I talked it over with my wife and . . . I feel under obligation to the

Department. It takes two solid months of training for a Radio Inspector to do any work at all. Besides, they have been very good there to me. My health has been a little bad lately. I have had a lot of boils due to a lack of iron in my system. I have to take special injections every day and they have kept me on at work in the city and not sent me away on any work."[25]

Julius had said enough for the case against him to be dropped. Yet even on his "good salary," all he and Ethel could afford to rent in 1941 was a small furnished room, with a bathroom down the hallway, in an old tenement building near Tompkins Square Park in the heart of the East Village. It was extremely basic and, according to all their friends, extremely messy, because Ethel was not a good housekeeper. Nonetheless, they appeared "happy as anything. Without a dime, they made marriage look like something wonderful. And there was always open house there on Saturday night, always people around sometimes sleeping on the floor. Julie'd give the shirt off his back and he'd never say 'no' to someone in from out of town or broke who wanted a place to stay."[26]

One friend commented on how they did not have a stick of furniture that was their own here, but "they were awfully happy in each other, very much in love and happy in their work."[27]

On June 22, 1941, while they were living in the East Village, Hitler invaded the Soviet Union. At a stroke, Operation Barbarossa broke the Nazi-Soviet pact and turned Stalin into a Western ally. Six months later, on December 7, the Japanese bombed Pearl Harbor, killing 2,403 Americans and bringing the United States into the war. But already in the summer of 1941 Ethel had started working night and day as a full-time, unpaid volunteer for the East Side Defense Council, an organization that campaigned for America's entry into the war against Hitler and raised funds for food and clothing to be sent to help the Soviet people now under attack. The offices of the Defense Council were directly opposite where Ethel was living. She apparently just walked in one day and offered her services. Carl Marzani, chief executive of the organization, a charismatic, well-traveled Communist Party activist and intellectual who had fought in the Spanish Civil War, immediately took Ethel on as his personal secretary. He later described her as "a cheerful, lovely, housewife type."[28] On another occasion he recalled "she mothered me to death,"[29] although he was three years older than her. Marzani was clearly grateful to find someone prepared to undertake uncomplainingly any amount of clerical work including typing, phoning, coordinating parades, and encouraging press coverage. Several of Ethel's fellow workers here described her as very active and efficient, a good organizer and easygoing. "When Mrs. Roosevelt sent us a letter commending our work, Ethel put it up on the bulletin board. She was especially energetic in helping to organize a mass blood donor mobilization."[30] Another former singer who volunteered alongside Ethel spoke of how they would often scour the secondhand music stores together on Fourth Avenue, looking for sheet music.[31]

Ethel's friends at the Defense Council spoke later of the euphoria they all felt once America was involved in the war, convinced that this would finally destroy Nazism and Fascism. Suddenly, not only belief in Communism was acceptable but so was praise of Russia, now seen as a brave and valuable friend whose manpower would be crucial in the battle ahead.

However, not everyone saw it like this. The strongly held views of isolationists in the country, some of whom also harbored equally strong anti-Semitic sentiments, did not simply wither away. The industrialist Henry Ford, for example, was one of the country's most virulent anti-Semites who, through the pages of his newspaper, *The Dearborn Independent,* constantly attacked Jews for being at the root of many of America's and the world's ills.* Similarly, Charles Lindbergh, the pro-German former aviator who addressed many rallies for the America First movement in 1941 urging America to stay out of the war, argued that the forces pulling America into war were the British, the Roosevelt administration, and American Jews. In one speech he argued:

---

* The newspaper had been closed down in 1927, but its influence went beyond the mere number of editions published as piles had been left in dealerships around the country and a copy had been placed inside every new Model T.

Instead of agitating for war the Jewish groups in this country should be opposing it in every possible way, for they will be among the first to feel its consequences. Tolerance is a virtue that depends upon peace and strength. History shows that it cannot survive war and devastation. A few farsighted Jewish people realize this and stand opposed to intervention. But the majority still do not. Their greatest danger to this country lies in their large ownership and influence in our motion pictures, our press, our radio, and our government.[32]

Although organizations such as America First, to which Henry Ford belonged, dissolved once war had been declared, many of the ideas behind them, such as anti-Semitism, isolationism, and American nationalism, remained, lurking never far beneath the surface. Americanism was often conflated with anti-Communism, which was dangerously close to hostility to Jews, a disproportionate number of whom were believers in Communism. Some Jewish organizations were so sensitive to these currents that one of the reasons given during controversial debates for not bombing the railway lines leading to Auschwitz was the consideration that it would give anti-Semites a reason to argue that America was fighting a Jewish war.

•   •   •

Julius was not at risk of being drafted because, as an engineer, he worked in a so-called restricted occupation that was critical for the war effort. Even if he had tried to enlist, though, it is likely that he would have failed the medical test due to his poor eyesight and asthma.

Julius had just been promoted to engineer inspector when the United States entered the war, a reassuring sign of the army's renewed confidence in him after his nerve-racking loyalty hearings. His higher salary enabled him and Ethel to move in April 1942 to a more salubrious apartment at 10 Monroe Street in Knickerbocker Village, a federal housing project on the Lower East Side. The man responsible for building this massive 1,600-apartment complex between the Brooklyn and Manhattan Bridges was Fred F. French, a self-made New York real estate developer who in

1925 had built Tudor City, at that time the largest housing development ever undertaken in mid-Manhattan. Knickerbocker Village, farther downtown, was financed by a loan from Roosevelt's Reconstruction Finance Corporation as one of the nation's first publicly subsidized urban redevelopment projects.

The rent-controlled building G boasted an elevator and electricity, and the Rosenbergs' apartment number was 11-E, prompting Ethel to refer to their new home as the General Electric. There was also a gas stove in the kitchen and the joy of heating in every room. By now Ethel was pregnant, and the three-room apartment seemed ideal for starting a family, with its river view, its own nursery school, playground, and laundry room. After tenement life, it felt like a palace. Julius was doing well.

The Rosenbergs made friends with some of the other young couples in the complex, many of whom were, like them, trying to get on in the world. They were especially close to Mike and Ann Sidorovich, who shared their left-wing views and lived on the floor above. Mike had been at school with Julius and then fought in the Spanish Civil War with the Abraham Lincoln Brigade. Ann, a dressmaker who took in tailoring to make ends meet, became a good companion for Ethel during her pregnancy, now that Julius was away so much on his wartime work as an engineer inspector.

•   •   •

On March 10, 1943, Michael Allen Rosenberg was born at the Long Island Physicians' Hospital in Jackson Heights, Queens. At the time, Julius was working at Orlando Field in Florida on a job for the Signal Corps. A week after the birth, with Julius still in Florida, his parents followed traditional Jewish custom and arranged for Michael to be circumcised. Julius's brother Dave, a pharmacist, and his wife Ruth, a nurse, were present and invited to be Michael's godparents.* Ethel's elder half brother, Sam Greenglass, now thirty-four, had come too, but stormed out following a violent

---

* This did not, however, mean that they were prepared to make themselves available as guardians when the boys needed them.

row with his sister over politics, vowing that he never wanted to speak to the Rosenbergs again. He was (almost) as good as his word.

Michael was "a delicate baby, a sensitive precocious child," recalled one friend.[33] In the first few months he was often awake and crying and Ethel gratefully resorted to help from Bertha Britain, a young Black woman who had worked for some of Ethel's cousins and helped with various aspects of housework as well as baby care. Ethel herself later movingly recalled those early days of being a first-time mother with a cranky baby who did not want to sleep and a husband who was frequently away. "It wasn't the usual thing of where a baby gets sick occasionally. It was practically every week in and week out."[34]

Michael was extremely demanding, possibly because he instinctively picked up on Ethel's nervousness about trying to do her best. In Ethel's view Michael cried too much, meaning she could never relax in the company of other young mothers at Knickerbocker. She could not bear to hear a child cry, any child, which may have indicated an innate reserve in Ethel. Her sense of isolation must have increased when Ann Sidorovich, the one woman neighbor with whom she had forged a close relationship, moved out of the city soon after Michael's birth.

And yet Ethel had an extraordinary amount of patience with Michael. As one acquaintance recalled: "Never did I see such patience as Ethel had . . . When my boy would return from their house he'd expect me to drop everything, even if I was in the midst of making a cake or sewing and 'play with us like Ethel does.'"[35] Another Knickerbocker Village mother told a similar story that showed Ethel in a less positive light. One day she invited Michael and Ethel to play with her son, Steve. "She [Ethel] sat down on the floor and played with the children. She did not say three words to me . . . I was just astounded . . . you would think she'd sit and talk and watch them . . . whatever toys my son brought out—the blocks—she'd help them build. She was there maybe two hours and I'm sitting there and I finally just took a book and read it . . . so she was a very peculiar girl."[36] Ethel, unusually, focused on the assigned reason for the visit: playing with the children. Most mothers organized such playdates in order to chat with each other.

Julius's sister, Ethel Goldberg, also criticized Ethel's mothering. In the summer of 1944 the Goldbergs rented a two-story house in Budd Lake, New Jersey, and invited various family relatives, including Julius, Ethel, and the almost eighteen-month-old Michael, to live there and share the cost. Ethel was exhausted, and although Julius could not be with them the whole time and they could barely afford their share of the rent, they thought that a chance for Michael to run around in the country air might be good for him. Instead, this holiday home only increased their stress. It did not help that the refrigerator did not work in the baking summer heat. Even worse, Ethel was suffering from constant, often intense, back pain, a legacy of her childhood scoliosis. Yet, far from showing sympathy, Ethel Goldberg later described that summer watching her sister-in-law and baby nephew as "miserable." In her version, Michael cried "twenty-four hours a day . . . He was a very nervous child; he would cry and scream; I couldn't stand it."[37]

Ethel Rosenberg suffered in silence for as long as she could, but when she and Michael returned to the city at the beginning of September she enrolled in mothering classes, believing these might provide a key to unlock her misery. She could have sought help from one of the other young mothers at Knickerbocker Village. Perhaps she was too proud or shy, or perhaps she was simply driven by a desire for knowledge and self-improvement. Instead, she discovered an advanced and highly theoretical course in child psychology titled "The Child from Birth to Six Years," which met once a week for two hours at the progressive and extremely prestigious New School for Social Research, and placed all her faith in her teachers there, Eleanor Reich and the Viennese-born psychoanalyst Edith Buxbaum. Buxbaum, who had studied with Anna Freud, was a refugee from the Nazis who had arrived in New York in 1937. When her first cousin, Bruno Bettelheim, also managed to escape the Nazis, he lived with Buxbaum for a while. Buxbaum was noted for her devotion to children, for her strong desire to improve the quality of their lives and thus better the world, by emphasizing the child's individuality and creativity—with more listening and less discipline. What Ethel would have learned here—that the mother must give way to the needs and demands of the child—would only have reinforced what she was already doing. Parents were encouraged to show guidance, not control, if children were to develop into happy, healthy, and successful adults.

Ethel Goldberg believed that Ethel exacerbated an already difficult situation by not punishing Michael. "He was such a disturbing child . . . I would grab him away from her and say 'you're gonna sit down and eat or you're gonna lie down for a while . . .' I couldn't take it; that woman was wearing herself down. Every little beck and call, she'd run to his side. That's how Ethel was . . . never punished him in any way. I punished my kids . . . But Ethel was different."[38] She was, however, pushing herself to the limit as she tried never to respond negatively to her challenging son.

Ethel was an avid reader of the childcare expert Dr. Dorothy Whipple's influential column in *Parents* magazine, a mass-circulation periodical that was packed with useful tips for modern young mothers like her. In 1944 Whipple published her bestseller, *Our American Babies,* which advocated: "Be natural and easy with your baby." Where previous generations had encouraged strict feeding schedules and letting babies cry to exhaustion, Dr. Whipple argued that feeding a baby when it was hungry and letting the baby set its own schedule might be a better idea. She insisted that love and understanding were what counted: "Nothing we can do or provide for a baby is more important."[39]

The classes might have offered Ethel more insight into her relationship with her son, but they did not solve her increasing back pain and headaches, which now forced her to take bed rest. As she recalled to the judge at her trial:

> It so happens that I have had a spinal curvature since I was about 13 and every once in a while that has given me some trouble and at that time [1944] it began to kick up again and occasionally I have to get into bed and nurse a severe backache. Through the bargain I developed a case of low blood pressure and that used to give me dizzy spells sometimes to the point where I almost fainted. I also had very severe headaches and it finally got so bad that I went to visit my doctor.[40]

He prescribed regular weekly iron injections, but it was more than just anemia that had to be treated. Ethel desperately needed emotional reassurance as well as practical help on the domestic front in this crisis. Although Julius was generally supportive, and it was agreed that decisions on child-rearing were Ethel's, he was out at work during the day. She was therefore recommended an older woman, Evelyn Cox, who came three times a week from ten until four p.m. at seventy-five cents an hour. Evelyn undertook all sorts of household chores and cared for Michael, who was also not well in the exceptionally severe winter of 1944. "The condition of my child was very poor. I had had a very difficult time ever since his birth, I mean with him," Ethel remembered.[41]

Home life during the war was tough for Ethel in other ways. Her extended family still played a large part in all her activities and traditional Jewish Friday nights at 64 Sheriff Street were a significant weekly reunion. Tessie had turned Sam's former bedroom into a dining room, allowing everyone to get together around the table. Ethel and Julius did not always attend, particularly if Sam was present. Even so, Ethel tried to be a good daughter, despite her difficult relationship with Tessie, now that she had become a full-time housewife and mother herself. She spent more time with Tessie, who occasionally babysat Michael when Ethel was busy or needed a break. Visits to Sheriff Street were also a chance for Ethel to see her much-loved sister-in-law Gladys ("Gladdy"), who was married to her brother Bernie, away fighting in Europe.

For all Ethel's efforts, she was becoming increasingly distant from her uneducated, illiterate mother, who distrusted her and could not keep up with her intellectually. By contrast, Ethel remained close to her mother-in-law, the more aspirational if equally uneducated Sophie Rosenberg. Yet as Ethel moved further into the Rosenberg family orbit, a sliver of envy between the Rosenbergs and her brother David and sister-in-law Ruth began to lodge deep into the relationship.

David had graduated from Haaren High School in February 1940 with moderate grades, then went to Brooklyn Polytechnic Institute to study mechanical engineering. But he lasted only a semester there as he failed all six technical courses and was asked to leave. Since he had no particular ambition in mind beyond marriage to his childhood sweetheart, he does not seem to have been too concerned and managed to get a job working night shifts at the Federal Telephone Company doing machine maintenance. Nobody in the family was especially surprised when David and Ruth married swiftly in November 1942, before David turned twenty-one, partly through fear that he might soon be drafted and sent overseas. "It was just understood we were to be married,"[42] explained David later, insisting that marriage was all Ruth's idea. Many young couples in wartime did the same. Ruth's family were very poor, while David, having been fired by the Federal Telephone Company, worked in a menial, low-paid factory job making parts for aircraft and weapons. As they embarked on married life, all Ruth and David could afford as a first home was a tiny walk-up, cold-water Lower East Side apartment on Stanton Street with primitive shared toilet facilities in the hall. This might have been what prompted David to try to get a raise by threatening his employers that he might enlist. If so, the ploy backfired: his demand was rejected and in March 1943 just as Michael was born, he was indeed called up by the army. David appealed, but was ordered to report to the Armed Forces Induction Center at New York's Grand Central Palace Hotel. He was dispatched for basic training as a machinist to an ordnance unit at Aberdeen, Maryland, and almost a year later to Mississippi. New weapons were being designed and tested and the army desperately needed machinists to work on repairs.

In the summer of 1944, around the time of the June 6 D-Day invasion, most of David's battalion were sent overseas. David never knew precisely why he was not included, but told Ruth that "it was a matter of politics. The First Sergeant didn't like me and, besides that, some of my politics must have reached his ears."[43] He may well have been right, because fellow soldiers who remembered David recalled above all his outspoken Communist views. Far more difficult to explain is why David was now dispatched to Oak Ridge, Tennessee, and then in August 1944 to the Los Alamos site to work as a low-level machinist on the top-secret atomic bomb development project based there. In all likelihood, David slipped through the security net because of an administrative oversight when all eyes were on the invasion of Europe.

Ruth, now alone in New York, naturally moved closer to Ethel and Julius. Once David had left, much of Ruth's free time was spent with them attending events such as the American Council on Soviet Relations rally on November 4, 1943, at Madison Square Garden, opened by Paul Robeson singing. But Julius was often away as well, leaving just Ethel and "Ruthie" together. Nine years younger than Ethel, Ruth looked up to her clever sister-in-law. However, Ruth had also been a high achiever at Seward Park High School, and what began as intense closeness gradually evolved into mild resentment on Ruth's part, possibly provoked by Ethel's superior status as a mother and her more comfortable home at Knicker-bocker Village compared with Ruth's miserable, cramped apartment on Stanton Street.

David and Emily Alman, who themselves had lived in Knickerbocker Village, observed in their book about the Rosenbergs that "just as there were marked differences in the educational and occupational backgrounds of her [Ruth's] husband and Julius, there were obvious differences between the cultural and matrimonial attainments of the two women. Both were strong women [and both had wanted to go to college but could not] but Ethel had become a singer and actress even if still at an amateur level and had married an engineer, which in their families and social circles elevated her status."[44] There were also jealousies projected into the future. Both couples were eager to improve their material circumstances, but somehow Ruth recognized that "Ethel's children would be raised amidst a modest sufficiency while her—Ruth's—children might always lack for something."[45]

The wartime letters seized by the FBI following David's arrest in 1950 make clear how, initially, both Ruth and David saw Ethel and Julius as something of a model couple whom they hoped to emulate. A tinge of bitterness crept in once they feared this might never be possible. This correspondence, mostly passionate love letters between two lusty youngsters, also shows how both Ruth and David were equally passionate believers in Communism and optimistic about the ultimate victory of Marxism.[46] Ruth would refer to people they were friendly with as being either "reactionary" or "re-educated," and also spoke of the need to get the Communist message across and raise the red flag everywhere.

In January 1944 she wrote to David: "I hope that our children will be brought up in a socialist world and our money will be useless. I look forward to that day when necessities and luxuries are to be had by all and sundry."[47] In May he wrote to her: "I love you with all the love of Marx and the humanity of Lenin, love Dave."[48] In a letter from Ruth to "Dearest Dave" (decorated with pictures of lips and lipstick kisses), she recounted their life at that time, which consisted mainly of going from one family to another, playing records, and enjoying warm family ties. She described "an especially nice day. I was with Eth and Julie . . ."[49]

But Ruth also betrayed her insecurity that perhaps their future children might not be as bright as the Rosenbergs' little boy, Michael. She wrote of him: "He's such a cute baby and really exceptionally clever. The kid amazes me. He's very friendly and full of personality . . . I'm not so sure he takes after you," she added, presumably since David had asked. "His parents may have had something to do with it. Don't feel badly sweetheart. All our kids will take after you. I'll guarantee it. I'll train them . . . we'll be proud of them."[50] Then the tone changed just slightly: "I traipsed around with the R's all day . . . and little Mike was the life of the party, he's such a doll."[51]

In another letter she wrote:

I had a very lovely evening at Eth's as you can imagine. Before we had supper Julie ran down for the paper and came back with hot dogs . . . no one could finish his supper and then we listened to records . . . and they have some really good stuff as you know. We spoke about several hundred things and in the course of conversation the question of homes came up. Julie said that he was counting on us for one of the families in this community of homes to be built after the war . . . he says that most likely it will cost $2000 to start with . . . that means we have to save $3000 if we're to have any furniture to put in our home . . .[52]

Ruth was referring to a scheme Julius was hoping to be part of that at this stage involved simply a down payment of $50 on a plot of land in

Yorktown Heights, thirty-five miles outside New York City. It never came to anything, but clearly indicates his postwar aspirations to provide for his family—a basic ideal endorsed by most Americans of the era, but one that might have led him astray from Communism.

•   •   •

Since August 1944 the Soviet Union had been receiving details about the development of the atomic bomb at the isolated site in the New Mexico desert, which they called Operation Enormoz, from a variety of Soviet sympathizers, British and American. So when David Greenglass was sent to work at Los Alamos around this time, Julius, although he had no particular knowledge about the bomb, felt strongly that the Soviet Union, as a key wartime ally, should benefit from all the information that he believed he could now obtain from David, a mere machinist with no scientific expertise, who was stationed there.

There are various accounts of how Julius began passing secret information to the Russians. Julius's former college classmate and fellow Communist Max Elitcher maintained that Julius told him he was making "a point to get close to people, people in the Communist Party . . . he kept getting close from one person to another, until he was able to approach someone, Russian . . . who would listen to his proposition."[53] Quite possibly Julius had been recruited on September 7, 1942, during a Labor Day rally, attended by as many as fifty thousand people, where he was introduced by his friend, the Communist labor organizer Bernard Schuster, to Semyon Semyonov. Semyonov was a Soviet intelligence officer working at Amtorg, the US-Soviet trading organization founded in 1924 and widely considered to be a front for Soviet intelligence operations. Julius's wholehearted enthusiasm for the Soviet Union was so sincere that when he was told by Semyonov that "America, in spite of its commitments, was hiding its latest technical innovations from its ally who needed them very badly, Rosenberg was quick to volunteer."[54]

But according to another account Julius was, by the time of the rally, already giving information to the Soviet Union. "Julius Rosenberg was the leader of a CP cell consisting of four other engineers and was supplying

data pilfered by himself and his comrades from their jobs in defense in-
stallations to [Jacob] Golos," concluded the historian Walter Schneir,
writing in 2010. Schneir explained that Semyonov considered that supervision of the output of this secret cell by Golos, a long-standing Soviet
spy, "was haphazard." So he checked the office files himself and concluded
that Golos's engineers were furnishing "desultory materials rated low in
importance," although he believed that the group had "great potential possibilities . . . He appealed to his boss . . . to transfer them to his control,
and around late summer or early fall 1942 this was done."[55]

The meeting at the rally may therefore simply have changed the pace
and seriousness of Rosenberg's work, as Semyonov considered his new in-
formant was "absolutely unripe in matters of working as an agent."[56] What
is clear is that Julius, having always wanted to be more involved in the fight
against Fascism, to prove himself and be valued, needed no persuasion to
pass on whatever information he could get his hands on. Semyonov remained Rosenberg's Soviet handler until 1944, when he was transferred
to thirty-year-old Alexander Feklisov, four years his senior, who had been
working in New York since 1940. Feklisov and Rosenberg quickly developed a warm relationship, meeting once every six weeks, even if briefly or
simply in a "brush pass" when Julius handed over documents. According
to Feklisov, who wanted to show Moscow how passionate Julius was about
helping the Soviet socialist cause, these included "immeasurably valuable
technical documentation of the radio device that allowed anti-aircraft de-
fenses to distinguish between friendly and unfriendly aircraft."[57] When
they began to meet for longer they exchanged stories of their childhoods
and upbringing and found many shared experiences and ideas. As with all
agents, Feklisov told Julius from now on not to advertise his party membership and to avoid any Communist rallies.

Julius's friendly rapport with Feklisov fed his enthusiasm to do more,
more daringly and more heroically. He reportedly confessed to Feklisov: "I
know you may not be aware of it, but our meetings are among the happiest
moments of all my life . . . I have a wonderful wife and a son whom I adore
but you are the only person who knows all my secrets and it's very important
to be able to confide to someone."[58] According to Feklisov, Julius also told

him: "I find it unfair that you should be fighting the common enemy alone. If I can do anything to help, you can count on me."[59] He never wanted money for his help, but craved acceptance from his Soviet friends that he was taking risks, just as a partisan soldier would, to secure a Communist future.

By late 1944, Julius was working so hard recruiting his friends for the cause that even the Russians, who had code-named him "Liberal," were worried that the burden of dealing with so many agents would be too much for him. In December 1944 he had "on hand eight people plus the filming of materials. The state of Liberal's health is nothing splendid. We are afraid of putting Liberal out of action with overwork."[60]

According to Feklisov, Morton Sobell was recruited by Rosenberg in the summer of 1944 when he was involved in radar engineering at the General Electric Company and had access to confidential documents that he agreed to microfilm. Sobell offered reassurance to Feklisov that this was not a problem, "since he knew photography quite well. At our next meeting I brought him a camera with the necessary accessories and a small stock of film."[61] Julius was involved in relaying the microfilmed documents.

Julius was so eager to please Feklisov (and Feklisov to keep him in this mood) that for Christmas 1944 Julius excitedly left a large, heavy carton as a present for his Soviet handler on a windowsill in a café and took home a much smaller package that the Russian had given him—a wristwatch, Feklisov later recalled, "to help him remember me long after we had parted."

Feklisov found it more difficult to choose something for Ethel since he had never met her and did not know her tastes. "But I knew how much Julius loved her," so Feklisov asked him for suggestions. When Julius suggested that Ethel would like a new, more fashionable handbag, Feklisov employed his own wife in the search. Mrs. Feklisov found Ethel a brown crocodile bag at the department store Gimbel Brothers; inside, the Feklisovs put a plush teddy bear, bought specially for Michael.

Where did Ethel think the crocodile bag, watch, and toy had come from? By giving Julius such presents for Ethel and Michael there must have been a tacit understanding with Feklisov that Ethel was aware of, and approved, her husband's espionage activities. They were partly a thank-you to Julius as his work involved him being away from his wife so much. But arguably the Russians were also buying the silence of his wife.

When Feklisov returned to the *rezidentura* and opened his heavy package he found a short-range proximity fuse detonator, reassembled from parts, including one that had been defective.[62] According to Feklisov, Julius pulled off this dramatic theft of an important military weapon— which could track, target, and then shoot down an enemy plane—by removing the heavy components out of the factory where he was inspecting parts at a time when all his fellow workers were thinking only of the Christmas holiday the next day. A week before or a week after it would never have worked.

Julius hoped he had something else valuable to offer Feklisov: the fact that David had just started working at Los Alamos. The Russians had already infiltrated the Manhattan Project, as it was known, and so additional information acquired by Rosenberg from his brother-in-law about such a key installation would have been welcomed by Feklisov. Soon after meeting Feklisov, Julius contacted Ruth, who was due to travel to New Mexico in November 1944 to see David and celebrate their first wedding anniversary. Julius wanted Ruth to ask David to supply as much information as possible about whatever it was that was going on at the base. David, a fervent believer in the Communist cause, agreed. He was not being asked to steal anything, simply to look, listen, and remember. He would be returning to New York in January 1945 on leave and the plan was for Julius to arrange for him to talk directly with some Russian nuclear physics experts.

On January 1, 1945, with the war still raging on all fronts, David returned home on furlough for eighteen days. This was a critical time for the Allies, who were finally gaining ground in Europe following bitter fighting at the Battle of the Bulge in December 1944. This turned out to be the last German offensive in the west as Nazi resources were by then stretched beyond their limits. On January 12, on the eastern front, millions of Red Army soldiers backed by thousands of tanks and aircraft lined up on the Vistula River and struck at the exhausted and inferior German armies. Notwithstanding this devastating defeat, an obstinate Hitler refused to accept that the war was over and began introducing new and terrifying rocket weapons. Even in retreat, the Germans posed a threat. The atomic bomb had to be built as quickly as possible in order, it was thought, to defeat Hitler for good and bring the war to an end. But then what? Western governments were uneasy as to how much of Eastern Europe would be claimed by the Soviet Union and to what extent that would unsettle the balance of power. Communists like Julius Rosenberg, however, believed that the courage and gallantry of the Soviet Union, which had played such a crucial role in the war, should be recognized and that if they too had access to atomic power the balance of power in Europe would be maintained.

Julius wasted little time in visiting his brother-in-law and, according to the Greenglasses, encouraging him to convey more information about Los Alamos, which he said he would come and collect the following day. Since they had no telephone, Julius took to arriving at their New York home unannounced, alone without Ethel. But he invited the Greenglasses to his place for supper when Ethel would be at home.

According to Ruth, it was Julius who encouraged Ruth to move nearer to her husband in Albuquerque so he could visit her on weekends, but with the intention that Ruth could act as courier. But Ruth needed little encouragement as she was lonely without him and they were trying to start a family. A few months later Ruth went to live in Albuquerque.

Yet Julius and David's budding careers as Soviet spies were now suddenly threatened with disaster. At the start of 1945, the FBI, thanks to a large network of informers who had infiltrated the Communist Party, received fresh evidence that Julius was a Communist Party member and in February he was fired from his job as an Army Signal Corps engineer inspector. Once again Julius was confident that he could win his appeal, especially when he was inadvertently shown the charges, which related to his membership in the left-wing labor union, the Federation of Architects, Engineers, Chemists, and Technicians. According to a memorandum of March 28, 1945:

Information has been received following your graduation from CCNY you became a member of FAECT allegedly controlled by the Communist Party and you attended federation school maintained by that organization. Your instructor at that school is reported to have been the director of the Abraham Lincoln Brigade and a member of the loyalist forces in Spain in the Civil War . . . it is further reported that you and your wife resided in an apartment owned by Marcus Pogarsky who is reported to have been active in student organizations affiliated with the CP during the time you resided in this apartment. Pogarsky's wife Stella signed a Communist petition and solicited signatures for a Communist Party petition . . . it is reported that your wife also signed a CP petition during this same period.[63]

In response, Julius made a statement under oath, most likely typed by Ethel, that he was not now and had never been a party member. He pointed out that the same charge had been dropped and the issue terminated when he had been previously investigated in 1941:

> It is difficult to understand why after four and a half years of conscientious and hard work this discredited charge should be revived as in 1941 there is no evidence presented, merely allegation rumor and reports together with totally irrelevant charges against other persons with whom I had not more than an incidental connection eg my employer teacher or landlord may have indulged in subversive activities . . . preventing me from making my contribution to the war effort as an engineer and from earning my livelihood in the established American way.[64]

Unlike in 1941, Julius's self-serving bluster and outright lies failed to win him back his job and the sacking caused a painful breach with his father, Harry Rosenberg, who had often argued with his son over politics. Julius and Feklisov's main anxiety was that the FBI had evidence about his double life as a spy, not his party membership, and so he was ordered by Moscow to lie low for the moment. Yet almost immediately Julius found an engineering job with the Emerson Radio & Phonograph Corporation, based in New York. It was another remarkable lapse by the US authorities. Emerson was the manufacturer of the proximity fuse detonator that Julius had given Feklisov as a Christmas present, and was engaged in other projects for the army and navy. In theory, Julius would have more opportunities to steal military secrets and technology. Even better, the pay was good. If he was prepared to work overtime, Julius could earn about $100 a week, an improvement on his previous salary. To celebrate his good fortune he splurged on a $30 watch for Ethel, a $21 table from Macy's, and a secondhand upright piano that they bought for $25 through an advertisement in the *Knickerbocker Village News*. Ethel was particularly thrilled with the latter as she could now sing with Michael.

•   •   •

On April 12, 1945, President Roosevelt died suddenly of a brain hemorrhage. Hitler took his own life two weeks later and on May 7 Germany offered an unconditional surrender. The war in Europe was over, but in Asia the Japanese fought on, seemingly willing to engage in a defensive war of attrition despite overwhelming US air, naval, and ground superiority. As the summer wore on and American losses mounted, everyone at Los Alamos began to suspect that the bomb they were working on would be used to force Japan's imperial government to surrender, by demonstrating America's ability to destroy whole cities and kill millions of the emperor's subjects. This was not the initial purpose, and controversy bubbled not far below the surface.

•   •   •

While Roosevelt's successor, Harry Truman, debated with his advisers whether and if so where to drop the first atomic bomb, Ethel had more mundane problems. For months she had been in poor health, mostly caused by back pain and broken nights thanks to Michael, and was still not fully recovered. She and Julius now decided to spend some of his extra money from Emerson to rent somewhere out of town for the summer, away from the city heat, in spite of Ethel's miserable experience the previous year staying at Julius's sister's house. This time, Julius and Ethel rented a bungalow just for themselves in Lakewood, a wooded holiday area in New Jersey, about fifty miles from Manhattan.

To their dismay, when they arrived they found the place so dirty and run-down that they could not stay. They decided instead to go to some friends they barely knew, Sonia and Ben Bach, who lived nearby at Toms River. The Bachs knew Julius a little through their cousins, who were fellow radicals, but they had never met Ethel. Nonetheless, they generously offered the Rosenberg family the use of a cottage on their property. Ethel liked Toms River so much that she and Michael eventually moved into a local rooming house, with Julius coming down on weekends from New York whenever he could. While Julius was alone in town he saw some of his old CCNY male friends. These included Max Elitcher, Morton Sobell's friend, William Perl, and Joel Barr: a small circle of clever, left-leaning twentysomething friends all of whom Julius believed, or hoped, would want, like him, to do their bit to help the Russians, wartime allies at this point. If women came too, they were kept on the edge of the circle. Julius had made contact with Max recently in Washington, so when he came to New York with his wife, Helene, they all joined up for a meal in a restaurant. But, as Max was later to tell Sobell, much to the latter's displeasure, he suspected that Helene knew about "this espionage business . . . If she knows she knows and I just can't do anything about it," he informed Sobell.[65] After dinner they went on to Barr's apartment, in the West Nineties, off Broadway, toward the river. They played some records and chatted for about an hour on a roof adjoining his apartment until his parents returned. Ethel was not part of this life; it was not that she was excluded, but she chose to stay in the country doing her best for Michael.*

Helene, a psychiatrist and influential member of the Communist

---

* Both Barr and Perl were recruited by Julius as Soviet spies in 1941. Barr fled to Paris, where he disappeared the day after David Greenglass was arrested. Perl did not flee and was found guilty on two counts of perjury for lying about his "acquaintance and association" with Rosenberg and Sobell. He served two concurrent five-year sentences. Elitcher was never indicted as a spy.

Political Association (CPA),* in charge of all trade union work in the District of Columbia, was to recall both this outing and another occasion in the summer of 1945 when she gave evidence to the grand jury five years later. On the latter occasion she recalled how a group of them again met up in New York City and Max suggested, rather than stay with her in-laws—a deeply unpleasant experience, as the mattress had bedbugs—they stay with "Julie," who was on his own. "Ethel spends the summer away and Julie 'baches' by himself in his apartment at Knickerbocker Village." Max rang Julius at the last minute to ask if they could sleep at his place and he agreed. By that time it was close to midnight, long after the Radio City show they had come to see had finished, "and we went there. Julie was by himself, and the apartment was obviously not being cared for by a woman during these months. That is, you could see a man 'baching' there."[66] But he welcomed them for the night, and they all went out the next morning to have breakfast at a nearby drugstore.

It was while she was at Toms River that Ethel learned with the rest of the world that on August 6 the United States had dropped the world's first atomic bomb on the Japanese city of Hiroshima, killing at least eighty thousand immediately but many thousands more died in the weeks following, and that her kid brother was working at the base where it had been made. Three days later another US bomber dropped an A-bomb on Nagasaki, killing a further estimated forty thousand people. It may have signaled the end of the war, but gave no clue as the nature of the peace.

---

* In 1944 the CPUSA dissolved and reformed itself into the Communist Political Association.

Three

Struggling

"Julius wasn't doing well,"[1] was Morton Sobell's frank assessment of his friend in postwar New York. According to Sobell, Julius had been unfulfilled by his work as a government inspector (well paid though it was) as it had involved no engineering, and now Emerson Radio & Phonograph had no further use for him in a postwar world where research on new weapons was less important and so contracts were drying up. Since his engineering experience was so slight and his political record so clouded by allegations of Communism, he knew that finding a new job was going to be tough. Julius's decision at the end of 1945, when he was twenty-seven, to start a small government surplus hardware shop, initially called United Purchasers and Distributors and based at 64 Sheriff Street, should therefore have made obvious sense. But it never got off the ground, and the name and the focus of the shop were soon changed to G. and R. Engineering once it was clear that Ethel's two younger brothers would also join, Bernie investing $5,000, David $1,000. Bernie had served since 1942 in the US Army as a tank commander on the African front, twice wounded, and had been decorated with five Bronze Stars, while David had been honorably discharged from the army on February 28, 1946, but had no idea what he was going to do. The new shop operated from rented premises at 200 East Second Street, the other side of Houston Street but not far from the family homes on the Lower East Side. It contained various pieces of machinery that had been bought from the War Assets Administration and the unoriginal name was chosen because R stood for Rosenberg and G both for Greenglass and Goldstein. (A friend of Julius's, Isidore Goldstein, an accountant and fellow Knickerbocker Village tenant, also put some money in the venture, as did Izzy Feit, Tessie's brother.)

But this business too never took off, either because of lack of orders or complaints about shoddy work—or possibly both. The shop lacked proper equipment, so some of the jobs had to be subcontracted to a company in the Bronx. Julius grumbled that David's supervisory and technical skills as foreman were poor and that he was lazy and continually shirking. David had a ready-made ideological excuse for despising the whole grubby business of making money. In one of several astonishingly frank and naive letters that David wrote to Ruth when he first joined the army, not worried about freely airing his Marxist views, he proclaimed: "Although we are materialists we base our materialism on humanity and humanity is love. It is the most powerful force in the world. It is causing us to win where we are outnumbered. The victory shall be ours. The Freedom shall be greater because of our great feeling that only democratic and freedom loving peoples can foster. Darling, we who understand can bring understanding to others because we are in love and have our Marxist outlook."[2]

David countered that Julius, as chief salesman, did not bring in enough work from his meager contacts, who were mostly former fellow students at CCNY or people at Amtorg, the Soviet trading company that acted as cover for Feklisov and other Russian intelligence agents. David later maintained that his brother-in-law took little interest in the business since all he was interested in was his "secret work."[3] In addition, Julius was preoccupied in the summer of 1946 with his father's illness and hospitalization. Harry had been in poor health for several years but was now declining rapidly. While Harry's older son David, wife Sophie, and daughters Lena, Ida, and Ethel (Goldberg) did little more than weep, his youngest child actually moved into the hospital, prompted by his wife Ethel, who had apparently told him: "Go, that is where you must be,"[4] words that had touched her mother-in-law greatly. And so, for the last week of July, Julius stayed by his father's bedside, healing the breach that had erupted a year previously over politics and his father's concern that, in spite of his intelligence and education, Julius—the son for whom they had nurtured such high hopes of a successful career that would lift him into the professional middle classes—did not even seem able to earn a steady living. On August 1, 1946, Harry Rosenberg died.

As the company went into debt, relations between the Rosenbergs and Greenglasses soured further. By 1947, the partners had concluded that they needed more capital and so they took in another investor, David Schein. Schein was a small-time entrepreneur and manufacturer of matzo, the traditional Jewish flatbread, sales of which flourished at the beginning of the twentieth century. This additional capital enabled them to relaunch from a new address, 370 East Houston Street, under a third new name, Pitt Machine Products. However, this company also failed to thrive. Somehow they just about made ends meet most of the time, but it was difficult for David to live off $55 a week, his salary when business was good. More often he took home less than $45 a week.[5]

David, recognizing that ideology did not pay the bills, was now less interested in Communism and the good of the world than in providing for Ruth and their baby son Steven, born in 1946. He and Ruth wanted to move out of their tiny apartment on Stanton Street, which was far too small to raise a family. While they were looking for a larger place, Ethel suggested they might want to stay at her and Julius's apartment at Knickerbocker Village while she took Michael away for ten days to recover from a tonsillectomy. David and Ruth declined Ethel's offer, perhaps because of David's fractious working relationship with Julius. They eventually found rooms a few months after Steven's birth above a grocery store on Rivington Street, only a slight improvement on their previous apartment but at least on the same street where Ruth's parents lived.

By October 1948, Pitt Machine Products was in such trouble that all the employees had to be let go, leaving only David, Bernie, and Julius working full-time to pay off the company's debts. David and Ruth managed by living off their dwindling savings and borrowing from the bank as well as from Julius. They hated owing him money and increasingly blamed him as the source of their woes. For his part, Julius was desperate to keep the company going, even if that meant sinking deeper into debt, so he sometimes accepted jobs that cost the company more than it made because he knew how difficult it would be for a suspected Communist to secure another job.

Ethel at this point had no job, and no activities beyond her small apartment and looking after her son, as was normal for most women at this time. But it meant she was totally dependent on Julius, both financially and emotionally, which was a complete reversal of how things had been at the start of their marriage. Although they were extremely hard up, some friends and neighbors believed that Ethel found poverty easier to tolerate than Julius. She was used to it, and in any case did not care about clothes or her material surroundings, while Julius felt responsible and frustrated but was unable to gain any traction with the business to lift his small family out of poverty and enable them to sample the joys of suburban consumerism that other young couples were discovering in these years. What Ethel could not tolerate above all was seeing her husband failing, and she asked at least one former contact to "do what you can to help Julie in the business."[6] They were so hard up that a neighbor in Knickerbocker Village commented that even though many of the residents had little money, Ethel "appeared to have less than the majority of them." She was always poorly dressed and now was forced to start asking for credit from the Village Grocery and Dairy just opposite. According to this neighbor, "Ethel occasionally borrowed small food items that she never returned and for which she never reimbursed them."[7] In spite of this being a low point in their marriage when both were struggling with tiredness, Julius because of the floundering business and Ethel because she was often up at night with Michael, by the autumn Ethel was pregnant again. Quite possibly it was an accident, but more likely it was a reaffirmation of their mutual love, which expressed a hope that a better life was in prospect. Ethel going out to work as a way of making more money for them was not discussed.

•   •   •

Julius did not even have the consolation of knowing he was still regarded as a valuable Communist spy by Feklisov, the Soviet handler he naively thought was his friend. Julius's espionage career had also stalled due to a number of events in 1945. In the first place, after he was fired from his civilian job with the US Army Signal Corps in March that year, Moscow feared that the FBI might know about his spying activities. He was therefore "released from his duties as a group handler" and warned that he should halt personal contact and be instructed "about the need to be careful, to look around himself."[8]

Then in November that year, Elizabeth Bentley, a forty-five-year-old Vassar-educated former CPUSA member and Soviet spy, finally defected after months of agonizing. Bentley was an unstable and lonely character, a long-standing alcoholic who had been passing information to the Soviets since 1938. But after her lover, Jacob Golos, chief of Soviet espionage operations in the United States, died suddenly of a heart attack in 1943, she lost any romantic illusions about the work she was doing. She had an affair with an American military officer (possibly an undercover FBI agent) and by 1945 decided to change sides. She gave her FBI interrogators almost 150 names of Americans she said had spied for the Soviet Union, some of whom were dedicated Stalinists, others "romantic idealists [who] wanted to help the brave Russians beat the Nazi war machine."[9] Moscow soon learned of Bentley's defection and instructed all station chiefs to cease immediately their connection with anyone who had known or worked with her and to warn all agents about her betrayal.

Julius had possibly spoken to Bentley on the telephone once, although she did not name him in 1945. But this was an extremely dangerous time for anyone involved in passing information; Moscow was already jittery about Julius being active following his dismissal from the Army Signal Corps and worried four months later that "he is slightly pained and suffers from the fact that he is left without people."[10] So now, as a precaution, Feklisov ordered him to stop all espionage activities. According to Feklisov, writing from memory some years after the events, this was for six months at the beginning of 1946. However, Julius had already been "deactivated." The problem, as Moscow saw it, was that Julius "can't reconcile himself to his relative inactivity. At every meeting he asks us to allow him to bring materials out of the plant and thus benefit us."[11] Feklisov considered that

Julius failed to grasp the gravity of the unfolding situation: "I told him to make the most of it and use his free time to take Ethel out on the town or to the country with little Michael."[12] Yet Julius looked not worried but sad, Feklisov reported.

There was worse to come for Julius. In August 1946, Feklisov was given a departure date for his return to Moscow. Having not seen Julius for at least the previous eight months, Feklisov decided he must take Julius out for dinner to give him the news in person:

"Once an agent is left hanging he may panic or decide to break with us. I knew there was no such risk with Julius but it was a very powerful argument for the Center [Moscow]," explained Feklisov. For this farewell dinner, Feklisov chose a place that would be an improvement on the usual cafeterias and self-service restaurants where he and Julius had met when Julius had been an active spy recruiter. Feklisov thought that "The Golden Fiddle," a good Hungarian restaurant on the West Side, would be "somewhere they could be comfortable and take our time . . . The band was excellent and created a happy atmosphere for Julius who was very pleased to see an old friend who knew everything about him and with whom he could open up completely, knowing he'd find security and understanding."

Finally, Feklisov, whom Julius craved as his friend, had to admit that he was about to leave the country. "Julius stopped, looking at me wide-eyed. A few long seconds went by. 'What do you mean,' he asked, 'you're leaving me? Why?'" Feklisov explained that the normal tour of duty for a man in his position was three to four years and he had been in the United States for five and a half. He could not stay longer without arousing suspicion and advised Julius: "Even for your sake it will be best to lay [sic] low for a while. In about six months one of my colleagues will contact you in the manner we have set up together."[13]

Julius had always refused any compensation, according to Feklisov: "All I could reimburse him for were travel expenses and restaurant bills he paid for his colleagues so I was lucky to get him to take $25.00 per month."[14] Yet Feklisov also knew how hard it was for the Rosenbergs to make ends meet every month, so "following instructions, from the Center, I gave him one thousand dollars for any unforeseen emergencies."

Was Ethel aware of the extra cash, money that enabled them to have household help and live in more comfort than her youngest brother? Or did Julius do as he was bid and keep it for an emergency? There is no way of knowing how much of this meeting, if any, Julius shared with Ethel. Yet if David knew that Julius had "friends" who could help out financially from time to time, it is unlikely that Ethel, whom Julius trusted, did not also have some knowledge, even though Feklisov never met her.

•   •   •

Extra cash was little help in Ethel's continuing battles with Michael. Helene Elitcher caught a glimpse of how seriously Ethel took her duties as a mother on the only occasion the two young women met, Christmastime in 1946. The evening began with a small dinner gathering at a New York restaurant where the Elitchers were joined by Julius, but not Ethel, who, pregnant again, was at home babysitting Michael. The group was completed by Julius's closest CCNY friend, Morton Sobell, and his new wife. Helen Sobell was a former teacher, member of the Young Communist League, and scientist who had worked as a technician for the US Bureau of Standards during the war. She had a daughter from her previous unhappy marriage to another Communist, Clarence Darrow Gurewitz, who came to live with her and Morton. William Perl and Joel Barr, both former CCNY classmates of Julius's, completed the party—a close-knit young group of engineers with Communist sympathies, most of whom were part of Julius Rosenberg's "spy ring."

Like Ethel and Julius, the Elitchers also had a baby. "The reason I mention it," Helene later told the grand jury in 1950, "is that it helps me to remember—it helps me to place it in time, because we were looking for *Evenflo* bottles, which were hard to get; there was a shortage at that time, and we would drop into drug stores any time we passed one, to ask if they had any, so I remember that."

After dinner, they ended up at the Rosenbergs' Monroe Street apartment in Knickerbocker Village: "There I met Ethel, Julius's wife, for the first and only time," Helene later recalled. She said she remembered the season because there was both a small Christmas tree and a Chanukah menorah—the two holidays generally occur at approximately the same time—and the discussion was about how to celebrate these two holidays, if you have Jewish kids.

That is, do you honor both holidays, or does it confuse the children, if they are Jewish, to celebrate Christmas for them as Christmas, or would it be better to celebrate just Chanukah alone; or, if you are not particularly religiously inclined, and let us say would not celebrate Chanukah yourself, do you let Chanukah go by the board, and celebrate Christmas because it has become a sort of national holiday?

Helene had a particularly vivid recollection of this discussion

because the two bachelors [Perl and Barr] were so sure of themselves, and all the married people with kids were so damned unsure of themselves, which would of course have been the camp into which Ethel fell. The bachelors had the feeling that you didn't have to worry too much about what the kids thought— they said, why do you worry about that? If it comes Christmas, it is Christmas, and you don't bother about it . . . and here we all had been reading the best on the subject—you know, Gesell[*] and so on—and I had a brand new baby and was sure I was going to run into a million and ten problems and I was trying to prepare myself unto the nth degree and they were very blasé about it.[15]

What is striking about Helene's stories is the picture that emerges of a group of young friends, most of whom had worked in government jobs during the war rather than serving abroad in the military, having fun in

---

[*] Arnold Gesell, a popular child psychologist widely read at the time, was considered one of the main proponents of permissiveness in the mother-child relationship.

postwar New York. They considered themselves patriotic, yet were aware that in helping Soviet Russia, albeit a wartime ally and in their eyes still a friend, they were acting outside the law. This group perfectly expressed the mood of the times that, as an entire issue of *Life* magazine on March 29, 1943, made clear, encouraged ordinary Americans to see the USSR as a new country still finding its way. "When we take account of what the USSR has accomplished in the 20 years of its existence we can make allowances for certain shortcomings, however deplorable," *Life* editorialized. But in general their thinking remained in this groove long after Russia ceased to be an ally and by 1950 admiring the Soviet Union was a dangerous admission. As Sobell admitted later: "I was deeply troubled by the worsening state of Soviet American relations and the possible use to which the work I was doing might be put."[16]

This was a group that had strong links to Julius and the Communist Party, but saw Ethel as something of an outsider. When she attempted to join in, her focus was almost entirely on discussions of babies and worries about how to be a better mother. Helen and Morton Sobell were also conscious of how all-consuming child psychology was for Ethel at a time of widespread belief in self-improvement books, especially on the subject of mothering. It was almost a new science for many women trying in the postwar world to be better than their own, often first-generation, immigrant parents. One of the best known of these was by the American pediatrician who was to become a household name the world over, Dr. Benjamin Spock. Dr. Spock's *Baby and Child Care*, first published in 1946, went on to sell 50 million copies in forty-two languages and clearly reflected the hunger of a generation of mothers, managing mostly without any household help, to be more successful parents. Spock, a left-winger in political matters, never afraid to buck the mainstream, told mothers they were probably doing better than they thought they were. He aimed to give them confidence by telling them: "You know more than you think you do."[17] This went against the prevailing orthodoxy of the previous generation, who had been trained to believe that the best way to prepare a child to be strong in a harsh world was not to pick up a crying baby and give it a hug or kiss but to leave it to cry, a philosophy with which Spock loudly disagreed.

Ethel never talked about studying Dr. Spock's ideas but it seems inconceivable, given her enormous appetite and interest in such matters, that she was not aware of them, either from talking to other mothers, from her reading of *Parents* magazine, or from her social workers. His were the ideas she was trying to espouse yet she felt, at least in her dealings with a headstrong and challenging baby such as Michael, that she was not succeeding.

Yet, however unsure Ethel felt as a mother, the likelihood is that they decided to try for a second child, a clear indication that she and Julius must have harbored a degree of optimism about their future. The nation that emerged victorious from World War Two believed that the postwar future offered more affluence for all. The aspiration to own your own home in which to raise a family, the raising usually done by a stay-at-home mother living in the suburbs, was a common experience for most parents of what became known as the baby boom generation. Ethel and Julius were part of this consumer-focused society, which saw a comfortable home, centered around happy children, as an accessible goal for all. They too were aspirational and did not see any contradiction in being loyal Americans while believing in Communist ideals. But the tide of mainstream America was swiftly turning against them; almost as soon as the war was over the domestic coalition that Roosevelt had put together started to come apart. In the 1946 elections, although Truman remained president, the Democrats suffered heavy losses as Republicans took control of both the House of Representatives and the Senate. George Murphy, an actor, singer, and dancer turned politician, captured the popular mood when he told a Republican fundraising event: "Party labels don't mean anything anymore. You can draw a line right down the middle. On one side are Americans, on the other are the Communists and Socialists."[18]

The Sobells also recalled from various social gatherings with the Rosenbergs that "Ethel was interested in child psychology, as was Helen, and this became an important topic of conversation when we all got together."[19] Revealingly, when conversation turned to politics, art, and the sciences, the Sobells considered that while Ethel may have been "more soft spoken" than Julius, "she expressed herself with a certain tentativeness which belied the fact that by this time her ideas were actually well formulated."[20] Yet she must have looked at these two other wives, both college graduates, with some envy. Helen Sobell was, like her, the daughter of Yiddish-speaking immigrants and yet Helen had overcome childhood polio, even more debilitating than scoliosis, to study physics at Rensselaer Polytechnic Institute and was about to embark on a MSc degree at Columbia University.

Quite why Ethel did not pick up the threads of her early ambition to go to college and have a career is not clear. Her mother, amid the general economic gloom of the day, had thwarted these ambitions initially in 1931, but she might have considered returning now, as a postwar mature student. Childcare arrangements, especially for a demanding infant, might have been a constricting factor—had she enjoyed a better relationship with Tessie, this would not have been such a problem—and worry about the general financial situation of the family and putting Julius under greater pressure to provide may have been another. But more likely this was an inner constriction, a result of having imbibed the overall ethos of the fifties. Several women who came of age during World War Two recalled in later years why, once the children arrived, they did not pursue career aspirations but sank into domesticity, cooking, cleaning, baby-minding, and sewing. They were told that unless it was an absolute necessity to work, doing so was demeaning for husbands. More important was to show how successful the husband was by not working and bringing up happy children in clean homes with balanced meals. Although Ethel never wavered in her political beliefs, she was like so many women of her generation, torn by the twin ideals of caring for her children and supporting her husband, which she viewed as her principal role in life.

Ethel's story is not unusual and is closely paralleled by that of Hilda Bernstein, a South African political activist and Communist Party member, also born (in London) in 1915 to Russian Jewish immigrant parents. Hilda, like Ethel, intelligent but largely self-taught, had left school and formal education behind at a young age; in Hilda's case sixteen. Like Ethel she learned "never to define herself by race or religion but as members of the human race."[21]

Yet by the time Hilda and her husband, Rusty, were arrested suddenly at 3 a.m. one night at their home in Johannesburg in 1960, her four children were older and so Toni, her sixteen-year-old daughter, was left in charge of the other three. Hilda was "lucky": she spent only three months in prison. But, as she explained years later, "this was the worst time for me, not because the prison conditions were so bad—disgusting food, chipped plates and mattresses without sheets—but I really suffered from being without my children . . . I couldn't bear even to think of them . . . I had wanted them, they were not accidents and I felt responsible for them." After the arrest Hilda escaped into exile in London, where she spent hours contemplating the price her children had paid for their parents' determination to fight for social justice, and was struck by depression, "a breakdown of sorts and suffered a real loss of identity." What mattered to Hilda was being a mother, but if imprisonment meant she was not able to look after her children properly then surely she was a failed mother? And yet, whenever Hilda had been pressed by others to consider the fate of her children, she would reply: "I do. In the long run the most important thing as far as the children are concerned is what sort of country they will have to live in."[22]

Both Hilda and Ethel, deeply compassionate women with a drive for social justice, agonized over how their political activities might impact the needs of their children. In Ethel's case she had given up activism of any sort and was concentrating on motherhood, probably through a fear of abandoning her children, but also as a matter of identity. Ethel identified as a mother and homemaker, and being a good one really mattered to her.

* * *

On May 14, 1947, the Rosenbergs' second son, Robert Harry, always called "Robby," was born. The name was chosen "in loving memory" of Julius's father. From the first day he was an easier child than four-year-old Michael, and Ethel enjoyed breastfeeding him. But the Knickerbocker Village apartment now seemed less palatial with two children to share it. Ethel and Julius decided to give up their bedroom for the boys and sleep on the sofa in the living room, an arrangement, however practical, guaranteed to encourage a feeling that in this household the children's needs were paramount. Meanwhile, Michael, like many firstborn, responded badly to the arrival of a little brother. From the time he could talk, Michael had always called his mother "Ethel" as part of her belief in children's rights. Her lack of authority over Michael was now amplified as their battle of wills after Robby's birth became more entrenched than ever. Michael recalled in adulthood that "if I fussed over meals she rarely made me leave the table; instead, she tried to make a game out of eating. I was a wild lion and she a lion tamer who danced around me and fed me scraps of meat as I 'performed.'"[23] According to Michael, she "generally dealt with me by giving me what I wanted,"[24] and tried her best not to reprimand him, sticking to the advice she had imbibed from progressive childcare experts like Dr. Dorothy Whipple.

Despite the stress she was under, which regularly resulted in back pain or migraines or both, Ethel decided to take a special course for teaching children music at the Bank Street School in Greenwich Village. She wanted to help Michael learn the piano and the school's progressive ethos chimed with her views. Founded in 1916, Bank Street aimed to educate "the whole child—the entire emotional, social, physical, and intellectual being—while valuing and reinforcing the child's integrity as learner, teacher, and classmate." The school saw in education "the opportunity to build a better society," which also met with Ethel's approval.

Her neighbors at Knickerbocker Village recalled how "music was a part of their daily home life with Ethel singing and playing on their old piano, songs for the boys and songs for 'Julie.' Records were almost a nightly ritual before the children were put to bed . . . ranging from Mother Goose to the Star Spangled Banner."[25] As soon as Michael was old enough, Ethel began studying the guitar in order to teach this instrument to him.*

On Saturdays it was Julius's turn and he would take Michael out for hours riding the subway, going to Bronx Park—a favorite—or the zoo,

---

* The strategy clearly worked as Michael has played the guitar all his life.

walking around Penn Station, or playing baseball, imaginative activities that did not cost much but that offered time to talk and explore together. Michael also recalled playing "a labor versus capitalist version of cowboys and Indians, which his father had invented and which involved crawling on all fours pretending he was a bridge while Julius pretended the blocks he rolled across Michael's back were American and Russian convoys . . . When a German 'convoy' arrived Michael would stand up. 'Hey,' Julius would say. 'Shake hands, bridge. You killed the fascists.'"[26] As Ethel would show in her earliest letters to Julius from prison, she not only loved him deeply but believed he was a wonderful father. After seeing him briefly in court she wrote:

> My dearest darling Julie, there were so many other things I might have said so let me say them now, my dear one . . . I couldn't ever say enough what pride and love and deep regard for you as an individual I feel. What you wrote to me about ourselves as a family and what the family means to you made my eyes fill. And yet at the same time there came to me such an abiding sense of faith and joy, such a sure knowledge of the rich meaning our lives have held that I was suddenly seized with an overwhelming desire to see you and say it to you and kiss you with all my heart.[27]

It was around this time, shortly after Robby's birth, that one of Ethel's closest women friends, Vivian Glassman, came up with a suggestion. During the war, Vivian had worked with Julius at the Army Signal Corps Engineering Laboratories in Fort Monmouth. Later, the FBI tried to prove that Vivian had belonged to Julius's "Soviet spy ring." Vivian, however, insisted that she and Ethel had first met in 1945 when she was canvassing on behalf of the socialist American Labor Party and knocked on Ethel's door at Knickerbocker Village. What is certain is that by 1948 Vivian and Ethel were good friends.

Vivian was a social worker with an interest in psychiatry, which was not something in which good Communists were expected to indulge since it was considered bourgeois and encouraged an examination of the individual rather than society. Nonetheless, Vivian decided she must talk frankly to Ethel about issues that were evidently threatening to engulf her friend now that she was the mother of two small boys. Vivian could see that Ethel needed professional help and urged her to make an appointment at the Jewish Board of Guardians, a charity that offered child therapy. In the autumn of 1948 Ethel agreed to apply.

There was a waiting list and Ethel had to promise a serious commitment, which she did. Fees at the Child Guidance Clinic were assessed on ability to pay and, based on income or lack of it from Julius's business, Ethel was accepted at the end of 1949 for a course of sessions. She was fortunate to be assigned a young woman therapist called Elizabeth Phillips, a graduate from Columbia University who had grown up in a single-parent family and, like Ethel, finished high school at fifteen. She became radicalized after spending three of the war years in Hawaii working with Japanese-American prisoners incarcerated in camps there, an experience that fostered in her a strong sympathy with anyone who she considered had suffered injustice. She believed she could help Ethel.

"I saw her in relation to Michael. He was my client. She was having trouble handling him and I could immediately see why," Elizabeth recalled with great clarity almost seventy years later:

> The first couple of sessions we used various kinds of play therapy and in those days we used "dictaphones" to record the sessions. Michael wanted to speak into it himself and play with it, and at the beginning we spent the sessions arguing as to why he couldn't use it. I let him do it for a couple of sessions.
>
> Some afternoons at 5 p.m., after the session, I had a headache, so I could identify with Ethel, and I was not the mother! He was so clever in what he was doing to get his own way. I would guess he was near genius level. We argued every session and he was running circles around me. But I had an advantage; time to think about things before the next session.

Although six-year-old Michael was her "client," Elizabeth also saw Ethel separately for one hour a week as part of the counseling. On these occasions she often brought Robby, now two, who waited patiently in another room while his mother saw Elizabeth. She recalled that Ethel craved this time alone with someone she looked up to and felt comfortable telling about the events of the week and how she had coped:

> She was so eager to learn and appreciative of being in a situation where she could talk about the kinds of things that bothered her . . . she was bright but had talents that were not ever supported . . . Ethel came from a background where she was not the cherished child . . . so she wanted to bring up her own kids in a way that would not inhibit them and would show her love for them. She gave in to them to show how much she loved them and that was where the trouble began . . . She wanted to be friends with her kids.

Elizabeth concluded:

> What I am telling you is not a criticism of Ethel. We know how important the first year of life is and she must have given those two boys so much in the very early years that it lasted them throughout the rest of their lives. But you have to create boundaries, and one of the things I did as a therapist was to give her confidence as a mother in her own instincts. She had to be able to stand up and say "no" and make that stick in places where it was important. She had to find ways to avoid locking horns with her kid. Isn't that the story of every mother's life? I could help her with a plan. She was not far off getting it right.[28]

Looking back on his relationship with Ethel, Michael recognized in adulthood that "I was tense and becoming very difficult to control. There may even have been some school problems when I was in second grade."[29]

Michael accepted that he was a demanding child who "had a tremendous sense of being the center of the universe." Ethel encouraged that, yet even so felt she sometimes failed, and on rare occasions her patience dried up in the face of Michael's "stubborn persistence."[30] He recalled one such occasion a few years after Robby's birth when "I tried against her orders to phone a friend who was away at summer camp . . . I picked up the phone to get the number. My mother replaced the phone on the hook and spanked me on the butt." Michael tried again and braved repeated spankings for this activity, not understanding that long-distance phone calls were a luxury for people like his parents and pushing her further "against her nonexistent limits."[31]

Ethel's acute awareness of the emotional warmth lacking in her own childhood was reinforced by the death in the hospital of her seventy-eight-year-old father in March 1949, after slipping and falling on an icy sidewalk. Barney Greenglass had never been sufficiently outspoken in his support of Ethel, but he had been close to his only daughter when she was young. She missed him now, as she felt family support sliding away from her amid all her other worries about being a good mother. The Greenglasses were so hard up when Barney died that Ethel's brothers Sam, Bernie, and David borrowed from Julius, who managed to come up with the money.

Barney's death was the catalyst for Ethel to consult a psychiatrist herself, possibly strengthening her drive to ensure her sons had a better childhood than she had endured. This time the Jewish Board of Guardians would not pay. Her need was so compelling that she scraped together the funds to afford three visits a week with Dr. Saul Miller, who was still completing his training as a psychoanalyst and therefore charged greatly reduced fees at his Upper West Side clinic. According to Michael, writing as an adult many years later, Ethel "was anxious and needed someone to hold on to while she sought to discover the sources of her anxiety." Michael interviewed Dr. Miller for the book he and Robert co-wrote about their parents, *We Are Your Sons,* first published in 1975. He concluded:

> In his [Miller's] opinion the root of the problem was her relationship with her immediate family. She felt she was "looked down upon" by her mother and brothers. Her mother had always

dominated the family and treated her brothers as the consequential human beings. My mother never felt her own mother really loved her. Though she was burdened by the demands we placed on her, our mother's problem was not related to the presence of children. Further the doctor remembered nothing to indicate that her marriage even slightly contributed to her unrest. She felt she had been short changed in the family relationships encountered since childhood.[32]

Ethel's early biographer, Ilene Philipson, also interviewed Saul Miller in the mid-1980s, describing him as having something of the European about him since he had received his medical education in Vienna and Lausanne. He was a short, stocky man in his early forties when he first met Ethel.

"From the start, Ethel was a 'good patient,'" reported Philipson, by which Miller meant that Ethel was keen.[33] Neighbors at Knickerbocker recalled that Ethel often looked smarter these days and was frequently busy, although they did not know the reason; she was rushing off for an appointment on the Upper West Side, where she consulted Miller:

She spoke freely, could recount her personal history in great detail, remembered her dreams, and never missed appointments. She seemed to be psychologically minded and was quick to point out that she believed her problems stemmed from her family of origin. She called her mother a "witch," felt that her brothers had "denigrated her," and although she liked her father the best, she thought of him as "namby-pamby."

Ethel also talked to Miller about what it was like to grow up in such abject poverty, which she resented fiercely when it meant that her brothers were given better educational opportunities. However, she did not discuss poverty in general in political terms nor disclose her sympathy for the American Communist Party. Miller said, according to Philipson, "she never spoke of anything pertaining to that organization or its activities."

Ethel quickly came to trust Dr. Miller, seeing both him and Julius as "saviors." In her view, as disclosed to Miller, both were "intelligent, empathetic men (not 'namby-pambies') who actively valued and respected her, and took her side in her internal and external battles with her family."[34]

There is another possible reason for Ethel's visits: her desire for self-improvement. "Had she lived longer, I think she might have become a therapist herself," Elizabeth Phillips came to believe. Elizabeth recognized that while Ethel had remained unwavering in her belief in Communism, she had started to think freely and independently through her psychotherapy sessions. It was this aspect of her intellectual development that became her predominant interest in the year before her arrest, as her other world with Julius and his failing business started to crumble.

•   •   •

Julius's financial situation was parlous by 1949. When David's wife Ruth cut her leg in an accident, they struggled to pay the doctor's bills and asked Julius for a loan. He refused, saying he was short of cash and would have to ask a friend. By now, David had abandoned Pitt Machine Products for a regular job working shifts at the Arma Engineering factory in Brooklyn, which manufactured aircraft parts. Toward the end of 1949, David stopped by the shop one afternoon to ask Julius to pay him out of his outstanding shares in the business. Once again, David found himself rebuffed by Julius, who did not have the necessary cash available.

According to David, Julius urged him instead to sign over the stock and wait patiently for Julius to pay him as soon as he could. David refused. Julius then warned David that he, David, and Ruth were "hot," suggesting the authorities had finally found evidence of David's espionage at Los Alamos during the war and that the net was closing in. Over coffee at a nearby luncheonette, Julius told David he should get passports and visas ready so that he and Ruth could slip out of the country, first to France and from there to Communist Eastern Europe.[35] David was shocked and knew he could not share this plan with Ruth, who was pregnant and would not want to leave New York.

Four

Unraveling

The year 1949 ended bleakly for Ethel, but worse was to come in 1950. Her life began to unravel in late January when the FBI came to interview David Greenglass at his Lower East Side apartment in connection with some uranium-238 thefts from Los Alamos. David lied to FBI Agent Lawrence Spillane, claiming that while he remembered seeing these hollow, golf ball–size hemispheres, he had never entered the tube alloy shop where they were refined. In fact he had sent his stolen uranium sample home in a sock, where it was still hidden in a cupboard. The day after the interview David hurled the sock with its contents into the nearby East River, without being entirely confident it would disappear without trace.

David immediately recounted what had happened to his brother-in-law, Julius. According to the Greenglass version of events, Julius urged him repeatedly to make plans to leave the country. But David and especially Ruth, as she was expecting the couple's second baby, did not want to flee the United States.

A week later, on February 3, 1950, Klaus Fuchs, the German-born anti-Nazi Communist scientist who had worked at Los Alamos on the development of America's atomic bomb, was arrested in England and almost immediately admitted that he was a Soviet spy. In 1933 Fuchs's father, a prominent and outspoken Protestant theologian, had been imprisoned by the Nazis, and after his mother and sister committed suicide Fuchs had made his way to Britain. He endured a short spell as an enemy alien, but was soon made a British citizen and in that capacity traveled to Los Alamos as part of the British mission involved in cooperating with the US Atomic Energy Commission working there. After the war, Fuchs returned to England and continued his work on the British atomic bomb project as head of the Physics Department at the Harwell Atomic Energy Research Establishment.

There are conflicting views as to how and why suspicion fell on Fuchs. The US government was shocked to detect that the Soviet Union had exploded its first atomic bomb in Kazakhstan on August 29, 1949. Two months later, in October 1949, the world looked bleaker still to American eyes when China finally became a Communist country after Mao Zedong ended years of civil war and declared the creation of the People's Republic of China. Washington had not expected that Stalin could possess nuclear weapons knowledge so soon. General Leslie Groves, the United States Army Corps of Engineers officer who had directed the Manhattan Project, had given a public talk in New York in March 1946 where he told his audience that the US did not need to worry about the Russians ever making a bomb. "Why," he said smiling, to thunderous applause, "those people can't even make a jeep."[1]

Many in the US political and military establishment believed the Russians must have been passed secret information. Under interrogation, Fuchs rapidly confessed and, following a hasty trial, was sentenced to fourteen years in a British prison.*

Fuchs revealed that he had used an American courier known to him only as "Raymond." By May 23, 1950, the FBI had identified and arrested Harry Gold, a middle-aged Jewish chemist from Philadelphia, as "Raymond." Gold in turn described an unnamed young soldier at Los Alamos with whom he had had contact at Albuquerque in 1945. According to Gold, this soldier had been a draftsman, machinist, or electrician, probably no older than twenty-five, "five feet seven inches, sturdily built, with dark brown or black curly hair, a snub nose and a wide mouth."[2] Gold also thought the man was probably Jewish and recently married and that his wife's name was Ruth.

---

* He served only nine and on release went immediately to live in East Germany.

By June the FBI had enough information to link Fuchs via Gold to Ethel's twenty-eight-year-old brother David, an army machinist, part of the Special Engineering Detachment (SED) that had worked at Los Alamos during 1944–5, and they knew exactly where he lived from the interview in January. In Moscow, Soviet intelligence was increasingly alarmed by the arrest of Fuchs and David's interview by the FBI. They now assigned new code names to three of the protagonists: "Zinger" for David, "Ida" for Ruth, and "King" for Julius—tellingly, there was no code name for Ethel—but otherwise simply watched and waited as the Greenglasses lived through their own private drama.[3]

February 1950 felt especially raw in New York, and the Greenglasses' shabby apartment at 265 Rivington Street had no central heating. It was often so bitterly cold that the couple sat in overcoats. One freezing evening, David returned late from work, turned on the bedroom gas heater, and left it on all night. The next day Ruth woke first, leaving her husband to sleep on while she looked after their three-and-a-half-year-old son Steven. By midmorning Ruth—now six months pregnant—decided it was time to wake David. Leaning over to shake him, the bottom of her flannel nightdress caught the bars of the heater. She screamed as her nightdress swiftly went up in flames, which finally woke David, who instinctively tried to beat out the fire with his bare hands and then smothered his wife in the bedcovers. While David managed to extinguish the flames, the charred nightdress pressed against Ruth's body caused devastating first, second- and third-degree burns with blistering all over her body.

David rushed Ruth to Gouverneur Municipal Hospital, the nineteenth-century institution built specifically to look after residents of the Lower East Side, where it was discovered that she desperately needed a blood transfusion. But Ruth's blood type was the relatively rare O-negative, which the hospital did not store. David, his own badly burned hands heavily bandaged, now made an urgent and highly emotional appeal for blood on New York's WOR Radio. In the course of his interview David explained that he and Ruth could not afford a steam-heated apartment and that, although they had applied for public housing, they had been rejected, apparently on the grounds that others were worse off.

Ruth pulled through and on May 16 gave birth to a girl they called Barbara. Mother and baby had to remain in the hospital for a further week and Ruth did not return home with her new daughter until May 23.

The following day Julius came around to their apartment with a copy of the latest edition of New York's *Herald Tribune*, to make sure David and Ruth understood the seriousness of developments. The headline on the front page read: "US Arrests Go-Between for Soviets in Fuchs Case."

Harry Gold was now publicly named and the article referred to an encounter between Gold and Fuchs in 1945 in Santa Fe, New Mexico, the nearest town to Los Alamos. Later, both David and Ruth maintained that they did not recognize from Gold's photograph that he was the man they had met in Albuquerque—a little farther from Los Alamos, where Ruth was then living—on June 3, 1945, the man who had given them $500 in exchange for information about research at the site as well as the names of the top scientists who worked there. Yet, based on Gold's description, by June 2 the FBI had identified David Greenglass, army serial no. 32 88 24 73, as Gold's contact inside Los Alamos.

According to David, on Sunday, June 4, 1950, Julius delivered a package of money, urging him once again to leave the country. David described the accompanying instructions as "a whole rigmarole [of] how to get out of the country and he asked me to memorize it and also he gave me a list of the route of how we were getting out, getting to the Mexican border . . . He told me he would give me a lot more money."[4] David said he was only half attentive to Julius because he had no intention of leaving, even though throughout the spring and summer of 1950 anti-Communist paranoia was rising to a fever pitch as unscrupulous politicians such as Senator McCarthy as well as FBI director J. Edgar Hoover regularly made speeches taking advantage of the increasingly grim world situation. Hoover had been instrumental in founding the FBI as a crime-busting agency in 1935, before becoming its first director. However, his own re-mit went far beyond fighting crime. He was a law enforcement officer who used, or abused, the extraordinary power he had built up to fight political activists and dissenters, arguably driven by deep political prejudice and by what many believed was his own repressed sexual drive as a homosexual.

In May 1950 Hoover gave a speech to New York State's Grand Lodge of Masons, declaring that "files had recently revealed there were 55,000 actual Communists in our midst and 500,000 hypocrites and moral swindlers. These groups work on a mass influence basis by constantly gnawing away like termites at the very foundations of American society. Then when caught they seek the protection of the freedoms which they constantly seek to destroy."[5]

Hoover's accusations of the numbers of Communists working in government touched a raw nerve in America at large.

The one key event of 1950 that seemed to confirm both conspiracy theories and genuine anxieties about nests of "homegrown Commies" penetrating the US government was the conviction of Alger Hiss. On January 21, Hiss, the patrician, well-educated, and well-connected former government lawyer and State Department official who had helped create the United Nations in the aftermath of World War Two, was found guilty of perjury charges relating to Soviet espionage. Hiss had been one of those named by Elizabeth Bentley when she defected. But for two years he had seemed utterly convincing in his confident, arrogant way as he denied ever having been a Communist. Now a jury had decided he was guilty and he was sentenced to a five-year prison term.

It took only days following his conviction for an emboldened Senator McCarthy to declare melodramatically that he had a list of 205 Communist Party members "known to the US Secretary of State . . . who nevertheless are still working and shaping the policy of the State Department." The claim was false, but that mattered little to McCarthy, a man well used to lying. He had claimed to have flown on thirty-two combat missions in the war though he had flown on no more than two, and that he walked with a limp from "ten pounds of shrapnel" when he had simply hurt his foot at a party.

Waving a paper in his hand, he asserted on February 9, 1950, during a speech at Wheeling, West Virginia: "Today we are engaged in a final, all-out battle between Communistic atheism and Christianity. The modern champions of Communism have selected this as the time. And, ladies and gentlemen, the chips are down—they are truly down."[6]

His message that the Democrats were soft on Communism and that sinister forces were at work against the country (and had been since Yalta) landed on ground that was to become increasingly fertile over the next four years. McCarthyism was born.

•   •   •

If the Greenglasses had not been so enveloped in their own private tragedies they might have had a better grasp of the anxiety of many American citizens in the summer of 1950, some of whom feared an atomic attack on the American continent itself. For the moment, David and Ruth, unable to move beyond their personal drama, simply stashed Julius's money in the chimney flue. But soon afterward they gave it for safekeeping to Ruth's brother-in-law, Louis Abel, a significant indication that David was now removing himself from contact with his sister and aligning himself instead with his wife and her family. David decided that his priority must be to look after his sick wife and that the cash would at the very least enable him to take a six-week leave of absence from his job at Arma Engineering. But on Monday, June 5, Arma turned down his request, narrowing his options further. Even with the FBI on his tail David nonetheless thought he might be able to hide in the Catskill Mountains, in upstate New York. When pressed years later by a reporter on *60 Minutes* as to why he thought this would have been a good idea, David replied: "I know the Catskills quite well."[7]

The next few weeks were fraught at various levels. The Greenglasses realized they were under surveillance after Ruth noticed a van from the Acme Construction Company parked outside their tenement building. She checked the name and found that no such business existed. By June 13 her burns had become infected and she had a severely swollen leg. She was taken by emergency ambulance back to Gouverneur Hospital, leaving David in charge of a baby and a toddler. In between visiting his in-laws, the Printzes, to keep them informed about their daughter's progress and visiting Ruth in hospital, David also went to bank some of the cash that he maintained Julius had given him. But he seems to have been dazed, with no clear plan, as if unaware of the seriousness of his and Ruth's predicament.

On June 15, two FBI agents again arrived at 265 Rivington Street and, in spite of having no search warrant, took away various personal items, photographs, college textbooks, and a bundle of handwritten letters between the childhood sweethearts, Ruth and Dave. Once a grandmother had been brought in to babysit, the agents drove David downtown to FBI headquarters, located in the Federal Court House in Foley Square, "to continue the conversation," as they politely put it to him.

Later that day Gold identified David and Ruth from a 1945 photograph as the man and woman he had met in Albuquerque. Immediately after David was told of Gold's identification he stopped his denials and confessed his guilt. At 1:32 a.m. the following morning David was placed under arrest, shortly to be charged with conspiracy to commit espionage on behalf of the Soviet Union. He phoned Louis Abel, asking him to engage a lawyer and to tell Ruth—still in the hospital—not to worry.

On June 16, Julius was surprised by officers while shaving early in the morning—before details of David's arrest had leaked out. He was swiftly brought in to Foley Square for a bout of questioning. During a six-hour interview, interrupted by a phone call from Ethel, Julius robustly denied everything and asked to talk to a lawyer. The FBI agent complied with his request to call the office of Victor Rabinowitz, the lawyer who had helped him in 1945 when he had been dismissed from his job working for the Army Signal Corps for allegedly failing to disclose membership in the Communist Party. Rabinowitz was not in, but a colleague in the office who took the call asked Julius if he was under arrest. When his FBI interviewer confirmed (perhaps an indication that they lacked evidence) that he was not, Julius made a 5 p.m. appointment to consult with the lawyer, politely put on his hat, and walked out. The following day Rabinowitz passed Julius over to a colleague, Emanuel Bloch, a radical attorney and well-known defender of left-wing causes. After the two of them talked on a park bench and then over coffee in an Eighth Street restaurant, he agreed to take on the case. Bloch did not immediately realize its severity.

Meanwhile, O. John Rogge, the lawyer Louis Abel had found to defend David (and Ruth if necessary), along with Rogge's colleague Robert Goldman, had their first meeting with David at the Greenglasses'

Rivington Street apartment. Ruth had been released from the hospital but was still bedbound. Several relatives also crowded in to offer support— Bernie, their war-hero older brother; Sam, their half brother; Tessie's brother Izzy Feit, and Louis Abel. Ruth had recently given birth and was still in pain from her burns. She was openly terrified that she might be arrested and separated from her children. She therefore volunteered to the lawyers insights into her marriage in the hope that revealing David as mentally unstable might be a useful defense. She had known David since she was ten years old, Ruth explained, marrying him at eighteen; her husband "had a tendency to hysteria, at other times he would become delirious and once, when he had the grippe, he ran nude through the hallways shrieking of elephants and lead pants . . . he would say things were so even if they were not. He talked of suicide as if he were a character in movies but she didn't think he would do it."[8]

Rogge discouraged this line of defense and outlined what he saw as the best options available to them. These included a proposal of cooperation whereby David would help the government prove its case against someone else as opposed to merely talking about his own involvement. In return, presumably, for Ruth's immunity from prosecution, Goldman noted that the Greenglass and Printz families had "a long discussion of JR"[9] at that meeting. As the two families found themselves plunged into discussions with lawyers for the first time in their lives, the first meetings any of these people had had with such senior American establishment figures, they became aghast at the consequences being spelled out to them and closed ranks. Support for Ethel and Julius swiftly ebbed away.

Why, during June, did Julius and Ethel not realize that David and Ruth would shift as much blame as possible onto Julius and try to leave the country themselves while they could? Alexander Feklisov, the Soviet case officer who had handled both Julius Rosenberg and Klaus Fuchs, wrote in his memoirs that Julius was so shaken by Ruth's accident and concerned about her pregnancy that he simply "couldn't abandon his sister-in-law."[10] Sam Roberts, the *New York Times* journalist who in 1996 tracked down and interviewed David Greenglass, also noted that concern for Ruth and belief in family loyalty played a part in Julius's inertia. But Julius's unfounded confidence that there was no evidence against him played a role too.

Julius's new attorney, Emanuel Bloch, was reassuring. Bloch's experience was defending prominent left-wingers or Communist sympathizers facing cases involving civil rights abuses. A native New Yorker, not yet fifty when he took on the case, Bloch was well dressed and well educated, having graduated first from City College, like Julius, followed by three years at Columbia Law School, where he gained his LLB degree. He worked as an attorney in New York City before being called up to serve in the US Army from 1942 until he was granted an honorable discharge a year later. He was married, not happily, childless and, according to the FBI file on him, a long-standing and "well known Communist Party speaker in Upper Manhattan in the 1930s." An informer told the FBI that "he recalled Bloch as openly indicating he was a Communist in his speeches and by his close association with known Communists."[11] In spite of his strong sympathies with Julius and Ethel, Manny Bloch was a civil lawyer, not a criminal lawyer, and had scant experience of trials of any sort. He agreed to help, convinced at this point that this would be "just another routine case."[12] However, a military crisis in Asia was about to make the case anything but routine, as US paranoia about the Soviet threat reached unprecedented levels.

On June 25, 1950, Communist North Korea, supported by the Soviet Union, invaded the South, which was supported by the United States. Within two days US forces were involved in a conflict that many feared might lead to a war either with the Soviet Union, now with access to its own atomic bomb, or newly Communist China. Suddenly, a Communist takeover of the world no longer seemed an irrational fantasy.

"It looks like World War III is here—I hope not—but we must meet whatever comes—and we will," President Truman noted in his diary.[13] Truman was determined to learn the lessons of history, one of which, he concluded, was that the situation he was facing now was similar to appeasement of Hitler and Mussolini in the 1930s. "I felt certain that if South Korea was allowed to fall, Communist leaders would be emboldened to override nations closer to our own shores. If the Communists were permitted to force their way into the Republic of Korea without opposition from the free world, no small nation would have the courage to resist threat and aggression by stronger Communist neighbors."[14] The Korean War was for many not just a war to prevent Communism but a war to protect the American way of life, a war in which nearly every day American soldiers were dying, and a war that many believed might never have happened if Russia had not felt strengthened by possession of atomic weapons. And it was a war that began disastrously for the Americans as the North Koreans were a formidable foe, not to be underestimated. In the first week as many as 3,000 American troops were dead, wounded, or missing; and by the third week of combat, of the almost 16,000 men who had been sent to fight, more than 2,400 were lost, either dead or missing.

•   •   •

In the febrile days of July following David's arrest, newspapers were reporting on the unfolding drama within the Greenglass and Rosenberg families alongside the dramatic world events, and that David Greenglass was cooperating with the government. Ethel could not fail to notice the hardening of a bitter family divide. Whenever she visited her childhood home at 64 Sheriff Street on the Lower East Side she was met with icy silence, particularly from Tessie, but also from Ruth. Neither of the Greenglass parents had ever been particularly interested in politics. They were too busy surviving. Sam Greenglass, trying to make a living selling watches, was fiercely anti-Communist and had always made fun of Ethel and Julius's beliefs. But Ethel was fond of her middle brother, Bernie, the decorated war hero. Bernie, however, was now consumed by worry over the health of his young wife, Gladys, who was dying of Hodgkin's disease, and related concerns for the future of the couple's two-year-old daughter Sharon. Ethel was fond of Gladdy, having become close to her during the war while Bernie was away fighting and Julius often absent at work. Early in July, Gladdy was released from the hospital amid high hopes that a new treatment might work. Ethel decided that she would take her children to see their aunt at her mother's house on Sheriff Street, as her two boys had not seen her for some time.

Ethel later recalled this occasion: "Well, while I was there, my sister-in-law Ruth came in and at that time I asked her how she was feeling and she said that she still had some difficulty in getting around because of the burns and then I asked, 'Well, how is Davy?' And she said 'all right,' and then she said to my mother, 'Ma, I have to pick up the baby; she is outside in the carriage near my mother's store. Goodbye,' and left very abruptly."[15]

On Saturday, July 15, Ethel went again to her mother's house in the hope that she might be able to join the family group going to visit her brother in prison. This might be construed as sisterly concern or, more likely, wifely concern on behalf of Julius, hoping she could stiffen David's resolve to deny everything. According to Ruth, Ethel brought a home-made pie and gifts for the children as an additional inducement.[16] Ethel found the house empty at first, so went to see the Printzes, who told her that Ruth and Tessie had already left to visit David. Before returning home Ethel went to Sheriff Street once more, and this time found her aunt, who had not been permitted to join the prison party (presumably a question of numbers). Ethel waited with her aunt until Ruth and her mother returned from visiting David:

> And when they came in I began to ply her with questions as to his health and how he was standing up in jail and when I might get to see him and my mother said: "Well look, Ruthie is very tired and hungry. Suppose we sit down and eat and talk later." So I did that. We sat down and had a bite to eat and afterward Ruth said that she was going to pick the child up. It was almost time for her bath, and when we got to her mother's house, to the store where everyone was with the carriage, she said; "You know it is such a nice day I think I will stay down with her another ten minutes then I will take her upstairs for a bath." So we began to walk, she and I, with the carriage around the block,

and I said, "Look Ruth I would like to know something: are you and Davey really mixed up in this horrible mess?"[17]

As Ethel continued with her account of the conversation, it became clear that Ruth was not keen on discussing the matter. "So I said to her, in order to encourage it . . . 'You know how I feel toward Davey. You know how I always felt toward him and how I have always felt toward you . . . I will stand by and help in any way that I possibly can. But I am his sister and I do have a right to know.'" Ruth responded angrily, asking: "What are you asking such silly questions for? He is not guilty and of course I am not guilty and we have hired a lawyer and we are going to fight this case because we are not guilty."

When the two women said goodbye Ethel recalled that she put her arms around her sister in-law and kissed her. "She remained rigid in my arms, didn't return the kiss, said 'Goodbye' coldly, turned on her heel and left."[18]

Ruth's response, that she and Davey were fighting the case, was fabricated, as Ethel and Julius were soon to find out. But so was Ethel's courtroom version of the conversation, maintaining that she knew nothing at all about David and Ruth's involvement. Ruth's memory of Ethel's visit and their subsequent walk around the block was that it was a naked attempt by Ethel to wring assurances from her that David would not talk. Ruth told her FBI interrogators that Ethel said: "It would only be a matter of a couple of years and in the long run we would be better off . . . She said that if David said he was innocent and Julius said he was innocent, it would strengthen their position; everybody would stand a better chance."[19]

On Monday, July 17, Julius Rosenberg was formally arrested and taken to the Federal House of Detention. Although the Justice Department now had more information provided by David and Ruth, strictly speaking the authorities still did not have enough evidence to search the Rosenbergs' small apartment. Nonetheless the FBI performed a search incidental to the arrest. This time the FBI agents ransacked the whole place and took away every photograph, letter, and bill they could get their hands on. They rifled through cupboards and drawers, took Ethel's typewriter and, when Ethel showed presence of mind by asking for their warrant and insisted on calling a lawyer, they told her to go into another room, later calling her request a "typical Communist remonstrance."[20]

Robby was sleeping during this search, but Michael was listening to his favorite radio program, *The Lone Ranger*. Only now he thought it was happening for real. Seeing Ethel's anxiety, trying to protect her children and fight for her husband's rights, the agents suggested they drive her and the children somewhere else. Where else could Ethel go? Her immediate reaction was to go to her mother for comfort. On the ride there, trying to be friendly, Michael engaged one of the agents in conversation, telling him he always listened to a radio show called *This Is Your FBI*.

But Tessie showed Ethel little sympathy. She had decided that in any battle between the Greenglasses and the Rosenbergs she would be on David and Ruth's side. Ethel knew she had to return home. She might have sought support from Julius's relations but, from now on, she said she did not want to drag others into her net. Ethel steeled herself to face the future utterly alone.

The following morning she called an impromptu press conference, summoning a group of reporters to her narrow kitchen at Monroe Street in Knickerbocker Village. There, in a sleeveless floral dress with dishcloth in hand, she protested she was totally unaware of how her husband could possibly be involved with Communist subversives. Some newspapers described her as "calm and unemotional," perhaps because she was trying not to betray her fear. She carried on with her apparent domestic duties, cutting up a chicken for the evening meal, occasionally stopping to pose and even smile for the jostling photographers. Perhaps being a good organizer, even to the extent of involving the press, was something she had learned in her youth as a trade unionist. It had worked for her once; she might have hoped it would again now. Or perhaps, with reporters banging on her door, she concluded she had no choice and it was better to show courage and invite them in.

But this was a situation in which she had lost control. The world in 1950 was far removed from the Depression era, and playing the role of an unassuming housewife, uninformed about politics and current affairs, did not convince. It was a clumsy attempt to portray herself as simply a poor 1950s American mother and homemaker, more concerned to make sure her children were fed and cared for than worrying about the "crazy charges" against her husband, which could not possibly be true. She even pointed at one stage to a stack of *Parents* magazines with page after page of advice and guidance for young mothers, hoping this would convey a silent indication of her devotion to motherhood. But she would have been better advised to keep a low profile, rather than up the ante in this way. Her statement that "neither my husband nor I have ever been Communists and we don't know any Communists"[21] was, in the event, provocative.

Why did Ethel's efforts to play the dutiful mother and housewife backfire? During World War Two large numbers of women went out to work, playing a vital role in the economy and even undertaking heavy-duty industrial jobs. But, almost at the moment the war ended, so did most employment of women: in the two years after the war approximately two million women lost their jobs. If there were now well-paid jobs to be had, then obviously they should go to the men. There was little encouragement for women from any class to pursue careers; instead they were pursued by advertisers to buy washing machines, dryers, freezers, blenders, and all the rest of the developing consumer culture on offer. They stayed home to make sure their husband's dinner was on the table as soon as he returned from work, and were encouraged to see their prime duty as keeping the family together. This should have made Ethel's tactics successful and win her sympathy. But she was not believed. Fear of Communism was the overriding emotion of the hour and so the image of a Communist wife, not telling the truth, who had allowed the family unit to be destroyed, meant that she was seen as a danger. None of this was said overtly by the male reporters who attended Ethel's botched press conference. But somehow that was the impression conveyed.

Her sister-in-law Ruth was soon dealing with the press as well. At first Ruth had not wanted to speak to any reporters at all. But Rogge urged her to, as a way of planting ideas and images in the public mind in advance of David's trial, and she was more successful than Ethel. She offered the influential anti-Communist *Jewish Daily Forward* newspaper an interview that appeared as a series of articles on August 29 and 30, and September 2. Ruth was interviewed both at home and over lunch and the resulting series portrayed her as a Jewish girl who, "aside from the misfortune into which she was drawn, we have no reason to be ashamed of."[22] She made the case that she and David had been gullible victims, sympathetic at first but led astray by the older couple, Julius and Ethel, who were ideological Communists. Ruth also pointedly described Ethel as the "dominant person" in the marriage, but in the wider family too. According to Ruth, Ethel was so blinkered that she would not "buy from a butcher or grocer unless he were an open sympathizer toward Soviet Russia. She considered everyone who was against Communism her personal enemy."[23]

In fact, David's outspoken Communist sympathies were so well known at Los Alamos that some of his fellow SEDs found him obnoxious. According to Benjamin Bederson, a Jewish physicist from the Lower East Side who, along with two others, had to share a room with David, "political arguments among the four of us gradually grew intemperate . . . Eventually they became so unpleasant that Bill [a friend of Bederson's] and I asked for and received permission to transfer to the second, newly constructed barracks."[24]

After her kitchen-sink press conference, Ethel tried to carry on as usual. She took Michael later that day for his regular session with Elizabeth Phillips, and confided that she was indeed worried. In addition, Ethel was trying to keep Pitt Machine Products running. Julius was sending her detailed instructions from prison suggesting that she bill all those who owed them money and try to sell as many small parts as she could before selling the whole business.

At the same time, Ethel found she was increasingly ostracized by her neighbors. She recognized that she must take the initiative in deliberately ignoring some of her oldest friends so as not to incriminate them. When she bumped into one such friend, Betty Birnbaum, outside Ohrbach's, the inexpensive clothing store on Union Square, Betty said Ethel rebuffed her suggestion that they make a date for a visit. "She couldn't wait to get away from me . . . she was uneasy and I knew that I had better stop persisting."[25]

Julius and Ethel had no way of knowing exactly what David and Ruth were saying to Justice Department officials. But for the moment Julius remained optimistic that Ethel would not also be prosecuted, even suggesting to her that she became both secretary and participant in his legal defense: "You realize that you will be an important witness in my case so take an active role."[26] On paper, the case against Ethel was weak or nonexistent without a confession from her. But the more obstinately Julius refused to cooperate, the more the authorities were instructed "to consider every possible means to bring pressure on Rosenberg to make him talk, including consideration of additional charges being filed against [Julius] Rosenberg at Albuquerque and a careful study of the involvement of Ethel Rosenberg in order that charges can be placed against her if possible."[27]

On the day Julius was arrested, FBI investigations chief Alan H. Belmont sent a memo to assistant director "Mickey" Ladd in which he clearly stated government concern about the case. "Relative to the subject Ethel Rosenberg, Mr. McInerney [Head of the Criminal Division of the Justice Department] advised that there is insufficient evidence to issue process against her at this time." He went on to say that, according to McInerney, the evidence against Ethel depended upon the statement of Ruth Greenglass that "Ethel talked her into going to Albuquerque to see David Greenglass to see if he would cooperate with the Russians in furnishing information. Mr. McInerney requested that any additional information concerning Ethel Rosenberg be furnished the Department. He was of the opinion that it might be possible to utilize her as a lever against her husband."[28]

A memorandum by Hoover to the attorney general, Howard McGrath, two days after Julius's arrest shows that Hoover too was happy to adopt the plan as he was desperate to get Julius talking: "Proceeding against the wife," Hoover wrote, "might serve as a lever in this matter."[29]

And thus the "lever strategy" hardened in the weeks and months before the trial. In a secret memorandum of February 8, 1951, about a meeting between Department of Justice officials, members of the Congressional Joint Committee on Atomic Energy, and officials of the Atomic Energy Commission, it became clear that the lever strategy was not simply a question of including Ethel in the charges. The strategy also encompassed "the prospect of a death penalty, or getting the chair, plus that if we can convict his wife, too, and give her a stiff sentence of 25 or 30 years, that combination may serve to make this fellow disgorge and give us the information on these other individuals."

The chairman of the meeting, Senator Brien McMahon of Connecticut, commented:

"He's pretty tough, isn't he?"

US GOVERNMENT LAWYER MYLES LANE: "It is about the only thing you can use as a lever on those people."

THE CHAIRMAN: "You think what you want to do is have Greenglass divulge somehow secret information on the chance that the death penalty would then result to Rosenberg."

MR LANE: "Yes."[30]

Ruth's interview with the grand jury had not provided them with the facts they needed, despite her portrayal of Julius and Ethel as rabid Communists. On August 3 she told her interrogators how she believed both Julius and Ethel were card-carrying Communists, how they had met at a Communist club, how in December 1944 Julius had come alone to see her at her home after she had returned from Albuquerque, where she had gone for a short visit to see her husband working at Los Alamos to celebrate their wedding anniversary. Ruth said she had relayed to Julius what David knew about the set-up there, adding that Julius had been pleased at receiving this information.

Q. "Didn't you write that down on a piece of paper?"

A. "Yes I wrote that down on a piece of paper and he took it with him."

Q. "In longhand?"

A. "Yes."

David's grand jury statement, given on August 7, 1950, but revealed only in 2015, was not especially helpful for the prosecution either. He clearly disassociated Ethel from any spy ring, commenting almost testily when he was asked if Ethel tried to persuade him to stay at Los Alamos to gather more information: "I said before, and say it again, honestly this is a fact: I never spoke to my sister about this at all."[31] There was certainly no mention of Ethel doing any typing of notes to be sent to the Soviets. Yet under US law in 1950, none of what David said on this occasion was available to Julius's defense team.*

The same day, August 7, Ethel was first subpoenaed to appear before the grand jury where—again in accordance with US law at the time— she had to testify without an attorney, indeed without any legal help at all. Ethel's hearing was brief and she responded to almost all the questions by refusing to answer in case she incriminated herself by pleading the Fifth Amendment, as previously advised by her lawyer. She was not challenged and was allowed to go home after the hearing to collect both Michael and Robby from her mother's house in Sheriff Street. As soon as she walked in, Tessie and Ruth abruptly stopped talking. Ethel admired Ruth's baby daughter Barbara, but Ruth did not respond. The conversation became tense and then Tessie slammed her hand down on the table, saying: "If you don't talk you're gonna burn with your husband."[32] Ethel protested that, having lived with Julius, she knew he was not guilty and went home.

Four days later, on Friday, August 11, Ethel was summoned to her second grand jury hearing. This time, as again it was during the summer holidays and there was no school, she left the two boys with a neighbor, not daring to risk her mother's wrath once more. It was an extremely hot and humid day in the city and Ethel had dressed carefully in a pale-blue

---

* Just seven years later, following the Jencks Act of 1957, they would have had to disclose this crucial evidence to the defense.

and white polka-dot summer dress with a full, tiered skirt and a brooch at the neck; she wore white gloves, white sandals with small heels, and carried a white handbag, an outfit with which she was to be forever associated after being greeted by a battery of photographers when she arrived at the courthouse.

Sitting on the bench outside was Vivian Glassman, who had been called to testify later that day and had already admitted to knowing Ethel. But for more than an hour the two women did not acknowledge each other in any way, acting as if they were complete strangers.

Once again, when Ethel was called she repeatedly declined to answer questions on the grounds that her reply might incriminate her. She repeated that response, verbatim, thirty times. But this line of defense led to a slightly more flustered performance. On one occasion, asked about a conversation between her and Julius, Ethel declined to answer on the grounds that it was a confidential relationship. The US government lawyer, Myles Lane, explained to her that her right to refuse to answer was not valid if there was a third party present—as there had been. Ethel requested the advice of a lawyer.

"For what reason?"

"Whatever the reason might be."

"No you have to give a reason for it."

"Obviously I want something clarified."

"What do you want clarified?"

"I'd rather wait to discuss it with my counsel."

"In other words you want to discuss the answer to that question, on the grounds of privilege between you and your husband, is that right?"

"I would like the advice of counsel."

"For what reason? For what reason? You have declined to answer. I mean do you want to answer these questions. Is that why you want counsel?"

"I have a right to ask for counsel before I go . . ."

And so it went on.[33]

After a bruising confrontation in which Ethel parried and persisted in her refusal to answer without any legal advice, Lane eventually withdrew the question as to whether or not she had ever heard her husband discuss with her brother either the atomic bomb or the work he was doing at Los Alamos. But then he immediately shot back with the same question differently phrased: "Did you ever hear David Greenglass discuss the work, his work, in connection with the atom bomb and nuclear fission?" "I decline to answer on the grounds that this might tend to incriminate me," Ethel replied once again.[34]

Among the few questions Ethel did answer in an interview that probably lasted less than an hour were an admission that she had written to David while he was at Los Alamos and that she had signed a Communist Party petition in 1939 in connection with elective office. At the end of the morning an exhausted Ethel was allowed to leave the courthouse. If she reckoned she had managed well in difficult circumstances by not giving anything away, this thought could not have lasted long. She was walking quickly across Foley Square to catch the subway home, a ride that would have taken her less than fifteen minutes as Monroe Street was not far away. She had an appointment booked that afternoon with the Jewish Community Homemakers Service to look into making long-term plans for her two sons. But it was too late. She was barely out of the building when she was suddenly and dramatically grabbed by two FBI agents, one of whom seized her arm and told her she was under arrest. She was marched back into a different part of the building she had just left, taken for fingerprinting, measuring, and mug shots. She asked to call a lawyer, but Emanuel Bloch, who was helping Julius, was on holiday, so his seventy-year-old father, Alexander Bloch, came instead. Ethel, like Julius, was now formally charged with conspiracy to commit espionage under the Espionage Act of 1917. She was specifically accused of two overt acts:

1. On or about the first day of November 1944, the exact date being . . . unknown at the Southern District of New York, the defendant Ethel Rosenberg had a discussion with Julius Rosenberg and others.

2. On or about the 10th day of January 1945 . . . at the Southern District of New York, the defendant Ethel Rosenberg had a conversation with Julius Rosenberg, David Greenglass and others.[35]

Alexander Bloch could see from these vague charges that the case against Ethel was weak and unsubstantiated. In effect, Ethel was being indicted for having conversations with her husband and brother. Bloch pleaded for bail so Ethel could at least go home and make arrangements for her children. However, this was set at a deliberately unattainable $100,000 (around $1 million today). Ethel then called seven-year-old Michael to tell him what had happened, prompting an agonized scream at the other end of the line. She was never to see her children at their home again.

Five

Prison

David's initial interview with the FBI at his and Ruth's apartment in January 1950 appears in retrospect as the catalyst that triggered Ethel's descent from a troubled young mother with a burgeoning interest in child psychiatry to a suspected Soviet agent at the heart of Julius's alleged "spy ring." But her arrest and imprisonment on August 11 on charges of conspiracy to commit espionage have to be seen against the paranoid Cold War backdrop of the previous years, which had now come to a head. The fear about "Reds" plotting to enable a Soviet attack on the United States that might even lead to all-out nuclear war was genuine. There was growing evidence to show that the Soviet Union, a brutal dictatorship, did have military and political ambitions that spread beyond its own borders and that the CPUSA was still loyal to Moscow.

Once Julius was arrested on July 17, Ethel had struggled to handle the crisis that now engulfed her. Her own deep distress about her perceived shortcomings as a mother, which had led her to seek the help of psychiatrists, may explain some of her missteps during the weeks between Julius's and her arrests, not least her misjudged press conference in the family's apartment. It is likely, too, that Ethel's fraught relationship with David and Ruth, combined with her mother Tessie's hostility toward her, had left her mentally and emotionally fragile when she most needed to have her wits about her.

Yet a woman less beset by personal and domestic pressures than Ethel would still have failed to avoid arrest, given the prevailing hysteria.

During these desperate summer weeks, as Ethel was without either money or friends, she had single-handedly had to look after Michael and Robby, and Julius's failing business. She had tried to find a buyer for the shop to raise some funds on which to live and to pay lawyers for Julius's defense, or at any rate to try to sell some of the equipment and spare parts from the shop to pay the bills that were pouring in. She lacked any support within her own family, nor was there anyone outside her domestic circle she could turn to for advice. Ann Sidorovich, the seamstress who was her one close friend at Knickerbocker Village, had moved to Cleveland shortly after Michael's birth and on August 3 her close friend, the radical social worker Vivian Glassman, was questioned by the FBI, which meant Ethel dared not visit or call Vivian, whose phone was almost certainly bugged.

When Julius wrote to her, "I want you to understand that you've reacted better than was to be hoped for considering the adverse conditions you are presently facing,"[1] this was probably code between them to help her stay strong and maintain silence. He cannot have had any conception of what intense pressures Ethel was actually facing.

Ethel stopped her psychotherapy sessions with Dr. Saul Miller, increasing her isolation. When he called her, having read about Julius's arrest in the newspapers, Ethel responded by telling him, "Oh you don't have to see me anymore." Miller tried to reassure Ethel that he was not worried about being "tainted." Ethel started crying, said she would be in touch, and hung up. According to Miller, he got the impression that Ethel was trying to protect him.

This was only partly true. She may also, even in her critical hour of need, have been desperately concerned for Miller only to see her being strong in the face of adversity. Ethel did continue to see her other psychotherapist, Elizabeth Phillips, for Michael's sake. Even now, Ethel's first priority was getting help for Michael and trying to be a better mother.

•   •   •

Immediately following her arrest on August 11, 1950, Ethel was taken to the Women's House of Detention in Greenwich Village without being able to say goodbye to Michael and Robby. The impossible level of bail set for her meant she could not even make any plans for their welfare. When the friend from Knickerbocker who was babysitting realized Ethel was not returning she deposited the children at Grandma Tessie's. Tessie tried to refuse, promptly telephoning Ethel's lawyer, Alexander Bloch, and complaining to him about the boys, saying they were unruly and she was far too old and unwell to look after them without help. But although she threatened to take them to a police station, a comment that "shocked" Bloch, there was no alternative and there they had to stay for the moment.

On August 12 Myles Lane, the chief assistant attorney for the Southern District of New York, told the press: "If the crime with which she, Ethel, is charged had not occurred perhaps we would not have the present situation in Korea."[2] The government was already emphatically stating its case, connecting Ethel spuriously to the global Cold War drama. It was determined to apply as much psychological pressure as possible, hoping Ethel would break and confess to whatever it was they assumed she knew.

The Women's House of Detention boasted that it was intended "to effect the moral and social rehabilitation" of the female inmates, "giving them a chance for restoration as well as for punishment," according to the first superintendent of the prison, Ruth Collins. Opened in 1932 at 10 Greenwich Avenue, it was a tall, multistory Art Deco building with an elegant exterior that might have been mistaken for a Greenwich Village apartment block had it not been for the narrow, heavily screened windows. The prison housed women awaiting trial or on trial who had either been denied bail or, like Ethel, could not afford to pay it.

"A less suitable location for a penal institution could hardly be found," declared Elizabeth Gurley Flynn, a Communist activist in her sixties charged with advocating the violent overthrow of the government who arrived at the prison shortly after Ethel. The two women did not overlap:

> On one side is Sixth Avenue (struggling to be called the Avenue of the Americas); on the other side is Greenwich Avenue. Ninth Avenue ends on its East Side and Christopher Street starts on its West Side. All are busy intersections. There was a constant flow of traffic—buses, cars, trucks and people passing on all sides, at all hours. The night noises of Greenwich Village, which apparently never goes to bed, deprived the inmates of sleep. There was singing, shouting, fighting, musical instruments—what have you. Never was there a quiet moment. Whistles came up from the streets to attract the attention of a particular inmate. Others would call her. Families, friends, sweethearts, pimps all arranged such contacts with the women on visiting days.[3]

Ethel's ninth-floor cell looked out over Greenwich Avenue. There were no facilities for exercise or fresh air apart from a small wire-enclosed rooftop. Gurley Flynn vividly described the cells and general conditions:

> [They were] open, with a short curtain over the toilet as a concession to privacy. In each cell there was a narrow iron cot with a thin mattress, a covered toilet which also served as a seat before a small iron table, a washbowl, and a couple of stationary wood hangers for clothing. The blankets were old and worn beyond all possibility of real cleanliness though they were disinfected regularly. It was a filthy place, overrun with mice and cockroaches. The food was indescribably revolting, unfit to eat. Watery spaghetti, half cooked oatmeal, coffee that was hardly more than lukewarm water, wormy prunes and soggy bread baked by the men on welfare island, very little meat and that usually an unsightly bologna are items I recall. There was never any fruit. Sugar and milk were scarce and both had to be bought in the commissary by inmates.[4]

According to Gurley Flynn, all new inmates suffered a humiliating strip search on their arrival at the prison. Once naked, wrapped in a sheet and taken to the showers, "we were ordered to take an enema and to climb on a table for an examination. All openings of the body were roughly searched for narcotics by 'a doctor'—a large woman who made insulting remarks about Communists who did not appreciate this country."[5]

Ethel never wrote about the strip search or the enema, possibly an indication that she could not discuss what obviously would have been such a brutal experience for her without revealing her pain. Although she was determined to remain strong, in her first letters to Julius Ethel could not hide her misery, but tried to keep cheerful and not complain. She wrote to her "Dearest darling" the day after her arrest, recognizing that he must by now have heard about her fate (he had, on the radio). "I wish I could say that I am cool, calm and collected but the fact is that although, contrary to newspaper reports, I have not been hysterical at any time, I have shed many anxious tears on behalf of the children."[6]

She was worried that she might not be able to write to Julius more than once a month, a rule that was in fact never enforced, but told him she cried every night as she had no idea what the future held for her boys and just hoped that the Blochs would be able to sort something out. She was not able to bring herself to write directly to her sons until August 15, when she promised her "Dearest Michael boy" that she thought about him and Robby all the time "and I know how you must be missing your Mommy and Daddy . . . When you're having a hard time of it try to re-member that I am wishing like anything that I were there taking care of you."[7] Michael admitted years later that although he could still hear his mother on the telephone telling him she was under arrest, he had completely blocked out his heartrending scream, which his mother never forgot and "which continued to give her nightmares the rest of her life."[8]

After little more than a week, Ethel told Julius that she thought over-all she was taking the situation fairly well, "but there are times when I'm terribly blue and depressed."[9] The following day, a Sunday, was a little better, as Ethel went to both Protestant and Christian Science services where she could at least sing. She had also attended the Jewish services on the previous Friday when there was no singing, only the rabbi intoning the prayers "so beautifully that I couldn't help but enjoy it."[10]

The other prisoners soon realized that Ethel knew how to sing professionally. As her reputation spread around the cells, she received requests to perform favorite songs, from Brahms's "Lullaby" to "Goodnight Irene" and the famous left-wing protest anthem "Peat Bog Soldiers." Although the rule was silence after lights out, with mail withheld for talking, the prison guards encouraged Ethel's singing as they thought this helped pacify some of the inmates. "One morning at breakfast I was pleasurably surprised to hear a number of girls in corridors other than my own away across the hall express their appreciation," she wrote to Julius on August 20.[11]

Singing offered Ethel only a fleeting escape from her agony about who would take care of her children and the frightening possibilities that lay ahead for them. Being taken to Grandma Tessie's at Sheriff Street was a time that Michael recalled as a torment for all concerned. "On one occasion I blurted out to one of my father's sisters who lived in the neighborhood that I wanted to run into the street and get killed by a car."[12] For Robby, too, Grandma Tessie and her sister Chutcha, who had now come to live in one of the upstairs bedrooms and with whom Michael had to share a bed, were cold and unfriendly: "Our parents' lawyers were made to understand that we were unwanted, a message also conveyed to Robby and me. I remember Tessie's home as a place where I did nothing but read comics, draw tracks and walk around the neighborhood. Referring to my parents, Grandma would say things to me like, 'You're lucky they're born here or they'd be deported.'"[13]

The entire Greenglass family wasted no time in siding with David, who was being held in the Federal Detention Center on New York's Lower West Side, and against Ethel and Julius. The Greenglasses blamed Ethel and Julius for leading David and Ruth down the Communist route and claimed that Julius's failed business venture was his own fault. The Rosenbergs were already barely on speaking terms with Ruth and David because of arguments over money, and Tessie made her own feelings clear when she visited Ethel at the Women's House of Detention. Tessie suggested that Ethel should divorce Julius and cooperate with the government. Ethel was outraged. "You are helping him [David] and you are killing me," she shot back, forbidding Tessie from any further visits.[14]

Ethel's younger brother Bernie was the only one of the family who retained some love for his sister. Quite possibly he understood her feelings of resentment, since he too had never managed to capture his mother's wholehearted affection in the way that David clearly had. But Bernie could no longer play an active role as intermediary between the feuding Rosenbergs and Greenglasses as he was grieving over the recent death of Gladys and caring for their small daughter. At the same time her older half brother Sam, in spite of his angry vow in 1943 to have nothing more to do with his sister, nonetheless visited Ethel in jail and begged her to cooperate with the FBI for her children's sake. When Ethel rebuffed him, Sam went home and wrote her a vicious letter:

> Dear Sis
> Today I visited Mom . . . I told Michael that I had spoken to you. His first words to me were "My Mother is innocent"—"She would not do anything that was wrong." Well you certainly built up a lot of faith in this poor child.—How can you have the bitter thought on your conscience to let this child down in such a horrible way. When a stranger walks into the house—his first question is "Is she from the child welfare or is she an investigator—I don't want to go to a foster home—I want to stay here."
> How can Mom keep those two children—they are wearing her away very quickly—I must say you have done and are still doing a very wonderful job—there is not much more disgrace you could bring to your family—but now your great problems seems to be—to get rid of them—one at a time—first Mom—then Chutch—the children in a foster home—your brother in jail—what an excellent job—
> In my lousy heart there is only contempt for you and your kind— but spurred on by the emotions and a Mother and Aunt who unselfishly give of their lives so that poor defenseless and innocent children can have a temporary shelter and comfort and protection—

For these I ask again——give up this wild ideology——come down
to earth, give yourself a fighting chance (I may be able to help you) so
that someday you may possibly be a mother to your two children—
and not a number in some jail——rotting away your years——I mention
again that I may be able to help you but I must have your cooperation.

Your brother
Sam[15]

The picture of Tessie that Sam drew was reinforced by Bernie's sister-in-law Jean, who nonetheless was sympathetic to Ethel's plight and urged her to rescue her sons from Tessie:

Your Ma reviles and rants about you and the situation you and Julie brought on her family and how much trouble the kids are and how bad they are and how bad you are and why don't you do what Ruthie did so you too could be with your kids . . .

When I see your kids pushed around, screamed at, have to listen to your being spoken about badly and cursed and your Ma talking bad about your in-laws and poor Michael going into temper tantrums when your Ma curses you I want to hit her over the head.[16]

Ethel did not see Michael and Robby throughout her seven months in the Women's House of Detention. She believed it would damage such young children to remember their mother behind bars and without their father present. Ethel's desperation to be a good mother, refracted through 1950s expectations of how she should behave, meant she was prepared to suffer agonies of loneliness and grief to spare her boys from seeing her in jail. She tried to fill some of the emotional chasm that had opened between her and them by writing Michael and Robby loving letters, reminding them of favorite activities, and saying how much she missed them and longed to see them again.

In November she wrote her first letter (or at least the first letter that has survived) to the boys, once they had been moved away from Tessie and sent to a children's shelter. Tessie had finally won her battle to insist that the boys must be removed before the winter, when the water in the toilets would freeze—an image that fascinated three-year-old Robby, who went looking for ice in the bowl. So that autumn they were sent unwillingly to the Hebrew Children's Home in the Bronx, a dire experience even worse than living with the grandmother who did not want them. Ethel had discussed the home with a social service worker but, as a remand prisoner awaiting trial, she was allowed no choice in the matter. Michael hated the home so much that in his anger he convinced himself that he was enduring a type of Nazi concentration camp.

After trying to reassure "Dearest Michael" about the strangeness of his new surroundings, explaining how that was a normal reaction—after all, "I am a grown-up and yet it was hard for me too to get used to new surroundings and new people and a new routine"[17]—she reminded him of the word games they used to play together. "Kiss 'Obby for 'Ulius and me," she wrote. "Wouldn't Mr. Witover [the director of the shelter] laugh about Grekhalkis and Grekmais!" These were all references to characters in stories that Michael would sometimes dictate to Ethel for her to type out.[18] It was here that Ethel's "Dearest Kitty Cats"[19] spent Christmas 1950 or, as Ethel wrote to them, "Merry Chanukah, Merry Christmas and Happy New Year to my dearest Michael and Robby, from your Mommy who loves you, no matter what day, month or year it is, no matter where she is xxx xxx xxx xxx xxx xxx xxx xxx xxxx."[20]

Then on January 22, 1951, she reminded them of the imaginary games they used to enjoy and asked whether Robby still called himself "Hop-a-long Cassery?"[21] A month later she wrote to Michael congratulating him on doing so well at school and urging him to believe that "we will do all that is [sic] we possibly can to be with you again" in response to his "sweet" message wishing her and Julius "good luck" in the forthcoming trial.[22] A week later she sent them a letter full of reminders about the songs they used to sing together; and then again on March 2, four days before her court appearance, she wrote in a tone striking as much normality as possible, asking them what they had been up to, and wishing Michael much happiness for his eighth birthday on March 10: "My lovely children," Ethel concluded, "I am hoping, and so is Daddy, of course, that we really will have the luck you wished us. Certainly we will do all we can to make things come out the way we all want them to and Mr. Bloch and his father are working very hard to help us do just that."[23]

But Ethel recognized that there was little she could do from prison to make life better for Michael and Robby. She discussed the situation with her lawyer, Emanuel Bloch, but had limited time with him and a case to prepare. She asked for help from Julius's widowed mother, Sophie Rosenberg, who was sympathetic to the idea of taking care of Michael and Robby. However, Sophie, although only sixty-two, was in poor health and her family did not think she could cope with having the children to live with her. Instead, Sophie offered the boys some respite by taking them out most Sundays. Sophie was convinced that Julius and Ethel were innocent, but she could not persuade any of her three other children to take Michael and Robby because they were frightened of guilt by association with Julius. Julius's sister Ethel Goldberg later explained that if Michael and Robby had stayed with her in the Maspeth neighborhood in Queens, a gentile area, her husband's grocery shop would have been attacked, threatening the Goldbergs' livelihood.

The one bright spot for Ethel during these early weeks in prison, as her family and in-laws abandoned her, was visits from Michael's psychotherapist Elizabeth Phillips. "Bless her," she wrote to Julius on August 20.[24] Elizabeth understood that reassuring Ethel that her sons were managing would be critical in keeping up her spirits. Ethel was most worried about Michael, who at first was still seeing Elizabeth for therapy sessions, and who she knew was miserable. "She [Elizabeth] told me that a very good homemaker is now helping my mother and that Michael has been coming to see her very willingly," Ethel reported in the same letter to Julius. "Last week she took him home in a cab after getting him a sandwich he asked for."[25]

Seventy years later, in 2018, Elizabeth Phillips remembered vividly Ethel's utter desolation:

She was so alone. She had absolutely no one. I was the only person she had and that was for just a few weeks. But it was a difficult relationship, as if Ethel strayed at all into discussing her imprisonment or thoughts about Julius I had to say, "You're going to have to save that for your lawyer, all of that, as I cannot keep a confidentiality." I hated having to say that. But it was necessary as the FBI cast a long shadow. Before the arrest Ethel was a client I liked seeing with a son I liked. After the arrests, I felt so helpless.

One of the prison visits Elizabeth remembered most clearly was when Ethel handed her a green sweater that she said she had asked a fellow inmate to knit. Yet in a letter to Julius, Ethel described knitting it herself but added, "Don't dare tell her." Elizabeth was overwhelmed: "I was enormously touched . . . I burst into tears when she gave it to me."[26] Knitting was a new skill that Ethel's friends on the ninth floor taught her and she embraced with excitement. She then started, but never finished, sweaters for her boys.

Elizabeth continued seeing Michael alone at 4 p.m. every Friday afternoon for just a few weeks. During these sessions, Elizabeth realized that Michael was living in a fantasy world that he muddled with reality. Initially, when he told her about his father's arrest, "he was enacting *The Lone Ranger* for me. This was performance, not therapy." Michael said he had seen "the good guys [the FBI] take away the bad guy [his father], a view he swiftly corrected since of course he did not believe his father was a bad guy. He was simply a confused child."[27]

Worried that Michael was not eating, Mrs. Phillips took him to a hamburger joint nearby, deciding this was more important than play therapy; so they had their session while he munched a burger. Suddenly, without warning, Michael's visits to Elizabeth were stopped. She was not initially told why, but he was sent instead to the charity Jewish Child Care Association for therapy and the woman he had grown to trust was not allowed to continue the treatment. "It was the craziest thing, just when he needed all the friends and relations he could possibly have . . . it must have felt like I had abandoned him," Elizabeth recalled.[28] Later she was given a reason: "My relationship was so strong that it would interfere with his relating to his new therapist . . . Such a misinterpretation of the therapeutic relationship given the reality."[29]

·   ·   ·

Even after they had been moved out of her home, Tessie piled more distress on Ethel by telling her, in a telegram, how utterly miserable both boys were at the home. Tessie said she had tried to visit them twice, but complained that on each occasion they had not seen her because they were in constant tears. She added that she wanted to come and see Ethel in prison, "but would not be able to take it. All broken up with heartache. Let me hear from you Love—Mother."[30]

In fact, Tessie did visit Ethel soon afterward, despite Ethel having made it clear that she did not wish to see her at the Women's House of Detention. The visit was a disaster. Most of the inmates were young Black girls charged with drug offenses and many of them received regular visits from their mothers, held in a big, square room divided into stalls. By contrast, Tessie was ushered into a separate room where she berated Ethel for not cooperating with the FBI and accused her of not doing enough to save "Davey."

Ethel had not requested a "private visit" and believed that it must have been arranged by the authorities in the hope that she would confess. She subsequently revealed to a fellow prisoner, Miriam Moskowitz, what Tessie had said to her: "Tell the FBI whatever you have to to save him. You and your husband you're killing him and you're killing me."[31]

Miriam was a suspected Communist agent, charged with conspiracy to obstruct justice. She was put in a cell on the fifth floor, four stories down from Ethel, in order to keep the jail's only two "political" prisoners apart. Like Ethel, a few months older than her, Miriam was a second-generation American Jewish woman with a deep love of music. "The police van became our unplanned social outpost," Miriam recalled years later. "We traveled together in it when we went to court, I to attend my trial, she to meet with her lawyer and with Julius to plan their court defense." In 1954, Miriam told the radical journalist Virginia Gardner that she could not forget how deeply Tessie had wounded Ethel: "Yet Ethel never spoke of her mother with hatred . . . only with sadness—but what sadness."[32]

Even at the age of 101, Miriam's memory of her prison time with Ethel was still sharp. "Ethel always remained full of hope, but she was also very serious. One of the most notable things about her was the effect she had on others. The other women were very free with their language. But in front of Ethel they were always very careful. They treated her like a lady."[33] There were no uniforms in the House of Detention and Miriam recalled how some of the women made crochet hats for Ethel, which were far from stylish but she wore anyway: "The women liked her, they accepted her and they gave her their endorsement. Ethel was not a fashion plate. She was not concerned with what she wore as long as it was clean and in style. She had naturally curly hair but she took trouble to comb it nicely, and then wore a home-made hat on it."[34]

Miriam's observation about Ethel's dowdy clothes was not as tart as it sounds. In an age when women were literally judged on their appearance, Miriam felt that Ethel did not understand the importance of how she looked in court and should have made more of an effort to dress well. Ethel had never been in the habit of buying nice or fashionable clothes; she could not afford them, nor did she think it mattered. What mattered to her more in prison—strangely, since she had not considered it important at Knickerbocker—was to be well liked. She decided that being nurturing to the other female inmates, pleasing them by wearing the odd assortment of hats and other accessories that they offered her, was somehow more important than appearing attractive to the jury or the press. There were even stories that Ethel paid for extra items of food from the commissary in case any of the other prisoners wanted something—especially at night—so her cell acquired the nickname of Rosenberg's Delicatessen.

•   •   •

The trips in the prison van were also a treasured opportunity for Ethel to see Julius. But, as Ethel wrote after one of these, oh Darling, even though we were able to spend some time together . . . it seemed to me when I had returned here that there were so many other ways I might have expressed my feelings to you, so many other things I might have said. So let me say them now, my dear one. And yet I couldn't ever say enough what pride and love and deep regard for you as an individual I feel. What you wrote me about ourselves as a family and what that family means to you made my eyes fill. And yet, at the same time, there came to me such an abiding sense of the faith and joy, such a sure knowledge of the rich meaning our lives have held that I was suddenly seized with an overwhelming desires [*sic*] to see you and say it to you and kiss you with all my heart.[35]

On these regular journeys for court hearings and meetings with lawyers, the men would be picked up first at the Federal Detention Center on West Street. Then the van drove to Greenwich Village to collect the women, who sat on the other side of a grate across the middle of the van that separated male and female prisoners. Miriam recalled in her 2010 book *Phantom Spies, Phantom Justice*:

By the time I joined this trek to court it had become the prisoners' practice to let Julius have a seat abutting the grate on the inside. The seat on the other side of the grate was left for Ethel. Inside the van it was pitch black when the door was closed but no one cared . . . once, when a prisoner lighted a cigarette in the flickering of the match we witnessed Ethel and Julius maneuvering to kiss through the grate. No one hooted or made coarse remarks, as they would have done with anyone else. The prisoners gave these two a sense of privacy; the gothic dimensions of the drama engulfing them seemed to touch everyone.[36]

All agreed on how overwhelming was Ethel's love and physical need for her husband.

Newspaper images of Julius and Ethel in the prison van show Ethel wearing a baggy coat with a triangular fur collar and an unflattering yoke, confirming Miriam's negative view of her dress sense. Julius looks as serious as Ethel, in suit and tie and handcuffs. These press photographs instantly embedded this "Red spy ring" couple in the public consciousness, as the saturation coverage of the Rosenbergs' case prepared the American people for their punishment. "FBI Arrests Woman as Atomic Spy," proclaimed the *San Francisco Chronicle*. "FBI Nabs Wife: 7th Accused in Red Spy Ring" was the *Chicago Tribune* headline. Across the country, few Americans doubted that the United States faced an existential threat from a nuclear-armed Soviet Union, abetted by "Red" traitors like Ethel and Julius. "If Soviets Start War, Atomic Bomb Attack Expected on New York First," the mass-circulation daily *New York Journal-American* splashed as its front-page headline on January 8, 1951, two months before the trial began.

Ethel and Julius's priority was to plan a defense strategy with Manny Bloch. Yet they did not know precisely what the prosecution would throw at them and Bloch, a sole practitioner, lacked the resources to prepare for every eventuality and to mount a case that could take on the US government. He and his father, Alexander, whose chief experience was as a small-time corporate lawyer specializing in the sale of bakeries and advising the Furriers' Union, were based in a modest office with a single secretary. He had approached other attorneys to assist him but they all declined to get involved. According to Ben Margolis, the highly regarded California-based civil rights lawyer, "They had tried to get some Left lawyers . . . and they'd all refused. The reason for the refusal that was given at least on confidential levels, was that they thought that it was a mistake for the Rosenbergs to be represented by a Left lawyer, that that would tend to make their position more difficult. And, of course, they ended up being represented by an unqualified Left lawyer, who did it. He wasn't so prominently known as a Left lawyer as the ones that had been asked to do this."[37]

And so Manny's only source of advice in the months before the trial was his elderly father, who technically became Ethel's attorney. But in practice the burden of Ethel's defense also fell on Manny, and Gloria

Agrin, a young attorney who became his lover and the woman he hoped to marry once he had divorced. Gloria volunteered to help. "Among Bloch's problems," she explained, "was that he had no investigative facilities and hardly any funds. We learned later that the Communist Party, which we mistakenly assumed would assist financially in the Rosenbergs' defense, did not do so."[38] Yet, even had the Communist Party paid for the defense, there is no guarantee that this would have helped Ethel and arguably might have damaged their case more. In the circumstances all they had to rely on was a small fee paid by the court.

Alexander and his son did not always agree on tactics, but there was never enough time to discuss serious procedural matters, let alone Ethel's emotional pain. Following her arrest, she had repeatedly asked Manny Bloch if he could arrange for Dr. Miller to see her. In a heartfelt, ten-page letter to the lawyer she barely knew, she had explained that "I find all attempts to minimize my emotional needs indeed all my efforts to pretend those needs are nonexistent . . . are to no avail." Ethel understood how every moment when she and Julius met their lawyer needed to be spent on preparing their defense. However, she disagreed with Bloch's decision not to involve Miller on the grounds that the prosecution might use her need for psychiatric help as a way to attack her character, or by the press as "evidence" that she and by extension Julius were untrustworthy. She pointed out that Bloch's lawyer father Alexander had said "they will do these things anyway whichever way you behave."[39] But Manny Bloch would not budge, compounding Ethel's isolation and despair.

Ethel's arrest, despite the lack of evidence against her, meant she could do nothing to support Julius as she had to focus on her own case. Her incarceration also compounded the problem of arousing any public support for the couple at a time when anti-Communist hysteria had reached fever pitch. Their very name, Rosenberg, to some people said it all. In the public mind most Jews were Bolshevik supporters and therefore of dubious loyalty to the United States. As a result of defending the Rosenbergs, Bloch not only lost clients but former colleagues would cross the street if they saw him coming rather than have to acknowledge the Jewish lawyer defending Communist spies. In their respective isolations,

Ethel and Julius failed to grasp how meticulously the prosecution's case was being prepared and rehearsed.

Ethel rejected the option of calling friends and neighbors as character witnesses, explaining to Bloch that, for the latter, association with potential Soviet spies would damage their job prospects and possibly also result in family destruction, just as it had for her and Julius. What purpose would it serve to bring in friends, most of whom were, like them, Communist sympathizers, and see them suffer in the same way just to tell a jury what a hardworking, upstanding woman Ethel was or how nicely she sang? In any event most of their friends had abandoned them in the aftermath of their arrests. Ethel and Julius decided their best course of action was to plead the Fifth Amendment, preserving their constitutional right to remain silent rather than incriminate themselves under oath. The obvious risk was that, once in court, their silence would reinforce the impression already projected by the press that they were hiding the truth about their spying activities—or in Ethel's case worse, that she was cool, unemotional, unmaternal, and a liar.

It was Ethel, who had never personally engaged in espionage, who was most vulnerable, since Julius certainly did have much to hide about his life as a Soviet recruiter during the war. Too proud or naive to look the part of a weak and helpless woman, Ethel's damaging indifference to the effect she had on those in authority was easily slotted into the prevailing narrative that now developed about her. In this version of Ethel, amplified by the press, she was the strong half of the partnership who had made the key decisions in their "Commie" marriage.

Six

On Trial

Ethel's trial began at 10:30 a.m. on March 6, 1951, at New York's Southern District Federal Court on Foley Square. It was a mild, overcast morning in contrast to the stiflingly hot August day the previous year when she had been arrested there. She arrived at the courthouse in a prison van, accompanied by Julius and guarded by a phalanx of stern-faced US marshals. Julius looked dapper in a dark double-breasted overcoat and patterned tie. Apart from his handcuffs, he could have been mistaken for a bank clerk or trader on nearby Wall Street. Standing next to him as they paused briefly for the press photographers, Ethel seemed in these chauvinist times the very model of a dumpy housewife who had let herself go. She was wearing her now familiar shapeless coat over a plain white shirt and dark skirt, the whole outfit topped by a wide-rimmed bonnet with a confection of flowers held in place by a mass of netting that was gathered at the crown and tied beneath her chin. Her leather-gloved hands were without handcuffs and she wore oddly spring-like black peep-toe sandals.

Ethel's outfit was arguably her first misstep, even before she had entered the courtroom. As her friend and fellow "political" inmate Miriam Moskowitz recalled to Virginia Gardner:

The clothes Ethel wore to trial broke my heart. Everyone put
on the best she could muster, borrowing a bag or a handkerchief
or hat occasionally to go to court. Ethel had one or two blouses
and at most two skirts . . . We girls used to worry, particularly those of us who had been before juries . . . a couple of
the women had crocheted hats for her in jail. I saw her in one
of them and I thought it was horrible on her. But she thought it
was lovely and said "Julie" thought it was lovely.[1]

Yet a closer look at the pictures of Ethel as she arrives for the start of
the trial makes it clear that she had, in her clumsy way, done her best to
please both Julius and the female inmates who had helped her put together
this outfit since she had neither money nor opportunity to buy anything
new. Peeping out from under the brim of her hideous hat, her thick black
hair had been carefully curled. And over her white blouse she added a
scarlet bodice, which she had been lent by a friend in the detention center, providing the "brightest dab of color in the great chestnut paneled
chamber."[2]

Massive steps flanked by large pedestals and Corinthian columns
fronted the imposing neoclassical entrance to 40 Foley Square, but the
defendants were led in through the back. By the time Ethel and Julius
were ushered into the august, marble- and wood-paneled Court Room
110, the largest in the Southern District of New York, it was already filled
with spectators and reporters eager to witness the trial of the century and
to get a glimpse of America's homegrown atomic spies. Julius and Ethel
were seated at the extreme end of the table with their lawyers, Bloch
father and son, to their left, and next to them Edward Kuntz and Harold
Phillips, the two lawyers for Morton Sobell, the third defendant. In this
way the lawyers could confer with each other while the defendants were
kept as far apart as they had been since the arrest. Sobell was Julius's
former engineering classmate and fellow radical at City College, who had
gone on to work in Washington during the war at the Navy Ordnance
Department. Following David's arrest in June 1950, he and his family had
fled to Mexico with a view to escaping to Europe. Following a tip-off, he

had been kidnapped in August 1950 by armed thugs and handed over to the FBI at the Mexican border. Now Sobell sat next to Julius and Ethel, facing similar espionage charges as part of the Rosenbergs' supposed "spy ring" but with a different defense team.

In front of them was the prosecution table. Here sat Irving H. Saypol, who headed the prosecution team, Myles Lane, his chief assistant, and then a number of young thrusting lawyers eager to make their names. Twenty-three-year-old Roy Cohn was the brashest and most eager. James Kilsheimer, a suave, dark-haired thirty-year-old, was one of the few non-Jewish lawyers at the trial and had served as a gunnery officer in the Pacific during the war. Ethel would not have known who they were, nor about the reputations that preceded them. But doubtless they looked intimidating.

Throughout the trial Sobell's wife, Helen, came early and took a seat in the first row of spectators ten feet behind the defendants. "I could turn around and look at her any time I wanted to. It was good that she was there,"[3] commented Sobell, recognizing how important such moral support was. Ethel and Julius had no one in court to whom they could turn and smile. Unlike her brother David—due to appear as the prosecution's key witness—Ethel had received no pretrial coaching and there was no one in her family to give her confidence and support. She agonized about not being able to talk to Saul Miller.

In their letters to each other from prison, Ethel and Julius had agreed that they must remain calm at the trial, and above all maintain their dignity. "Your dignity, decency and wholesome character has set me an example to emulate," was just one such reference from Julius to Ethel.[4] But Ethel's interpretation of dignity in court, possibly in an attempt to conceal her nerves, was to try not to smile, resulting in a stony expression that some interpreted as lack of contrition or a failure to show emotion, a look that according to some "radiated disdain,"[5] while others believed that her refusal to show emotion revealed a "cold and unfeeling" woman whose "contempt for the proceedings was barely concealed."[6]

"She would throw back her head, arch her eyebrows and set her face into a visage of stony imperiousness," is how one historian described her defensive posture.[7] A juror commented later that, by not revealing the emotion and turmoil inside her, she came across as "a steely, stony, tight-lipped woman. She was the mastermind. Julius would have spoken if she had permitted him. He was more human. She was more disciplined."[8]

Both Ethel and Julius were charged under the Espionage Act of 1917 with conspiracy to commit espionage from 1944 until 1950 by communicating to a foreign government, in wartime, secret atomic and other military information. The time period was significant. Their last alleged overt act relating to atomic secrets was in mid-September 1945, but World War Two officially ended on September 2, 1945. However, other aspects of the conspiracy continued into 1950, and the oral indictment read out in court deliberately described this crime as having been committed during the early years of the Cold War, even though this was technically peacetime. Yet, amid the bloody stalemate in Korea and the frenzied building of nuclear fallout shelters around New York City, Ethel and Julius were cast as traitors who had helped Stalin steal the secure future that most Americans believed they had won in 1945.

Behind the scenes, the authorities knew that actual evidence of Ethel's "espionage" was nonexistent, while without a confession by Julius the evidence against him too might not be enough to convince a jury he was guilty and send him to the electric chair. But the charges against them both were the same. A month before the trial, on February 8, the government lawyer, Myles Lane, had told a closed-door meeting of the Joint Congressional Committee on Atomic Energy: "The case is not strong against Mrs. Rosenberg. But for the purpose of acting as a deterrent, I think it is very important that she be convicted, too, and given a stiff sentence."[9] Indicting Ethel on the same charge of conspiracy to commit espionage as Julius served another purpose for the government, which feared that the two key prosecution witnesses, Ethel's brother David and his wife Ruth, would buckle under cross-examination. The prosecution hoped that Ethel's plight would wring a confession out of Julius, who knew she was innocent as charged and might therefore see admitting his guilt as a means to save her life.

Ten days before the trial, the prosecution received a boost when

David and Ruth's version of events significantly changed. After his arrest in June 1950, David had told his interrogators that Ethel's involvement in his and Julius's espionage had been limited to two episodes: a conversation in November 1944, when Ethel had asked Ruth to let David make up his own mind if he wished to offer Julius information from Los Alamos; and Ethel's presence in the kitchen during David's furlough in January 1945, when Julius had cut up a Jell-O box to be used as a recognition signal.

As the trial approached, David and Ruth suddenly remembered a new story that made Ethel appear as an active participant. Ruth now stated that in September 1945, Ethel had sat down at a typewriter that she had placed on a bridge table in the living room and typed out the information from Los Alamos that David had given to Julius. Ruth's new testimony flatly contradicted David's earlier statements that Ethel had not witnessed any of the occasions when he had given Julius information. It also clashed with her own grand jury testimony, where she said she herself gave information to Julius. "I wrote that down on a piece of paper . . . in longhand."[10] She may indeed have invented this entire occasion if Julius Rosenberg was no longer on active duty for Soviet intelligence.[11] But from now on David stuck by his wife's account. Ethel and Julius were not informed of this new version of events.

·   ·   ·

At 10:30 a.m. Judge Irving Kaufman, a large US flag hovering behind his right shoulder, called the courtroom to order and the trial began. Kaufman, forty, known by the New York press as the "boy judge," was a short, stocky man with slicked-back, pomaded black hair. His father was a manufacturer of humidors for keeping cigars fresh, and, although the family was Jewish, Kaufman had studied law at a Catholic college, New York City's Fordham University, where he was nicknamed "Pope Kaufman" for his excellence in the compulsory Christian doctrine classes. Clever and ambitious, Kaufman had alternated between private practice and working as a New York public prosecutor in the 1930s. He married the daughter of his first law firm's boss (coincidentally called Rosenberg) and became a personal friend and admirer of FBI director J. Edgar

Hoover. The previous November, Kaufman had been the judge in the trial of Ethel's fellow "political" prisoner Miriam Moskowitz and Miriam's lover Abraham Brothman, who were suspected of being Communist spies. Lacking firm evidence of espionage, the authorities had charged both Brothman and Moskowitz with conspiracy to obstruct justice, for which they had respectively received seven- and two-year jail sentences from Kaufman. The ambitious judge had then used all his considerable legal and political connections to get appointed for Ethel and Julius's trial, recognizing its significance in standing up to Communists at the height of the Cold War. He intended to stamp his mark on proceedings from the moment he first banged his gavel.

The chief prosecutor in the Moskowitz and Brothman trial had also been forty-five-year-old Irving Saypol, "the nation's number one legal hunter of top Communists," according to *Time* magazine.[12] A self-made man, with thick lips and a jutting chin, renowned for his quick wit in court, Saypol was the son of Russian Jewish immigrants who had put himself through night school to become a lawyer. Saypol's other scalps since the war as attorney for the Southern District of New York included most of the senior leadership of the CPUSA, who were jailed for five years after a trial that ended in 1949. Their crime was violating the Alien Registration Act, which made it illegal for anyone in the United States "to advocate, abet, or teach the desirability of overthrowing the government." Following the trial of Moskowitz and Brothman, Saypol had secured the conviction in February 1951 on perjury charges of William Remington, a government economist who had been named as a Soviet spy by the defector Elizabeth Bentley. Saypol's deputy at the Remington trial had been an up-and-coming young attorney in his office called Roy Cohn. As chief assistant prosecutor, Cohn was now appointed to perform the same role again at Ethel and Julius's trial. The well-connected Cohn was distantly related to Saypol, but, more significantly, his father was a senior New York judge who was friends with Kaufman, and Cohn later boasted that he had pulled strings to ensure Kaufman was assigned to the Rosenberg case.[13] Given his subsequent notoriety, it is easy to see Cohn, the precociously clever son of a judge, as the incarnation of pure evil. He certainly looked menacing in court, with slicked-back hair, sunken eyes, and a fleshy nose with a mysterious scar down the center. In fact, his mother, Dora, was so obsessed with her only son that she had arranged a nose "improvement" job for him when young that left him permanently disfigured. Yet in 1951 Cohn was still on the make, hoping to use the Rosenbergs to claw his way further ahead of Saypol's other young assistants in the chief prosecutor's ferociously competitive office.

Cohn had already proved his worth to Saypol as his assistant in the trial of Moskowitz and Brothman. In the weeks before Ethel and Julius's trial, it was Cohn who had applied pressure on David Greenglass to incriminate Ethel directly in David and Julius's espionage. According to Cohn, he told David "that we knew he was protecting Ethel and that unless he told us what he knew about her activities we could not guarantee that Ruth his wife would be safe from prosecution . . . such was my message to him and he responded with alacrity."[14]

Seated side by side at the defense table, Ethel and Julius had no idea that Cohn had got David to add the typewriter story. As far as they knew, the flimsy case against Ethel rested entirely on the same allegation as at the time of her arrest: conferring with her husband, brother, and sister-in-law. Ethel was aware that, if convicted, she faced life imprisonment or even death by electrocution. In her ignorance, however, she believed the prosecution did not have anything resembling "proof" to find her guilty. Adding to her and Julius's disadvantage, their legal team would soon be exposed as ill equipped to confront Saypol and Cohn.

Manny Bloch was, at forty-nine, older than Kaufman, Saypol, or Cohn; arguably his graying hair, thinning and receding at the temples, and his deadly earnest pallor, made him seem older still. This had become much more than a case for him. He was emotionally involved in fighting for all four Rosenbergs and it was exhausting. Ethel and Julius's defense team was further weakened by a fundamental disagreement between Manny and his father about the wisdom of both Rosenbergs pleading the Fifth Amendment wherever necessary. Based on his previous experience acting for Communists, Manny was convinced that the defense had to disprove, or at least cast doubt on, the prosecution's linkage of CPUSA membership with espionage. From this perspective, Manny argued that Ethel and Julius were best advised to remain silent, rather than risk cross-examination about their alleged membership. Alexander Bloch was adamant that it was preferable for the couple to come clean about their Communism, rather than appear to be hiding the fact from the court. "Let's assume you were Communists," he told Ethel and Julius before the trial. "It would sound better to a jury if you said so in that case."[15]

Julius and Ethel, nursing not only a pride in their constitutional rights but a long-standing faith that their political beliefs were a private matter, were unconvinced by the elder Bloch's reasoning. They agreed with Manny, who was about to discover if his strategy was correct as Kaufman called the courtroom to order for the trial to begin.

•   •   •

The court clerk read out a list of 102 possible witnesses whom the prosecution claimed they intended to call. The list contained leading scientists and military personnel at Los Alamos from when David Greenglass worked at the site, including the physicist and "father of the atomic bomb" Dr. Robert Oppenheimer, who headed the research laboratory, and General Leslie Groves, the overall head of the Manhattan Project.

Onetime friends of Ethel and Julius also appeared on the list: people such as Julius's fellow college radical Max Elitcher and Max's wife, Helene, who had hung out with the Rosenbergs and Sobell during World War Two; Mike and Ann Sidorovich, the left-wing couple who had lived upstairs from Ethel and Julius in Knickerbocker Village; and Vivian Glassman, the Communist social worker who had urged Ethel to seek psychiatric help. Some former friends did not even know that their names were on this list before they were read out in court. In reality, Irving Saypol was not planning to call most of them as prosecution witnesses. His purpose was to strike fear into Ethel and Julius about what these people might say, none of whom had seen the couple since their arrests.

There followed almost two days of protracted wrangling over jurors. About one-third of New York City's population was Jewish, so it seemed no coincidence to Manny Bloch that the judge, both prosecuting attorneys, the defense team, and of course the Rosenbergs were Jewish as well; yet Saypol and Cohn, with Kaufman's compliance, succeeded in empaneling a jury without a single Jewish member.

According to Cohn's posthumous biographer Nicholas von Hoffman, Cohn, Saypol, and Kaufman regarded themselves as establishment or "good" Jews who were determined to prove they were superpatriotic and far removed from Lower East Side Communist Jews whose allegiance to America was shaky at best. Cohn was proud that he "disliked all Communists but Jewish communists most of all," von Hoffman wrote.[16] Whether or not von Hoffman was correct, the prosecution believed that a non-Jewish jury would be more likely to find Ethel and Julius guilty as charged. They were probably correct. However, the Jewish response to the Rosenberg case was confused from the start, reflecting deep anxiety about Jewish identity in a post-Holocaust Cold War America. From 1945 onward, many well-known Jews—scientists, scholars, and intellectuals—were not merely non-Communist but anti-Communist, concerned about the stereotype of the radical Jew, even though many Jews in postwar America had moved to the suburbs and embraced middle-class materialism. With memories of violent anti-Semitism so fresh in Jewish minds, the Rosenberg case, however much it evoked sympathy among some American Jews, produced anger in others toward the Rosenbergs for "taking advantage of America, the one country that had been good for Jews, for being stooges of the Communists."[17] As William Zukerman, a reporter for *The Jewish Advocate,* noted, no other trial in recent years had so deeply moved American Jews while at the same time evoking regrets and anxieties so that "at first there was a reluctance to discuss the case in the Jewish press even while it was the subject of conversation in every Jewish home."[18] The trial exacerbated all these responses but only later, by which time it was too late, did a public discussion begin in the Yiddish press.

However, the absence of Jews from the final jury may have had almost as much to do with process and demography as with artful fixing by Saypol and Cohn. As the journalist Ted Morgan later explained in a 1975 article for *Esquire* magazine, the final twelve were selected from a record number of three hundred prospective jurors, known as "PJs," whose names were taken from lists of registered voters. Kaufman, having rapidly established an aura of efficiency and authority in his impressive black gown, allowed the defense thirty challenges to the government's twenty on the grounds that there were multiple defendants on trial: Ethel, Julius, and Morton Sobell. Many PJs had in fact already asked to be excused by the time the challenges began, for the reason that they would not be able to keep an open mind because of their views. It was here that Kaufman's guidance had a crucial bearing on the final composition of the jury.

Kaufman urged all potential jurors that they were not to consider the eventual punishment as a factor in their suitability, even though this might involve the judicial killing of a mother.[19] In effect, anyone who was opposed to the death penalty was thereby excused from being a juror. Furthermore, as Kaufman made clear, any juror who believed that information concerning atomic energy should be shared with Russia, or who disapproved more generally of atomic warfare, was similarly excused. PJs were also probed on whether they had ever belonged to one or more of scores of supposedly suspect organizations going back to the 1930s, including the Abraham Lincoln Brigade, the American League Against War and Fascism, the American Jewish Labor Council, the School of Jewish Studies, the Joint Anti-Fascist Refugee Committee, and scores more. When Kaufman asked if anyone had attended, or had family members who had attended, City College, where Julius had studied, Manny Bloch politely went to the bench to object. It was too late to prevent the idea being circulated around the court that CCNY was somehow a dubious institution.

Kaufman's extensive guidance certainly increased the chance of Jewish PJs being excused or disqualified, given that many New York Jews had left-wing or "progressive" opinions. Yet according to Morgan, a more significant reason for the absence of Jews among the final twelve was that the PJs were selected from across the entire New York Southern District, including counties in New York State where Jews were less heavily represented than in the city.[20]

Cohn reportedly claimed later that the prosecution had focused its challenges not on Jews but on housewives who might sympathize with

Ethel's plight as a mother. If true, the strategy worked, because only one woman made the final selection. On the defense side, Manny Bloch and his assistant Gloria Agrin recognized that, in the circumstances, all they could do was try to eliminate any PJ with obvious anti-Communist sentiments. They were not certain that having Jewish jurors would help either, for fear that a Jew would be afraid to be seen to go easy on a fellow Jew.

Overall, the twelve volunteers who eventually composed the jury were broadly representative of the country, but not of the city of New York. Five lived outside the city in leafy suburbs such as White Plains, Dobbs Ferry, and Mount Vernon; they included two accountants, three auditors, an estimator, a sales manager, a caterer, a restaurateur, and a retired civil servant. The jury was completed by one Black man, an electrician, and the sole woman, fifty-year-old Mrs. Lisette Dammas, a former switchboard operator whose daughter had married a member of the National Guard. Without exception, all supported the death penalty.

Late in the day on March 7 Irving Saypol rose to open the government's case. Saypol declared that the defendants had joined "in a deliberate, carefully planned conspiracy to deliver to the Soviet Union the information and the weapons which the Soviet Union could use to destroy us."[21] He instantly conflated Ethel and Julius's alleged wartime activities, when the Soviet Union was a military ally, with the terrifying present, when many New Yorkers feared that Stalin was poised to drop an atomic bomb on the United States, destroying the American way of life. From the outset, Saypol alleged that Ethel and Julius had committed treason, a charge he and his prosecution team would repeat eighteen times during the trial. By heavy implication, this was the crime on which the jury would ultimately be expected to deliver a verdict, not merely "conspiracy to commit espionage," as the formal indictment stated. Saypol thus skirted round the awkward fact that Ethel and Julius could not be charged with treason under US law, because the country was not at war with the Soviet Union at the time of the thefts by Julius and David of military secrets.

From the moment he began his opening remarks, Saypol's style was aggressively adversarial, based on a grim determination to "win" by all possible means. He did not even pay lip service to the legal conceit that prosecution and defense were engaged in a search to determine the truth, known as the "English style" of courtroom procedure. Instead, Saypol set out to portray the defendants as Communist subversives who had plotted to destroy the country that had nurtured them: "A conspiracy is very simply an agreement and understanding between two or more people to violate some law of the United States," Saypol informed the jurors. "When any one of the persons who have entered into this agreement and understanding . . . does any overt act, that is, any physical act to help along the conspiracy . . . then all those other persons who had entered into this agreement and understanding with him become guilty of the crime of conspiracy."[22]

In slow, measured tones, so the jury could be in no doubt, Saypol continued: "therefore in this case proof of only one such overt act by any one of the conspirators would be sufficient to complete the conspiracy . . . the law wisely holds . . . that the particular acts that any one of the conspirators may have performed or did perform to help along this conspiracy binds not only the doer of the act, but also his partners in crime. That is so because he is not acting for himself alone, but with all of them, as well as for himself."[23] Winding up this opening salvo, Saypol announced: "the evidence will show that the loyalty and the allegiance of the Rosenbergs and Sobell were not to our country but . . . to Communism, Communism in this country and Communism throughout the world."[24]

At this moment Bloch interrupted with a point of order—his point being that Communism was not on trial here. Kaufman agreed, but allowed Saypol to continue, which he did in dramatic terms: "We will prove that the Rosenbergs devised and put into operation . . . an elaborate scheme which enabled them to steal through David Greenglass this one weapon that might well hold the key to the survival of this nation and means the peace of the world, the atomic bomb."[25]

According to *The New York Times,* Ethel seemed calmer throughout Saypol's ominous address than the two men.[26] "Her husband kept drumming the counsel table with long nervous fingers. Sobell's hands moved over his jaw and he was twitchy." In contrast, the newspaper reported, Saypol's accusations "brought no outward sign of emotional reaction" from

Ethel. Her gaze remained fixed on the jury box as it would be for much of the trial, believing that the best way to demonstrate her innocence was to look the jurors in the eye.

Bloch's father, Alexander, attempted to separate Ethel from the alleged conspiracy in his opening remarks by describing her as a wife of twelve years' standing and a mother raising two young sons. "She was a housewife, basically a housewife and nothing more," Bloch senior insisted. "She did not transmit or conspire to transmit any information to any government . . . she was dragged into this case through the machinations of her own brother and her own sister-in-law, who in order to transfer and lighten their burden of responsibility, accused her of being a co-conspirator."[27] Once the jury grasped that Ethel was nothing more than a housewife, she could be "sent back to her family to take care of her children."[28]

The eighth of March 1951 was dry and chilly and Max Elitcher, the first witness called by the government that day to open the trial, equally so. Elitcher, Julius and Morton Sobell's college classmate and fellow radical at CCNY, a man Julius had considered his friend and ally when he had visited him in Washington, had now chosen the path of cooperation with the government. Most likely he did so to avoid prosecution for perjury based on falsely denying membership in the Communist Party on a questionnaire he had completed in order to work as an artillery specialist for the Navy Ordnance Department. His testimony was damning as he told the jury of Julius Rosenberg's visit to his home in Washington, DC:

> Yes, he called me and reminded me of our school friendship . . .
> After a while, he asked if my wife would leave the room, that he
> wanted to talk to me in private. She did. Then he began talking
> about the job that the Soviet Union was doing in the war effort
> and how at present a good deal of military information was being denied them by some interests in the United States, and because of that their effort was being impeded. He said there were
> many people who were implementing aid to the Soviet Union
> by providing classified information about military equipment,

and so forth, and asked whether in my capacity at the Bureau of Ordnance working on anti-aircraft devices, and computer control of firing missiles, would I turn information over to him?[29]

Julius apparently also told him that "any information I gave him should be taken to New York to him and he would have it processed photographically" and would be returned overnight, so it would not be missed. He said that this would be done in a very safe manner.[30]

Elitcher continued by claiming that Rosenberg informed him his good friend Sobell was one of those who were getting military information for him and then related an occasion in June 1948, when he moved from Washington to New York, and he noticed he was being followed on the way to Sobell's home. Elitcher said he expressed his concern about this to Sobell when he arrived there and that initially Sobell was angry:

> However a short time later he . . . said he had some valuable information in the house, something he should have given to Julius Rosenberg some time ago and had not done so. It was too valuable to be destroyed and too dangerous to keep around. He said he wanted to deliver it to Rosenberg that night . . . He said he was tired and he wanted me to go along. He might not be able to make the trip back. Upon leaving I saw him take what I identified as a 33 millimeter film can.

Elitcher then recounted how they drove to Catherine Slip. He parked the car facing the East River while Sobell left with the can. He came back about a half hour later. "As we drove off, I said, 'Well, what does Julie think about this, my being followed?' He said, 'Don't be concerned about it; it is OK.'"[31]

The following day, Friday, March 9, David Greenglass took the stand. The jurors could immediately see the physical similarity between David's round, chubby face and Ethel's; but there all resemblance ended between the two siblings in court. David had clearly taken some trouble to look his best for the jury. He was wearing a pinstripe suit, white shirt, and patterned tie and his thick, curly black hair had been recently cut. He smiled repeatedly, perhaps from nerves. Meanwhile, Ethel maintained her impassive expression as the brother she had once loved so dearly took the oath.

Cohn, not Saypol, now rose to examine David, since it was Cohn who had pressured David into "remembering" more incriminating evidence against Ethel. As he began to testify, David was at his most vulnerable, positioned deliberately by the government between his guilty plea for espionage the previous June and his sentencing, which would follow his sister and brother-in-law's trial. At a minimum, David believed the government would not renege on what he hoped was a deal to secure future immunity from prosecution for his wife Ruth and a short prison term for himself. His and his family's fate depended on how he performed under examination and cross-examination.

At first, David gave simple answers to Cohn's factual questions about his education and upbringing and his time in Los Alamos. But David's replies kept falling away to whispers so that the court could barely hear him, and he had to be repeatedly admonished to "lift his voice." Cohn then turned to David's relationship with Ethel and Julius, asking whether he used to have discussions with them concerning "the relative merits of our form of government and that of the Soviet Union."[32] Both Blochs were instantly on their feet to object. Cohn had done his homework, citing a previous treason conviction to justify his line of inquiry. Kaufman agreed that this was admissible testimony.

Cohn explained to the jury that he wanted to show how Ethel and David had discussed Communism over a number of years from 1935 onward at the family home in Sheriff Street. After Ethel's marriage, Julius had joined them. In response, David made it clear that during these sometimes vehement discussions his sister and brother-in-law had preferred "Russian socialism."[33]

Cohn now turned in more depth to David's time at Los Alamos. Duly rehearsed by the prosecution, it did not take David long to involve Ethel directly in the case. He said that while he was away in Los Alamos, Julius and Ethel had invited his wife Ruth to dinner. "There was a conversation between the three present," David explained.[34] "It went something like this: Ethel started the conversation by stating to Ruth that she must have noticed that she, Ethel, was no longer involved in Communist Party activities." Once again, Bloch objected to the reference to Communism and Kaufman overruled him. David went on with his story. "The reason for this," Ethel supposedly told him, "is that Julius has finally gotten to a point where he is doing what he wanted to do all along, which was that he was giving information to the Soviet Union." According to David, it was Julius who informed Ruth "that I was working on the atomic bomb project at Los Alamos and that they would want me to give information to the Russians. My wife objected to this, but Ethel said . . ." Bloch again objected to the reported speech of a conversation at which David was not present, but it was too late. Ethel had been placed firmly at the center of the story.

The New York Times reported melodramatically that David's account of Ethel's declaration to Ruth caused Ethel to turn "deathly pale."[35] At one point she "pressed tight fingers against her eyeballs, her head lowered to her bosom. Her brother kept avoiding her fixed stare."[36] Shortly afterward, the court adjourned for the weekend. Ethel and Julius returned to their respective prison cells, dreading what further revelations David had in store for the jury.

On Monday, March 12, David Greenglass moved on to describe his furlough in Manhattan in January 1945. He explained how Julius had come to his and Ruth's apartment, where David had given his brother-in-law some sketches of flat-type lens molds that he had prepared based on those he had apparently seen at Los Alamos. David then produced a sketch of the lens mold, government exhibit two, which he admitted under questioning was a copy he had prepared the previous day, since he had given Julius the original. Bloch was furious at this reconstruction being used as evidence, which Kaufman ruled was admissible. David continued with his story. He said that Ruth now joined in his conversation with Julius to say that his handwriting was so bad it would need interpretation: "Julius said there was nothing to worry about as Ethel would type it up, retype the information."[37]

According to reporters, Ethel sat impassively as David continued to implicate his sister. He recalled how he and Ruth had gone to dinner with Ethel and Julius a few days later at their apartment in Knickerbocker Village. According to David, Ethel had introduced him and Ruth to her neighbor Ann Sidorovich, who was at the apartment in the early part of the evening. In David's account, Julius had then said Ann would come out to meet the Greenglasses in Albuquerque, in order to receive information from David about the atomic bomb.[38] But what if Ann could not come? David claimed to have asked Julius, who replied: "Well, I will give you something so that you will be able to identify the person that does come."[39] Ann Sidorovich had flatly denied to a grand jury that she was present that evening, or that Julius had ever asked her to act as a courier.

Sticking to his script, David next explained how Julius, Ruth, and Ethel went into the kitchen while he was in the living room. They emerged a few minutes later with the side of a Jell-O box cut in a particular, irregular way. "I said 'Oh that is very clever.' Because I noticed how it fit and he said 'the simplest things are the cleverest.'" To add to the drama, Cohn now repeated the ruse with another newly cut-up Jell-O box to show how it would work as a means of identification. For further theatrical effect, Cohn then asked David on the witness stand to cut a new box in the way that he remembered it that night, just like two pieces of a puzzle. These two pieces were then handed to the jury to inspect.

When Cohn asked if there was any further conversation that evening between the Greenglasses and the Rosenbergs David picked up his cue. He said "the Rosenbergs" (deliberately repeating the plural) told Ruth that she would not have to worry about money "because it would be taken care of."[40] David emphasized that Julius said it first, "and Ethel backed it up."

From here, David segued into how Ruth had supposedly said to Ethel that she looked tired: "and Ethel remarked that she was tired between the child and staying up late at night, keeping—typing over notes that Julius had brought her—this was on espionage." David clarified that those were not Ethel's precise words. She had said "in this work" and that "she didn't mind it so long as Julius was doing what he wanted to do."[41]

David then withdrew as the government called Dr. Walter Koski, an explosives expert at the Atomic Energy Commission. Koski explained to Saypol that whereas "a glass lens essentially focuses light, an explosive lens focuses a detonation wave or a high-pressure force coming in."[42] Saypol then asked Koski if the information relating to the lens mold and the experimentation to which he had testified continued to be secret information. Koski said it still was secret, except as divulged at this trial.

Throughout this exchange, Bloch had been objecting wherever possible: sometimes regarding the form of a question, if it concerned what someone other than Koski might be thinking; or if, for example, Koski, who was a scientist, was asked by Saypol to pronounce on political matters. Bloch made little headway with Kaufman, who at one point reprimanded him severely when he forgot what he was going to say. "You constantly interrupt me before I am through, Mr. Bloch," Kaufman snapped.[43] Increasingly flustered, Bloch neglected to question how David, whose academic career consisted of six months at Brooklyn Polytechnic, where he failed eight courses, would have understood the lenses' technical significance.

Dr Koski had made his point for the prosecution. The information the court was being shown would be extremely valuable to another nation trying to construct an atomic bomb.

In the afternoon, David took the stand again, Cohn examining. David said he had offered Julius a detailed sketch of the atomic bomb, including a cross section that he had handed over to Julius in Ethel's presence. Suddenly, Bloch stood up and asked the court to impound an exhibit "so that it remains secret to the court, the jury and counsel."[44] Bloch may have intervened out of frustration, for even Saypol found this "a rather strange request coming from the defendants."[45] Furthermore, Bloch had not discussed his intervention in advance with either his father or his assistant Gloria Agrin. "Bloch had a very real problem," Agrin later told the journalist Ted Morgan. "Saypol had told him at the start of the trial, 'If your clients do not confess they are doomed.' We knew we were facing the death sentence. Bloch wanted to show the court—we are just as patriotic as the others. He was trying to avoid the death sentence by lifting the stigma of treason. It was a courtroom decision made on the spur of the moment."[46]

As Saypol realized, Bloch had simply reinforced the prosecution's contention that the information David had allegedly given to Julius in Ethel's presence was highly sensitive. In fact, the Atomic Energy Commission had ruled in advance of the trial that the sketches were declassified material. Bloch tried to get around this awkward fact by telling Kaufman that he was "not at all sure in my own mind . . . whether or not even at this late date this information may not be used to the advantage of a foreign power." It was a grave misstep, making precisely the opposite point from the one Bloch should have made: that nothing a lowly machinist who had failed school exams and dropped out of college could get his hands on at Los Alamos and understand was of any serious value.[47] Bloch had violated the defense lawyer's canon never to concede anything the prosecution had not yet proven.

Kaufman eventually allowed proceedings to continue, after considerable discussion about whether the court should be cleared. David returned to the stand and to his story, which seemingly damned Ethel as an active co-conspirator. He claimed that when Julius had finished reading the information handed to him, Julius had said: "'We ought to have this typed up immediately' and my wife [Ruth] said 'we will probably have to correct the grammar involved . . .' so they pulled—they had a bridge table and they brought it into the living room plus a typewriter."[48] "Who did the typing, Mr. Greenglass?" asked Cohn. "Ethel did the typing and Ruth and Julius and Ethel did the correction of the grammar," David said smoothly.

•   •   •

Bloch finally got his chance to cross-examine David. He worked hard to demonstrate that David was at best an unreliable witness or at worst a liar, despite Kaufman repeatedly asking him to be more concise.

Why did David continually smile? Bloch inquired. David replied that he didn't realize he was smiling.[49] Bloch reminded David that he had been prepared to ignore an oath when he joined the atomic bomb project; so why should he be believed now, having taken another oath?

"You realize the possible death penalty in the event that Ethel is convicted by this jury do you not?"

Repeating the question Bloch asked: "And you bear affection for her?"

"I do."

"This moment?"

"At this moment."

"And yesterday?"

"And yesterday."

Bloch continually pressed David to admit that he had not mentioned Ethel when he was initially questioned by the FBI after his arrest; and that he only called for a lawyer to defend his wife Ruth once he realized the implications for her of his confession; and that he was now lying in order to save his wife, who was at home with their two children. Bloch failed to break him. David refused to admit anything beyond accepting that he had failed all eight courses at school.[50]

Once Bloch got into his stride he fired detailed questions at David:

"Was the name Harry Gold mentioned in the conversation you had with your lawyer . . . on the morning of June 16, 1950?"

"I can't tell and I don't remember . . . You are asking me about a period of time that was very confused for me, and it was a wonder that so much stayed with me about it."[51]

"You don't remember that?"

"No I don't remember that."

"What happened in June 1950?"

"No."

"But you do remember everything that your wife told you back on 29th November . . . 1944?"[52]

Nonetheless the jury was expected to believe that David Greenglass's memory was good enough to produce complex lens sketches for an atomic bomb, more than four years after he had apparently created the original drawings and without any assistance.

On Wednesday, March 14, David's final day as a government witness, he acknowledged to Bloch that he was color-blind and might not have been able to remember the exact color or flavor of the Jell-O box in question. Bloch reminded David of his quarrels with Julius over their failed business. According to Bloch, David had hit Julius on one occasion. "I—I don't recall if I actually hit him," David simply stuttered in reply.[53]

David's cross-examination finally ended. Bloch had landed some telling blows to undermine David's credibility, notably regarding his memory, without ever forcing David to alter the substance of his testimony. The government now called David's wife Ruth, its next key witness in the prosecution's attempt to persuade the jury that Ethel had actively assisted Julius and David's espionage for the Soviet Union. Like her husband, Ruth came to the witness stand looking her best. This twenty-six-year-old "buxom brunette," as she was described by the press, wore a pearl necklace over her smartest dark dress and plenty of lipstick; her hair was swept back in two big "victory rolls" either side of her face in the fashion of the day. She could have been going out to the theater or a restaurant rather than making an appearance in court.

Beneath this confident facade Ruth was nervous, so eager to tell her stories about Ethel and Julius that she had to be told to slow down. Once she composed herself, she gave a more confident, polished performance than her husband, repeating some of his stories but telling them firsthand.

In answer to James Kilsheimer's questions, she started by explaining that Julius had wanted her to undertake espionage work "because if all the nations had this information then one nation couldn't use the bomb as a threat against another."[54] Ruth swiftly added that she had initially disagreed with Julius's reasoning. "I said that the people who are in charge of the work on the bomb were in a better position to know whether the information should be shared or not."[55]

Ruth then placed Ethel at the heart of the story. "Ethel Rosenberg," she began deliberately, "said that I should at least tell it to David, that she felt that this was right for David, that he would want it, that I should give him the message and let him decide for himself . . . Julius and Ethel persuaded me to give my husband the message and they told me the information."[56]

Ruth went on to corroborate all the stories David had told about Ethel and Julius's neighbor Ann Sidorovich and the Jell-O box; and about going to live with David in Albuquerque for a year from March 1945, where she used the side of the Jell-O box to identify their courier for the stolen secrets, the American Communist Harry Gold. Prompted by Kilsheimer, Ruth concluded by recalling her visit to Ethel and Julius's apartment in September 1945, shortly after the United States had dropped two atomic bombs on Hiroshima and Nagasaki. Ruth claimed this was the reason why she now told the Rosenbergs that she opposed David giving Julius any more documents and material from Los Alamos. However, David had just passed Julius further information and "he wanted Ethel to type it right away . . . And Ethel got out a typewriter and sat down to work on the notes."[57] With devastating fluency Ruth said the typewriter was a Remington portable that Ethel had put on the bridge table. She said that she and Julius had helped Ethel with the phraseology when it got a little too lengthy and "then Julius burned the notes in the kitchen and flushed the ashes in the bowl."[58] She continued that Julius allegedly wanted her to persuade David to stay working in Los Alamos. According to Ruth, Julius reassured her that money would not be a problem as he could get enough "from the Russians" for them to be comfortable.[59]

Ruth eventually came to Julius's alleged visit to her on May 24, 1950, the day after Harry Gold's arrest. On that occasion she alleged Julius had handed over $1,000 (roughly $11,000 today), but then on June 4 "he gave my husband a package wrapped in brown paper and said it was

$4,000, that there would be more money available in Mexico when we got there."[60] Ruth continued: "I asked him what he was doing. He said he was going too, that he would not leave at the same time, and would meet us in Mexico. We would see him there, and I asked him what Ethel thought about it and he said Ethel didn't like the idea of it herself but she realized it was necessary and they were going to go."[61]

Ruth rounded off her testimony by focusing on Ethel. She insisted that Ethel had visited her after Julius's arrest on July 17, 1950, bringing pie and baby presents. According to Ruth, Ethel "said her counsel advised her to see me personally and get assurances from me that David would not talk. She said it would only be a matter of a couple of years and in the long run we would be better off . . . That if David said he was innocent and Julius said he was innocent . . . everybody would stand a better chance;"[62] "and she said 'Do you think it is a dirty shame for David to take the blame and sit for two?'"[63]

Alexander Bloch now rose to cross-examine Ruth. The elder Bloch could not get Ruth to admit that she had committed a crime in accepting the $4,000 that she said Julius had given her on June 4. "We had no particular love for the $4,000. We weren't trying to get money,"[64] she asserted. Ruth maintained that her husband had initially suggested "he wanted to tear it up and flush it [away]."[65] But then they decided to hand it over to her brother-in-law, Louis Abel. Why, she was asked, did she give it to her brother-in-law and not put it in the bank? Wasn't it so that in the event of David's arrest it wouldn't be found in her possession? "I don't think we thought of that at the time," Ruth replied disingenuously.[66] Try as he might Ruth evaded his answers until Saypol objected, "I think there has been enough of this now,"[67] an objection upheld by the judge, who commented that it felt as if they were going around in a circle.

Both Blochs tried to show that Ruth too was an unreliable witness; it was particularly striking, they contended, that she remembered some events in great detail while others seemed hazy to her. Alexander Bloch inquired directly at one point: "Did you ask Mr. Rogge [David and Ruth's lawyer] whether you had any chance to escape punishment in case you testified for the government?"[68] Ruth requested permission to ask her lawyer before responding.

Bloch senior was continually prevented from pursuing this line of questioning by Kaufman or the prosecution, who repeatedly raised points of order. Alexander Bloch persisted in the face of these interruptions, pointing out that Ruth was named in the original indictment as a co-conspirator and yet had not been arrested. His goal was to make the jury understand that a defendant was being called as a government witness, a tack that Saypol clearly did not like.

"It is always difficult for a prosecutor to decide when to raise an objection because of the latitude allowed in cross-examination. I think however at this point I should say it has gone much too far and I ask the court to control it," Saypol demanded.[69] The argument did not end there, but although Ruth was occasionally evasive she never lost control, even when acknowledging that she too had bought a typewriter with some of the money Julius had given her, and especially so when discussing the details of a Jell-O box, telling Bloch curtly: "I can tell you how to cook Jell-O."[70]

·   ·   ·

Ethel had now heard the worst. She had listened unflinchingly to the brother she had cared for like a mother and his wife accuse her of crimes that could result in her own death. David and Ruth had been so well rehearsed by the prosecution that Manny and Alexander Bloch had failed to find discrepancies between their recollections of the same alleged events. The defense had good reason to feel gloomy as the prosecution prepared to call a succession of witnesses to reinforce David and Ruth's potentially lethal testimony.

Seven

Destruction

After Ruth had told her story, the prosecution called several witnesses to corroborate various elements of the Greenglasses' story. They included Ruth's brother-in-law, Louis Abel, who testified that he had received the $4,000 that Julius had allegedly given Ruth and David when he urged them to flee after Harry Gold's arrest. Doctor George Bernhardt, a family friend as well as the family doctor, who sometimes allowed Julius to visit him at his home in Knickerbocker Village rather than at his medical office for allergy shots, was also called. Ethel and Julius had believed he was a political sympathizer, so seeing him as a prosecution witness was a shock. He said on the stand that Julius had called him around this time to inquire about inoculations for Mexico. Most likely, the FBI had told him that his telephone conversations had been wiretapped in order to persuade him to cooperate.

Harry Gold, the former courier at Los Alamos and admitted perjurer, was currently serving a thirty-year prison sentence in Lewisburg Federal Penitentiary. He had pleaded guilty to committing espionage and admitted that he had been working for the Soviet Union since 1935 when he was called to testify for the government. Gold, a short and stocky man with heavy-lidded eyes that gave him a permanently shifty look, was a forty-year-old laboratory chemist, the son of poor Jewish immigrants from Ukraine who had settled in Philadelphia during the Depression. He had a degree in chemical engineering, had never married and, after spending the last ten months in prison, appeared, perhaps not surprisingly, pale and unemotional as he gave evidence "as precisely and matter-of-factly as a high-school teacher explaining a problem in geometry."[1] Prompted by Myles Lane, Saypol's chief assistant prosecutor, Gold now swore that he had met the Greenglasses in Albuquerque at their apartment after identifying himself to them with the oddly cut cardboard half-box of Jell-O.

According to Gold, the meeting took place on Sunday, June 3, 1945, at about 8:30 a.m. as he had come from New York, tried to meet them the night before only to find they were out, so had to stay overnight in a hotel:

> I went again to the High Street address. I was admitted and I recall going up a very steep flight of steps, and I knocked on a door. It was opened by a young man of about 23 with dark hair. He was smiling. I said "I come from Julius" and I showed him the piece of cardboard in my hand, the piece of cardboard that had been given me by Yakovlev [the Soviet former consul and intelligence officer]. He asked me to enter. I did and Greenglass went to a woman's handbag and brought out from it a piece of cardboard. We matched the two of them . . . it appeared to be from the same part of the same packaged food from which the piece of cardboard that I had had originally been cut.[2]

However unlikely it was that he would have said, "I come from Julius" (real names were rarely used), Gold had thus established in one clear answer the link between the absent but indicted Soviet contact agent Yakovlev, Julius Rosenberg, David Greenglass, and Los Alamos. And, "despite abundant evidence suggesting that Harry was endowed with an agile imagination,"[3] the Blochs declined to cross-examine him. It is not entirely clear why they let him off the hook in this way, since a sharp interviewer could easily have revealed inconsistencies in Gold's testimony—in particular, how could such a consummate liar be trusted that his alleged unlikely greeting "I come from Julius" was what he actually said? But equally Gold might blurt out something even more damaging, true or not. Nowhere is Bloch's difficulty more clearly revealed than in this lapse. He took his clients on trust and was as convinced as anyone that they were innocent in the broadest sense. But there must always have remained a sliver of doubt that perhaps there were some details he would never know for certain.

Elizabeth Bentley, the former Communist and spy who had abandoned the party in 1945 and defected to the FBI as a professional informer, was one of the last witnesses for the prosecution. As she told the court, she had degrees from both Vassar and Columbia, while her elegant demeanor and articulateness spoke for itself, making her a formidable witness. The media had turned her into a famous personality, calling her "the Red spy queen," and she provided an interesting contrast to the usual Jewish leftists with Russian roots. But the truth was that her background was neither monied nor privileged, and her embrace of Communism can partly be explained by loneliness. In 1934, living in Florence, she had been a supporter of Mussolini and Fascism but soon changed her views following a brief affair with an Italian anti-Fascist. When she returned to America she joined the CPUSA and, once she met Jacob Golos and began a relationship with him alongside spying for the Soviet Union, her life became meaningful. But then, following Golos's death and her defection to the US authorities, her personal life became increasingly tumultuous: she drank heavily, was involved in car accidents, and was said to have had a relationship with a man who beat her. But none of this dramatic backstory was apparent on the witness stand, where she was invariably calm and professional and extremely knowledgeable about the CPUSA, to which she had belonged for a decade since 1935.

Bentley explained how after the death of Jacob Golos she gave orders to Earl Browder (CPUSA head from 1932 to 1946): "transmitted orders from Moscow to him and he had to accept them. Sometimes he would fight against them, but he ended up by accepting them."[4] These were, Bentley explained, implicit instructions understood by all CPUSA members "in the sense when you realized you were serving the International of Moscow and refused to carry them [orders] out, you were immediately expelled."[5]

Manny Bloch repeatedly objected to this line of questioning, which he argued was an attempt to make membership in the Communist Party the issue. But Bentley insisted that anyone who was a member of the CPUSA had "an almost adhesive relationship to the Communist International." In the circumstances, the best Bloch could do was try to discredit Bentley by pointing out that she had just written a memoir about her life as a Communist, *Out of Bondage,* from which she hoped to earn royalties; furthermore, Bloch noted, Bentley made money from lecturing about former Communists.

Judge Kaufman allowed Bentley to continue with her explanation because it showed, he claimed, "the causal connection that we have been talking about between the membership in the party and intending to give an advantage to a foreign government, to wit the USSR."[6]

At this juncture, the Blochs had not expected the government case to be over for another four or five days, as Saypol had previously indicated. Yet suddenly, on Friday, March 16, the prosecution announced that it did not intend to call any more witnesses. None of the renowned scientists who had been listed as ready to testify were going to be summoned. Manny and Alexander Bloch, together with Gloria Agrin, therefore had only a long weekend to prepare the defense's rebuttal. In vain, the Blochs complained to Kaufman that their clients were rarely available for discussion, as on most days the proceedings finished at 4:30 p.m. and the defendants were returned to their cells at 5 p.m. Even worse, Ethel and Julius were not available at all on Saturday and Sunday. "This we think is fatal," Manny Bloch inadvertently declared. Saypol interjected: "You do not want to go so far." Bloch, correcting himself, said his clients' availability was "vital to the presentation of the defendants' defense."[7]

Kaufman maintained his previously stated opinion about "the need for this case to proceed with dispatch."[8] As a seeming concession, he then ordered that Julius and Ethel should be made available for as long as they were needed "today and tonight." But he warned that he did not accept that the defense had been caught out. Kaufman said he felt he had given the Blochs ample opportunity to prepare, more advance notice than did many judges, for whom he insisted it was usually a question of "they finish and you start."

It was late afternoon when, on March 22, Julius Rosenberg finally took the witness stand. He had dressed once again in his best suit, with a white shirt and silver and maroon tie, looking smart as he spoke clearly, showing respect to the court by addressing all as "Sir." He began well enough as Bloch junior led him through an account of his life, places of education and work, and he answered straightforwardly and concisely. Bloch then turned to the sensitive subject of Julius's views about the Soviet system of government as compared with that of the United States.

"First of all," Julius said, "I am not an expert on matters on [sic] different economic systems, but in my normal social intercourse with my friends we discussed matters like that. And I believe there are merits in both systems. I mean from what I have been able to read and ascertain." He went on: "In the first place I heartily approve our system of justice as performed in this country, Anglo-Saxon jurisprudence. I am in favor, heartily, in favor of our constitution and Bill of Rights and I owe my allegiance to my country at all times."

"Do you owe allegiance to any other country?"

"No, I do not."

"Have you any divided allegiances?"

"I do not."

"Would you fight for this country?"

"Yes I will . . . And in discussing the merits of other forms of governments, I discussed that with my friends on the basis of the performance of what they accomplished and I felt that the Soviet government has improved [the] lot of the underdog there, has made a lot of progress in eliminating illiteracy, has done a lot of reconstruction work and built up a lot of resources. And at the same time I felt they contributed a major share in destroying the Hitler beast who killed six million of my co-religionists and I feel emotional about that thing."[9]

Julius's speech, while undoubtedly rehearsed, sounded as if it came from the heart. There was more in this vein as Bloch asked Julius specifically whether he approved of the "Communistic" system over the "capitalistic" system. Julius replied that he believed each country should choose its own system: "If the English want a king it is their business. If the Russians want Communism it is their business. If the Americans want our form of government it is our business."[10] He was expressing precisely the sort of ideas that *Life* magazine had made famous in its March 29, 1943, edition, devoted to explaining the USSR in a positive light when it suited the government to ensure that ordinary Americans were made aware why this once barbaric country was an ally.

Julius was speaking sensibly when Judge Kaufman abruptly intervened. He had heard enough. The judge asked Julius if he had ever belonged to any group that discussed the system in Russia.[11] "Well, your honor," Julius responded flatly, "I feel at this time that I refuse to answer a question that might tend to incriminate me." With one ill-considered answer, Julius had spoiled the impression that Bloch had been carefully trying to create of a somewhat naive but patriotic young American who had nothing to hide.

Bloch resumed, taking Julius back to the fateful night in January 1945 when Julius had allegedly cut up the Jell-O box and assigned his and Ethel's left-wing neighbor Ann Sidorovich as his choice of courier to receive whatever David stole from Los Alamos. Fed by Bloch, Julius denied everything that the court had just heard from David and Ruth about this purported episode; according to Julius, it simply never happened. When Bloch asked if Julius had access to the large sums of money alleged by David and Ruth, Julius said that he had bought Ethel a fur coat for $80 about eight or nine years ago when he had received a check for some work he had been doing for the government. "We remodeled it a couple of times and she still has it," he added.[12] Otherwise Julius said Ethel bought her own clothes and had spent a maximum of about $300 over the last ten years. Looking at Ethel's drab clothes, the jury would have had no difficulty in believing that statement.

Julius also denied ever having met Elizabeth Bentley or Jacob Golos. He denied ever discussing the nature of David's work at Los Alamos or even knowing at the time that an atomic weapon was being built there. For several more hours, Bloch put leading questions to Julius about every significant episode in the prosecution case. Each time, Julius emphatically denied the alleged facts that had been presented to the court. None of Ruth and David's allegations were true, said Julius, offering an alternative scenario of how David had approached him for help with money. According to Julius, when he had told Ethel about meeting David, she had replied: "What's the matter? Is Ruthie nagging Dave again for money?"

As Julius made clear, he and Ethel did not live the life of a top spy funded by another country; they did not have any spare cash for anything more than a make-do lifestyle. Occasionally he would take Ethel out for dinner at inexpensive restaurants such as Pappas or Nicholaus on Second Avenue.

After a brief recess, once Bloch declared he had no more questions, Saypol launched into cross-examining Julius. Ethel was proud of her husband's performance. He had been courteous but given away nothing. He had stuck to the script agreed between them, but she must have realized that the next few hours would be crucial. Saypol tried to elicit who Julius's friends were at CCNY and whether he had belonged as a student to any Communist group. Almost immediately, Julius fell back on his constitutional right not to answer the question. Julius did concede that he and Ethel had supported the Joint Anti-Fascist Refugee Committee; Saypol retorted that the US attorney general had deemed the committee to be a subversive organization.

Saypol next showed Julius a collection tin for "Save a Spanish Republican Child," which investigators had taken from his home. Did he do more than contribute to this cause? Saypol inquired. Julius insisted he had not.[13]

There followed a lengthy discussion about wristwatches, and whether or not Julius had ever bought any from his brother-in-law Sam, a wholesale watch dealer. He said he had not. Saypol asked Julius to clarify his views expressed earlier as to why he felt that the Soviet government had improved the lot of the underdog there and what newspapers had given him this information.

"Various newspapers," said Julius.

"You mean the *Daily Worker?*"

"On occasion," Julius conceded.

Saypol then asked him to clarify what he knew about the Soviet Union eliminating illiteracy or doing reconstruction work. When Julius insisted he did not know details, but "that is what I read the newspaper reports on," Saypol asked: "Did you read anything about the request of Russia for the atomic bomb? Would that be perhaps a resource that you had in mind?"[14] Julius denied that this was what he had in mind, but Saypol suggested that regular reading of the *Daily Worker* was the source of his information. "Were there some occasions that your wife got the *Daily Worker* when you didn't . . . is it fair to say that you or your wife got it every day?" Saypol persisted.

And from then on Saypol continually needled Julius as to how much he discussed with Ethel, how much he shared with her either about the uranium theft or about David coming to ask him for money and help with vaccination certificates:

> Saypol: "Well you are not answering my question. I am asking you when you told your wife, his sister, about this demand, or these demands, that he had made on you, in discussing it with her did you remind her perhaps of the conversation with Ruth Greenglass in 1945 when she told you she was worried because he wanted to steal something from that army?"

Julius: "Well I don't remember if I reminded her on this occasion but it was either this occasion or the second time I spoke to David Greenglass that I remarked about that incident."

Saypol: "Well now, coming again to this $2,000-small pox-Mexico incident, you told her, your wife, and she said, 'Maybe Ruthie is nagging him for money again?' Have you told her about the 1950 incident involving the questioning about the uranium?"

"I don't recall . . ." Julius offered lamely.[15]

And so it went on, with Saypol going over the same ground, repeating statements Julius had made earlier, and asking him to clarify precisely when he had discussed matters with Ethel. Exasperated, Julius answered: "I have already answered that, Mr. Saypol, a number of times."

But it was not yet over. A little while later Saypol returned to the question of David asking Julius again for money.[16]

Saypol: "Didn't you tell us before in response to your lawyer's question that it was after you went to his home and he told you he was busy, he had company, to come back in a few days that you then went and told your wife, 'Davey is in some kind of trouble he is acting peculiar?' Is that what actually happened?"

Julius: "Yes, Sir."

Saypol: "And your answer a little while ago in response to a similar question was not accurate? . . . Do you remember having told us a little while ago that you didn't say anything to your wife about it?"

Julius: "Well I did say something to my wife about it."[17]

Overall it was a bruising confrontation as Saypol continually asked the court to read out testimony that Julius had previously given, in an attempt to catch him out. Julius came across as slippery, unable to re-member dates precisely or explain convincingly why, for instance, he had suddenly splurged on a new watch for Ethel.

There was little Manny Bloch could do to rescue his client, although he intervened frequently, even to state, for example: "Just a moment I just want to get my objection for the record. Same objection your Honor."[18] When Julius admitted that David had threatened blackmail after Julius had refused to lend him money, Saypol pressed the point home with ease. "Did he say he would go to the authorities and tell them you were in a conspiracy with him to steal the atom bomb secret?"[19] Saypol asked. No, Julius insisted. But, battered by Saypol's relentless assault, he no longer seemed like a defendant who could be trusted to tell the truth.

•   •   •

Finally, on the afternoon of Monday, March 26, it was Ethel's turn to take the witness stand. She seemed to have paid more trouble than usual to her appearance, for today she was wearing some carefully applied lipstick to go with her plain pink blouse and black skirt. Although she appeared calm as she sat in the high-backed chair in a booth to the left of the judge, she must have been nervous as she took the oath and prepared to answer Alexander Bloch's questions. She had spent the past two weeks sitting silently in court, looking away as she endured her brother's accusations. This was her chance.

Inez Robb, a former war correspondent turned syndicated columnist, wrote an astute account of Ethel's appearance that also gave her millions of readers the frisson of uncovering the "real" woman beneath her bland exterior. Ethel resembled any woman you might meet in the supermarket, Robb wrote:

> There are 50,000 "Ethel Rosenbergs" on the subway any workday morning. This 34-year-old woman sits at the defen-dants' table in court wearing the tired uniform of the clerk or

stenographer—a dark wool skirt, a whitewash blouse and a white wool sweater.

Hers is a dish-face complexion, pasty and features undistinguished. It is difficult to imagine this ordinary-looking woman, slightly dumpy, mixed up in anything as dashing as espionage for she looks about as dashing as bread pudding.

She does not even make the best of her naturally curly dark hair. Her bob is neither long nor short and it needs shaping.

All in all she looks innocuous and vacuous until you come to her eyes.

They are not only her best feature but probably the clue to her being. They are large, dark and extremely intelligent. There is no way to camouflage them or the mentality that lies behind them.[20]

Ethel began straightforwardly by giving her age and educational achievements. After she explained that she had graduated from Seward Park High School before she was sixteen, she went on to say: "I became the youngest member of the Schola Cantorum under the directorship of Hugh Ross,"[21] an almost imperceptible note of pride intruding.

Step by step, Alexander Bloch guided their exchanges toward the substance of the prosecution case against her. He asked her first to describe the furniture and household effects that she and Julius had owned. Eventually Ethel came to the Remington portable typewriter that David and Ruth had claimed she had used to write up the notes that David had jotted down at Los Alamos. "I was a member of the Clark House Dramatic Group and one of the actors in the group had the typewriter and wanted very badly to get rid of it. So he sold it to me for $30.00 and I had it ever since."[22] Ethel spoke freely about all the typing she had done over the years for Julius, starting with his college homework and ending up with his business correspondence: "I used to type up all the bids for various government surplus material," she recalled.[23]

Kaufman now intervened to ask Ethel about the charges leveled against Julius in 1945 by his employer, the US Army Signal Corps, that he was a member of the Communist Party, and the typing she had done for him in that connection. In particular, Kaufman asked her, "And he was dismissed for that reason?" As Kaufman intended, Ethel misunderstood the question. She could have said yes, while making it clear that the government had failed to prove its allegation that Julius was a party member. Instead, she refused to answer, citing her constitutional right to remain silent. She had evidently thought Kaufman had wanted her to confirm Julius's party membership.

Kaufman had tripped her up and Ethel now suffered the embarrassment of being advised by Bloch senior that she had to answer the question. Ethel admitted under duress, "Well they gave that as a reason, that is right." Kaufman followed up by asking Ethel if the reply she had typed in 1945 denied that he was a Communist.[24] Once again, Bloch was objecting, but it was an unwinnable situation. The judge had made Ethel look like a liar who was concealing the fact that Julius was a Communist.

Use of the Fifth Amendment to protect a defendant against possible self-incrimination was and is a basic constitutional privilege included in the United States Bill of Rights. Yet it had become highly technical, and by 1951 lawyers often needed to consult guidelines as to its use. However, it was certainly not intended that anyone who legitimately exercised the right subsequently had to justify it, since evidently that made a mockery of the privilege. But when Judge Kaufman ruled that Ethel had to answer a question and that it was for the jury to consider the question of her credibility, the jury was effectively being told that it is inconsistent for a person to plead the Fifth Amendment before a grand jury and then to answer the question in a manner consistent with innocence before a trial jury.*

---

* In 1956 Judge Jerome Frank wrote: "No one who legitimately exercises the constitutional privilege ought to be so placed that he must subsequently justify it to a jury." See https://caselaw.findlaw.com/us-supreme-court/353/391 .html. Four Supreme Court judges agreed with his view that questioning a defendant at a trial about an apparent contradiction between taking the Fifth Amendment before a grand jury and subsequently asserting one's innocence at a trial effectively stripped that defendant of the amendment's protections.

It took Bloch some time to regain control of his examination of Ethel. He objected that the court was failing to distinguish between the circumstances where a witness involuntarily appeared before a tribunal, as in the case of a grand jury proceeding, and a trial where a witness voluntarily took the stand and asserted her innocence. Kaufman ordered him to proceed without responding. Bloch eventually returned to Ruth's claim that Ethel had tried to persuade David to undertake espionage work. Was this true, Bloch asked? No, Ethel replied.

Bloch now asked Ethel whether she had typed up any information concerning Los Alamos or the atomic bomb, as Ruth had alleged, and whether she had said that she was used to David's handwriting and could easily copy it. Several times Ethel emphatically denied both allegations.

Next, Bloch asked Ethel in turn if she had known Julius's alleged Soviet handler, Alexander Yakovlev; Elizabeth Bentley and her Soviet handler, Jacob Golos; Harry Gold or the atomic spy Klaus Fuchs. Each time, Ethel confidently replied that she had never met these individuals. In fact she did not know any Russians at all.

Bloch now tried to build a different, more sympathetic picture of Ethel for the jury by asking her about her health problems and her struggles as a young mother. Ethel spoke of her spinal curvature and how, shortly after Michael's birth, her health had deteriorated and she had often needed twice-weekly iron injections. She also described her worries about Michael's continual poor health. "I had had a very difficult time ever since his birth . . . he was given to severe colds and sore throats with high fever. It wasn't the usual thing of where a baby gets sick occasionally. It was practically every week in and week out."[25]

At this point, Saypol objected to Bloch's line of questioning and Kaufman agreed, cutting short Bloch's attempt to present Ethel in a softer light as just another ordinary, careworn housewife.

Encouraged by Bloch, Ethel then gave her account of meeting Ruth following David's arrest in June 1950. Ruth said she had told Ethel that "he is not guilty and we have hired a lawyer and we are going to fight this case because we are not guilty."[26] According to Ruth, she and Ethel had walked together a little way, talking about money and how little they had. However,

Ethel pointedly added a farewell scene that Ruth had not mentioned: "As we reached East Houston Street I put my arms around her and kissed her. She remained rigid in my arms, didn't return the kiss and said 'Goodbye' coldly, turned on her heel and left."[27] Ethel further insisted that she had not asked Ruth for an assurance from David that he was not going to talk.

Alexander Bloch's examination of Ethel was almost over. He questioned her about her wristwatch, which she said her husband had given her for her birthday in 1945.

"Did anybody ever tell you or intimate to you that this wristwatch came from the Russians?"

"No."

"Or that the Russians paid for it?"

"No."

And then his son Manny said he had just one question for Ethel. It concerned when he became Ethel's lawyer as well as Julius's. "Did I ever advise you to go to see Ruthie Greenglass and tell Ruthie Greenglass to tell her husband to keep his mouth shut?" Manny then had to explain to the court why he was asking: Ruth had testified that Ethel Rosenberg said her lawyer sent her. Ethel answered:

"No, you never told me to do any such thing . . . you told me to stay away from them."

"Did I tell you I believed that they were your enemies?"

"Yes, you told me that."

"That is all," said Manny and sat down.

Saypol began his cross-examination without a break. Ethel had endured a grueling session with frequent interruptions from all sides, questions repeated, and had had to be advised by her own legal team on occasion that she should answer a question. Now, with barely even time to draw breath, she braced herself for a further onslaught.

Saypol, his bushy eyebrows brimming over his rimless spectacles, began by asking Ethel for details of when and how Julius had lost his wristwatch. Then followed a discussion between the lawyers about whether a particular document that Ethel had admitted bore her signature was relevant, and whether or not Ethel correctly understood her rights about refusing to answer any questions if the answers might tend to incriminate her.

Saypol then asked her about her grand jury appearance on August 11 when, in reply to being asked if she had signed a Communist Party nominating petition in 1939, she had already admitted that she had. Ethel now responded: "I refuse to answer on the grounds that this might tend to incriminate me."

Manny Bloch regularly intervened, recognizing the difficulty that Ethel had created for herself. He argued to Kaufman that Ethel could subsequently assert her right to remain silent regardless of her earlier testimony. Kaufman responded by proposing: "Supposing he [Saypol] were to ask, 'Did you tell the truth before the Grand Jury?'" Saypol accepted Kaufman's invitation and asked Ethel exactly this question. Once again, Ethel refused to answer on the grounds of self-incrimination.[28] Unavoidably, she had created the impression that she had something to hide about her own Communist sympathies.

After this disaster for Ethel, Saypol moved on to her relationship with David. Ethel could have used this opportunity to reveal how much she had loved her little brother. Instead she answered warily: "I had always helped Davey in the past and I continued to feel the same way about anything involving Davey." "Did you help him join the Communist Party?" Saypol inquired.[29] Bloch objected and almost at the same time Ethel stated: "I refuse to answer." The lawyers continued to argue until Ethel again said: "I am going to refuse to answer on the grounds of self-incrimination."

It was, as Morton Sobell commented, "Legal Mayhem."[30] When asked if she had disclosed to her lawyer everything she knew about the matter of theft of atomic material or defense secrets she replied: "I didn't know anything about the theft of atomic secrets so how could I discuss it?"[31]

Saypol continued to tie Ethel in knots about whether everything she had told the grand jury was truthful. He asked in particular whether she had declined to answer anything then on the grounds that it might tend to incriminate her, and if so, did she still feel that way? "It is not necessary to explain the use of self-incrimination,"[32] Ethel answered defiantly.

Then Saypol asked Ethel specifically about her answer to the grand jury on the subject of her relations with her brother and her refusal to answer as to whether she had spoken to him about his being investigated just prior to his arrest. "How would that incriminate you if you are innocent?" he asked. "It wouldn't necessarily incriminate me, but it might," she parried. Manny Bloch was interjecting: "Just a moment . . . wait a second."[33] But Kaufman stated: "Let her give her own reasons as to why she answered it that way." So Ethel pressed on: ". . . and as long as I had any idea that there might be some chance for me to be incriminated I had the right to use that privilege."[34]

Saypol was so sure he was making headway with the jury that he pursued this line of inquiry about Ethel's use of the Fifth Amendment in relation to various questions. Kaufman also regularly intervened, mostly to respond to Bloch's objections, effectively conducting a two-pronged attack with Saypol. Repeatedly, Ethel was accused not simply of inconsistency but of not telling the truth. "It is not a question of it being true," Ethel herself had said at one point.[35]

Soon after this, when Saypol asked her "Was that truthful?" she replied authoritatively: "When one uses the right of self-incrimination one does not mean the answer is yes and one does not mean that the answer is no . . . I simply refused to answer on the grounds that that answer might incriminate me."[36] But it was a response that was unlikely to have won her sympathy from the jurors. Eventually, Kaufman felt obliged to remind the jury that there was no inference to be drawn from a witness pleading the Fifth Amendment, adding, however: "It is something the jury may weigh and consider on the question of the truthfulness of the witness and on credibility."[37]

Morton Sobell, watching Ethel's cross-examination from the defense table, believed the jury did not understand her constitutional right to remain silent. From Sobell's point of view, Saypol's cross-examination of Ethel amounted to her "crucifixion:" "It was a wonder that through it Ethel remained calm and collected, never once becoming emotional . . . Manny Bloch, who should have helped balance the struggle, was mostly ineffective . . . he should have screamed about what was being done to Ethel."[38]

Bloch had, though, repeatedly objected, only to be met by a patronizing response from Kaufman: "Have you thought of another grounds for an objection?" But Bloch carried on explaining why he was so upset by "the method of trying to import an unlawful act to a person who has asserted the privilege against self-incrimination [which] destroys the privilege and undermines and takes away the person's right under the Fifth Amendment."[39] However, he failed to make his point to the jury. He simply had not been able to protect his client in their eyes.

At last Saypol told Ethel, "That is all." His cross-examination was over and she was excused. Sobell's wife, Helen, watching from the public benches, later recalled:

> When she [Ethel] was on the stand she was just horribly bad gered. She was incredibly strong. It was a most, most difficult situation and the government attorney was extremely provoking and irritating in every kind of way and nasty and to all of this she remained a thinking person. It would have been so easy just to have become completely numb . . . you could see she would be almost provoked into something and then she would pull back. She was manifesting sheer will power.[40]

•   •   •

The day was not yet over, however, and March 27 finished with the prosecution calling two surprise witnesses of little or no consequence. One was Mrs. Evelyn Cox, the African American woman who had worked as a part-time maid at the Rosenbergs' apartment in Knickerbocker Village and who was questioned as to the use of a small table that the prosecution wanted to prove had been used for secret filming of documents. She insisted she had been told by Ethel that the console table was a present from a friend and not bought from Macy's. Ben Schneider, a professional photographer, described how he had taken passport photographs for the Rosenberg family one summer Saturday in 1950. Schneider had no negatives or invoices to prove his visit took place, but he told Manny Bloch that he remembered it well, because Saturdays were generally quiet and "not a rushing business."[41]

"Did you say 'a Russian business' or 'rushing business'?" Saypol interjected facetiously.

"I didn't know that Mr. Saypol was a punster," Bloch retorted.

"You mean you haven't found it out after all these weeks?" replied Kaufman, as if it was Bloch, not Saypol, who was out of order.

Edward Kuntz, Sobell's lawyer, was required to restore some gravity to the proceedings. "It seems to me, Judge Kaufman, in a case like this, that humor is out of place," Kuntz remarked soberly.[42]

And so, on that anticlimactic note, the last of the witnesses left the stand and the jury was excused until the following morning. Alexander Bloch immediately asked for a mistrial, "upon the grounds that the frequent questioning by the court [Kaufman], not intending harm of course, of witnesses especially of the defendants, had a tendency of unduly influencing the jury to the prejudice of the defendants and depriving them of their constitutional right to a fair and impartial trial."[43]

Manny Bloch joined in to say that the defense was asking for a mistrial "in the utmost good faith and without in any way trying to impugn the court . . . as I for one and I think all my counsel feel that you have been extremely courteous to us."[44] Yet again, Manny Bloch showed excessive politeness verging on subservience to Kaufman, who—to no one's surprise—rejected his and his father's request on the grounds that he considered he should have made his objections at the time and that doing so now "I think is purely an afterthought."[45] Manny Bloch made one further attempt before the session was wound up but got only as far as "If the court please . . ." to be met with a deep and sarcastic sigh from Kaufman, who exhaled, "Oh, no no no . . ."[46]

•   •   •

Manny Bloch rose to give his closing address on the morning of Wednesday, March 28, shortly after 10 a.m., to a packed courtroom. He had labored hard over his speech and used every ounce of heartfelt energy to make the jury see that this was essentially a case of the Greenglasses against the Rosenbergs.[47] David was beneath contempt, Bloch argued: "Any man who will testify against his own blood and flesh, his own sister, is repulsive, is revolting . . . and all the while he smirked and he smiled."[48] As for Ruth, she had admitted to being a co-conspirator but had never been arrested, never indicted, and never sent to jail. "Doesn't that strike you as strange?" Bloch asked.[49]

"Ruth Greenglass got out," he went on. "She walked out and put her sister-in-law in. That was a deal that the Greenglasses planned and made for themselves . . . they may not have made it by express agreement with the government and I don't think the government would countenance anything like that, but tell me, do actions speak louder than words? Is the proof of the pudding in the eating? Is Ruth Greenglass a defendant here?"[50]

Bloch returned to David: "Dave Greenglass loved his wife. He loved her more than he loved himself . . . and ladies and gentlemen this explains why Dave Greenglass was willing to bury his sister and his brother-in-law to save his wife."[51] The Greenglasses "would do anything for money. They would murder people for money," Bloch concluded his portrait of this sinister, scheming couple.[52]

Bloch moved on to Julius and Ethel, seeking to persuade the jury that, in contrast to the Greenglasses, the Rosenbergs were a wholesome

American couple, despite their left-wing sympathies. Julius's political views were hardly extreme, Manny insisted; indeed, they simply represented the kind of philosophy embodied in Franklin Roosevelt's New Deal, "but boy when you do that today it is different."[53] He painted a portrait of Julius as "a steady, hardworking man. He had a little business. He tried to make a go of it."[54] The Rosenbergs were a hardworking couple "who lived in a Knickerbocker Village apartment at $45 a month . . . who had two kids, and they had a terrible struggle and they had to go and borrow money, and he scraped together $1,000 in May 1950 to buy stock in the Pitt Machine Company, and he had to give notes for $4,500 for the balance of the purchase price; tell me, does that square with your idea of a pay-off man?"[55]

"Now look at that terrible spy," he said, pointing to Ethel, who—like Julius—was listening to Bloch's closing argument intently. As a *New York Times* reporter noted, Ethel's only change in demeanor when concentrating was to wrinkle her forehead and knot her fingers together.[56] "Look at that terrible spy and compare her to Ruthie Greenglass, who came here all dolled up, arrogant, smart, cute, eager-beaver like a phonograph record." To prove his point, Bloch merely asked the jury to compare Ruth's account of the conversation she alleged she had had with her husband on November 29 and November 30, 1944, in Albuquerque with her nearly identical version under cross-examination: "You will find that [Ruth Greenglass] repeated, almost word for word, if not word for word, the whole business; and she wants you to believe that she didn't rehearse this story with Dave and Dave Greenglass didn't rehearse this story with her. Cute, cute. Maybe some of you are more acute in sizing up women than others, but if Ruth Greenglass is not the embodiment of evil, I would like to know what person is?"[57]

"Nobody is looking for sympathy here," Bloch continued, belying the whole tenor of his appeal to the jury. He tried to show that when Ethel approached Ruth after David's arrest, she was simply displaying the love of an elder sister who wanted to help her kid brother. No, Bloch reiterated, he and his father were not going to look for sympathy; even though, "believe me, ladies and gentlemen, there is plenty of room here for a lawyer to try and harp on your emotions, especially as far as Ethel is concerned. A mother, she has two children, her husband is under arrest." Yet, as Bloch explained, "if these people [Ethel and Julius] are guilty of that crime they deserve no sympathy."[58]

Nonetheless, reminding the jury that "in your hands human lives are at stake," Manny had reached his peroration: "No, we want you to decide this case with your minds, not with your hearts, with your minds . . . I say that if you do that, you can come to no other conclusion than that these defendants are innocent and you are going to show to the world that in America a man can get a fair trial."

And yet, as so often during the trial, Emanuel Bloch had fumbled his lines. It had not occurred to him to remind the jury that in Cold War America it was also questionable as to whether a woman could get a fair trial.[59] It was a simple misstep not to say "man or woman," but a strong reminder that the language of the day was male.

Manny sat down, exhausted. Now it was Saypol's turn to close for the prosecution. He began by reminding the jury of the meaning of a conspiracy:

> [It was] merely an agreement between two or more persons to violate some law of this country—in this case the espionage law. The law actually need not be broken, as it was here. The agreement alone to break the law would be enough. Every person whom you should find entered into this agreement becomes guilty of the crime of conspiracy. If any one of the members of the conspiracy commits any overt acts, any physical act to further the objects of the conspiracy, all are guilty.[60]

Julius, by passing on atomic secrets to Russia, "had realized the ambition of his life. He had gone from one Communist Party contact to another until he had achieved the coveted status of a Communist Party espionage agent."

Saypol then drew Ethel into the conspiracy, countering Manny Bloch's sketch of a humble, dutiful mother and wife with his own lurid image of a treacherous witch, aiding and abetting David and Julius's dastardly plot:

> On David's September furlough Rosenberg got from him the cross-section sketch of the atom bomb and a twelve-page description of this vital weapon. This description . . . destined for delivery to the Soviet Union, was typed up by the defendant Ethel Rosenberg that afternoon at her apartment at 10 Monroe Street. Just so had she on countless other occasions sat at that typewriter and struck the keys, blow by blow, against her own country in the interests of the Soviets.[61]

Saypol's imagery was cleverly designed to strike home with a jury, almost entirely male, who held the same fixed attitudes toward women and the Soviet threat as did most mid-twentieth-century American men. On the one hand, here was Ethel the typist, a mere female aide to her husband. On the other hand, the very act of typing made her a fully fledged, active member of a conspiracy that had given Stalin the power to destroy the United States. "No defendants ever stood before the Bar of American justice less deserving of sympathy than these three," Saypol concluded bombastically of Julius, Ethel, and their fellow conspirator, Sobell.[62]

The prosecution rested its case. Kaufman now spent more than an hour advising the jury about their legal duties; in particular, the fact that their verdict must be unanimous and that they should not discuss any possible punishment in the event of a conviction. At 3:37 p.m. on March 28 the jury were sent out to deliberate, while Ethel, Julius, and Sobell were taken to separate holding cells beneath the courtroom. The jury, who had not been sequestered during the trial, went under close supervision to a restaurant just off Foley Square. At 6 p.m. they returned and were led into a room behind the jury box that was empty apart from a long oblong table and twelve chairs. Vincent Lebonitte, a Macy's sales manager, was "appointed" foreman by virtue of randomly having been put in chair number one.

They looked again at the indictment and the list of witnesses and started discussing any point that had made a particular impression on them. After a couple of hours the jurors were asked to write their verdicts on pieces of paper and hand them to Lebonitte.

On the first vote "one, possibly two did not vote for guilty," according to Lebonitte. The jury asked to see Ruth Greenglass's testimony a second time, then resumed their deliberations. A second vote was taken. This time it became clearer-cut; the issue was not guilt but the question of clemency. But the juror urging clemency was not the sole woman, Lisette Dammas. She was convinced of Ethel's guilt and, according to her daughter years later: "My mother never wavered in her opinion in her life"[63] that the Rosenbergs were both guilty. The one juror holding out against a death sentence for Ethel was a forty-eight-year-old accountant called James A. Gibbons, with two children of his own.

"This particular individual," Lebonitte recalled twenty-five years later, "was squeamish about the possibility of a woman being put to death . . . He also brought out the mother angle. It was not a dissent on the evidence. It was a dissent for sentimental reasons. The idea that a mother with two children could be put to death was revolting to him." Lebonitte remembered a general belief among the jurors that the death sentence was unlikely to be imposed on Ethel. But Gibbons, the accountant, held firm.

As midnight approached, Lebonitte informed Kaufman about the problem. Kaufman reminded the jury of his earlier advice that punishment was not their concern. It was now so late that arrangements were made for the jury to spend the night at the aptly named Knickerbocker Hotel at 120 West 45th Street, which offered twelve single rooms on the same floor.

Next morning, March 29, the jury returned to court and Lebonitte immediately got to work on the obstinate Gibbons. "Look," Lebonitte recalled telling him, "possibly this woman that you want to save will someday be a part of a conspiracy to transmit secret information to a foreign power that would result in your own doom and the destruction of your wife and children."[64] According to Lebonitte, Gibbons was finally won over by this nebulous image of a terrifying future—or perhaps he was simply worn out by his solitary attempt to save Ethel from the electric chair.

At 11:01 the jury returned to the courtroom, already jammed with spectators eager to witness the final act of this drama "apparently sensing the note of doom in the atmosphere."[65] Some had attended the trial so regularly that they had made friends with each other or the court guards. They were, mostly, detached observers whose "very detachment seemed to chill the atmosphere."[66] But on this the final day their mood changed. "One man, nodding familiarly to one of the guards, made a brushing movement with his hands saying, 'Well today we finish 'em off!' And as the Rosenbergs were led into the courtroom, and Ethel was seen to say something encouraging to Julius, a woman turned to her companion and said: 'Look at her smiling, the bitch! I wonder if she'll smile while she's hanging.'"[67]

The clerk of the court asked Vincent Lebonitte:

"Mr. Foreman have you agreed upon a verdict?"

"Yes, your honor, we have."

"How say you?"

"We the jury find Julius Rosenberg Guilty as charged, Ethel Rosenberg Guilty as charged, Morton Sobell Guilty as charged."

Vincent Lebonitte had delivered the jury's unanimous verdict on all three defendants just as the government had hoped. But Gibbons recalled in 1975 to the journalist Ted Morgan that he had felt at this moment "like Pontius Pilate washing his hands," even though he had believed in Ethel's guilt.[68]

Ethel, according to *The New York Times*, "Took the verdict stoically without changing expression." The eyes of reporters and spectators were all focused on her, as if waiting for some sign of weakness, but she remained utterly still, her face mask like.[69]

"I never saw any two people so devoid of any emotion," Lebonitte told Morgan. "I don't think they changed their expression once during the entire length of the trial."[70] David had also seemed less than human to the jurors, yet Manny Bloch's strategy to paint him as repulsive had backfired. According to Lebonitte, his fellow jurors sided eventually with the Greenglasses' version of events "precisely because they could not believe that anyone could turn in their own flesh and blood and be lying in the bargain. To do something that terrible to his own sister, they reasoned, Greenglass had to be telling the truth. The alternative was too shameful to contemplate."[71]

Kaufman then thanked the jury. More surprisingly, so did Manny Bloch: "I feel satisfied by reason of the length of time that you took for your deliberations . . . that you examined very carefully the evidence and came to a certain conclusion," Bloch said, perhaps hoping by his emollient words that even now the death sentence could be avoided.

One week later, on the morning of April 5, Judge Kaufman announced the sentence. Julius and Ethel listened, "their chalk-white faces frozen into grimaces of incredulity," the *New York Mirror* reported.[72]

Kaufman opened his sentencing remarks by stating that "because of the seriousness of this case and the lack of precedence I have refrained from asking the government for a recommendation."[73] This was untrue. In fact, as became evident later, Kaufman did discuss sentencing with the prosecution team and the government. FBI director J. Edgar Hoover argued strongly against imposing the death penalty on Ethel. Hoover had no hope that the Rosenbergs might be induced to testify against others in exchange for Ethel's life and he did not favor clemency for its own sake. However, he recognized the reputational damage that executing Ethel would cause to the United States and urged a thirty-year prison sentence instead. "This woman is the mother of two small children," he wrote. "As the wife of Julius Rosenberg she would, in a sense, he presumed to be acting under the influence of her husband."[74] Cohn, on the other hand, was intent on showing that Julius had been influenced by Ethel and therefore urged the death sentence for both of them. It was this view that eventually prevailed.

Before sentencing both Rosenbergs and Sobell, Kaufman, resorting to fear-inducing, apocalyptic language, made sure he set their crime as firmly as possible in the context of the contemporary fear of the Soviet threat. "It is so difficult to make people realize that this country is engaged in a life-and-death struggle with a completely different system," he stated.[75] He was at pains to make clear how he had "deliberated for hours, days and nights," and said: "I have carefully weighed the evidence."[76] Kaufman in fact revealed an inadequate grasp of the reality of the situation.

"I consider your crime worse than murder," Kaufman opined, addressing Ethel and Julius directly:

> Plain, deliberate, contemplated murder is dwarfed in magnitude by comparison with the crime you have committed. In committing the act of murder, the criminal kills only his victim. The immediate family is brought to grief and when justice is meted out the chapter is closed. But in your case, I believe your conduct in putting into the hands of the Russians the A-bomb years before our best scientists predicted Russia would perfect the bomb has already caused, in my opinion, the Communist aggression in Korea, with the resultant casualties exceeding 50,000 and who knows but that millions more of innocent people may pay the price of your treason. Indeed, by your betrayal you undoubtedly have altered the course of history to the disadvantage of our country.[77]

To declare that the Rosenbergs put the A-bomb in the hands of the Russians was a grotesque exaggeration, as all experts and many of the public knew. The activities of Klaus Fuchs and Alan Nunn May, who had both confessed to espionage, were of much greater significance, while to blame the Rosenbergs for Communist aggression in Korea in 1950 was something no one in authority seriously believed. The aggression took place for a number of reasons but possession by Stalin of a deliverable bomb, even if the Rosenbergs had helped this, was not one of them.

In effect, Kaufman had condemned Ethel and Julius for treason. Yet according to US law for treason there must be two witnesses to the same overt act, which must consist of giving aid and comfort to an enemy nation in time of war. Russia had been America's ally during World War Two, when the Rosenbergs were said to have passed on secrets.

Kaufman continued:

> The evidence indicated quite clearly that Julius Rosenberg was the prime mover in this conspiracy. However, let no mistake be made about the role which his wife, Ethel Rosenberg, played in this conspiracy. Instead of deterring him from pursuing his ignoble cause, she encouraged and assisted the cause. She was a mature woman—almost three years older than her husband and almost seven years older than her younger brother. She was a full-fledged partner in this crime.

Kaufman's emphasis on Ethel's age was a crude attempt to cast her as a domineering woman rather than the typical American mother and housewife portrayed by the defense. The judge then drove his point home by criticizing Ethel as a mother: "Indeed the defendants, Julius and Ethel Rosenberg, placed their devotion to their cause above their own personal safety and were conscious that they were sacrificing their own children, should their misdeeds be detected—all of which did not deter them from pursuing their course. Love for their cause dominated their lives—it was even greater than their love for their children."[78]

Kaufman now pronounced the death sentences on Ethel and Julius, describing them as "principals in this diabolical conspiracy to destroy a God-fearing nation" just as a nearby church clock struck twelve noon. Newspaper reports differed about how they reacted. One correspondent thought they just stared straight ahead; another wrote that Ethel's "right hand clamped a white-knuckled grip on a chair before her,"[79] while a "wan smile" creased Julius's face. It was as if the press was searching for something remarkable to say about this couple who seemed too ordinary and humdrum to fit the public's conception of treacherous "Commie" spies. Such was the focus on Ethel and Julius that it almost seemed like an afterthought when Kaufman sentenced Sobell to thirty years in jail for his part in the Rosenbergs' conspiracy. There was no evidence that he had been involved in passing atomic secrets.

Eventually, Ethel and Julius were escorted out of the courtroom through a side door, arm in arm, followed by a scrum of reporters. In the lobby Julius asked Ethel how she felt. "Fine," Ethel replied. "I'm all right as long as you are."[80] They were taken downstairs to adjoining basement cells as they waited to be transported back to their respective prisons. To keep up Ethel's spirits, Julius struck up a raucous tenor rendition of the "Battle Hymn of the Republic." Ethel heard him, and in her beautiful soprano voice serenaded Julius with "Un bel dì, vedremo," Puccini's famous aria in which Madame Butterfly yearns for the return of her beloved husband.

"Julie you're a low-down son of a bitch," a prison guard reportedly told Julius, as Ethel sang on. "But you're the luckiest man in the world because no man ever had a woman who loved him that much."

Eight

Isolation

"Think of it this way," Julius replied to the guard, as Ethel sang on. "I just got the death sentence because I'm a big shot in an espionage ring. Yeah, I pass out $1,000 here, $1,500 there, toss $5,000 to my brother-in-law but I never had the money to train that voice. I never had the money to do anything for her. Think of that."[1]

Within minutes, he and Ethel went their separate ways—Julius to the Federal Detention Center on the Lower West Side and Ethel back to the Women's House of Detention in Greenwich Village. On her arrival Ethel was moved to a cell on the fifth floor, where her friend and fellow political prisoner Miriam Moskowitz was also held. "Welcome to hell," Miriam said as the two women embraced.[2]

The prison matron, seeing Ethel's dazed look that first night after receiving her death sentence, offered her a sedative. Ethel refused. Next day, her brother David received a fifteen-year jail term for his espionage—his reward for incriminating Ethel under oath. David's wife Ruth, apparently furious and surprised that he had been given such a long sentence, "almost toppled from her front-row seat on the left of the courtroom," *The New York Times* reported. "After a stiffening shudder, the defendant's twenty-seven-year-old wife dropped her bare head forward to the rail and gripped hard with her right hand to steady herself."[3] Ruth herself was not charged at all and remained free to look after their children.

Ethel's cell was at the end of the corridor nearest the guards. She interpreted this as a sign that the Department of Justice wanted to be sure she did not kill herself, which, as she told Miriam, was "the least likely thing she could ever do."[4] Miriam was still awaiting transfer to another prison, following her conviction and two-year jail sentence in November 1950 for conspiracy to obstruct justice. She and Ethel now became close friends. Miriam recalled:

> There were ten cells in a corridor, and at certain times of day they were left open so that the inmates could visit . . . she talked about her children constantly . . . She was concerned about their music lessons, day-to-day events . . . We floated free then for those few moments in a more benevolent world— until a guard would yell across to us as we finished the last of our coffee: "Hey you two! You're not in the Waldorf, ya know, time's up for commissary."[5]

During their time together, Miriam and Ethel could enjoy what they called "free-world food"—sandwiches and cake that were brought in from outside—and try to blot out the grim prison environment. "We used to stand up on the roof together looking out toward the west, imagining that we could see the flagpole flying over the men's house of detention . . . we talked one time about how we would celebrate with one big blast of a party when we got out."[6]

In these first days after the trial, Ethel managed most of the time to display an outer calm. She admitted that she was barely sleeping and when inmates inquired further she replied: "Oh nothing's wrong. I just heard that scream again last night," referring to Michael's howl of anguish down the phone line eight months earlier when she had told him that she too had been arrested. Several former inmates recalled that Ethel would seize any opportunity to discuss children, both hers and those of the other prisoners. Indeed, the gossip at the Women's House of Detention during

Ethel's trial was that she had been "more concerned with the children than with her own defense."[7]

Without warning, on April 11, 1951, Ethel was woken early and taken from her cell, ostensibly to answer questions. In fact, she was being transferred from the House of Detention to the maximum-security Sing Sing Prison in the town of Ossining, much harder for any visitors to reach. She was given no chance to say a brief goodbye to Miriam or the other prisoners who had befriended her and planned farewell gifts for her. Ethel's execution had been provisionally scheduled for May 21 and was then immediately "stayed" when Manny Bloch gave notice that Ethel and Julius were appealing both convictions. But her fellow prisoners concluded that the reason for the move was simply to take her to a prison with an execution chamber to emphasize the reality of her impending death sentence. As soon as Ethel was out of the cell, guards stripped it of all her few possessions—photographs, letters, toiletries, and clothes—carefully collected since her arrest.

Miriam was distraught at Ethel's abrupt removal. On a political level, she considered Ethel a "deeply sympathetic person" who had never done more than support Julius's idealism, motives, and actions. Miriam shared the same ideals. But she also cared for Ethel as a fellow human being and shared her pain. "When they took Ethel, that was really dirty . . . cruel trickery," Miriam recalled in 2018, a few weeks before she died.[8] Seventy years after the event, she was still grieving that she "never got to say goodbye to Ethel." Ironically, Miriam and the other prisoners did not know that Ethel's transfer to Sing Sing may have been accelerated because the matrons at the Women's House of Detention, who would have heard Ethel crying privately at night, were worried about her ability to hold up.

Manny Bloch heard the news of Ethel's move from a press contact and rushed across town straight away. He had had no time to prepare a formal legal objection. He argued in vain with officials that her transfer to the "Death House" wing of the prison, where the electric chair was located, was "unnecessary and vindictive" while appeals were pending. He found Ethel remarkably calm and analytic. "They expect me to break under the strain because I am a woman," she told him. "They think that in the Death House I will be haunted by images, alone, and without Julie I'll collapse. But I won't."[9]

As she was driven away from the Women's House of Detention, Ethel was visibly determined to put on a brave face. Hearing one inmate scream, "Good luck Ethel, we love you," from behind her cell window, and others yelling farewell, Ethel smiled and waved at a press photographer who snapped her through the car window. Her features, so stonily impassive during the trial, were transformed. While it is impossible to know if the jury would have dealt with her more sympathetically had she smiled during the trial—they might have concluded that she failed to show any remorse for her crimes—it nonetheless seems clear that Ethel's face when smiling showed a warmth that might have endeared her to them as it clearly did to others who knew her well, such as Carl Marzani and Elizabeth Phillips.

Sing Sing Prison, overlooking the east bank of the Hudson River, was a grim maximum-security jail that had changed little since it first opened in 1826. Ethel, ticketed as prisoner 110510, was to remain the only prisoner in the women's wing and her spirits swiftly sank when she was locked up in one of three identical small cells on a single ground-floor corridor. The cell boasted a narrow iron bed, a chair, a metal table, toilet, and washbasin. Ethel's mattress, a mere three inches thick, filled with cotton bunting and covered with black-and-white-striped ticking, was hardly likely to be beneficial to her back. Initially, Ethel had none of her personal possessions, which the authorities had delivered to Julius's mother, Sophie, designated by Ethel as her next of kin, not her own mother, Tessie. She signed a waiver that permitted her to receive mail in return for having it inspected and tried to settle in.

The women's sector of Sing Sing had been vacant since the execution just a few weeks previously in March of Mrs. Martha Beck, the so-called Lonely Hearts murderer. The thirty-one-year-old single mother of two had been found guilty of one murder but was known to have committed several others together with her lover, Raymond Fernandez. The couple targeted women through lonely hearts advertisements and then killed them for cash. The warden, Wilfred Denno, had had to rehire the four matrons who had attended Mrs. Beck to watch over Ethel, in relays, at a cost to the taxpayer of $40 a day, as *The New York Times* informed its curious readers.

Ethel's only company was this team of matrons who sat outside her cell of whom only one became a friend, an Irish American woman called Bessie Irving, to whom she soon became deeply attached. As a condemned prisoner Ethel was not allowed to work, and for exercise there was just a yard, fifty feet wide by sixty feet long, enclosed by a high wall. She remained in solitary confinement for three days until finally, on Saturday, April 14, Manny Bloch was permitted to see her. It seems likely that the authorities hoped that this inhumane treatment would break Ethel and force her into naming those who were part of their circle, or simply people whom Julius had known and worked with. If she sat in isolation for long enough, so the argument went, surely any mother would decide that not admitting her and Julius's guilt was too high a price to pay in exchange for avoiding the electric chair. But, as she had promised Manny, she did not buckle under the strain.

Manny Bloch was fulfilling multiple roles as lawyer, go-between, and surrogate father. He had become almost possessed by their case. Although technically he was Julius's lawyer, while his father Alexander represented Ethel, from the start their fates were intertwined. As soon as he was allowed, clutching some of Ethel's possessions that he had managed to retrieve, he met his client in a second-floor room set aside for visitors. She was wearing a prison housecoat and slippers and seemed listless. Ethel told him about the horrors of her isolation and Manny tried to reassure her that he was doing all he could to improve her conditions at Sing Sing or, preferably, have her returned to the Women's House of Detention. Once again, Ethel implored Manny to arrange for her to see Dr. Saul Miller, her personal psychiatrist. Manny had rejected her request before the trial, fearing that Miller's testimony might be used against her in court. Now, seeing her distress, Manny said he would contact Miller.

Manny's visit had been "a shot in the arm" for her, Ethel wrote to him on the following Monday.[10] "Even though I was inclined to be a bit tearful after you had gone, I was also greatly encouraged."[11] She added that she had not yet written to Julius at the Federal Detention Center in Manhattan because she was "still trying to catch my breath and so far I think I've made progress."[12]

Most of Ethel's first letter to Manny concerned how best to arrange a visit with her two young sons, Michael and Robby, whom she had not seen in eight months. At the Women's House of Detention, Ethel had confided to Miriam that "she wanted to wait. She didn't want the children to visit her in one jail and then visit their father in another . . . She felt they would find it less of a shock if they saw their parents together." Her decision "required the most rigid self-denial," Miriam told Virginia Gardner in 1954.[13] Once at Sing Sing, all alone, Ethel changed her mind, her earlier decision having been based on the hope that they would not be found guilty and that her children would never have to remember seeing their parents in prison. However, now that she realized they were not coming home anytime soon she was determined that Michael and Robby's first visit to their mother behind bars should feel as natural as possible and somehow be a positive experience for them.

"How can any of us know how we might feel in such circumstances?" the child psychologist Elizabeth Phillips wondered almost seventy years later in 2018. "I saw her [Ethel] as a gentle, sweet person. I wasn't sure how strong-willed she was until Julius was sent to prison. I believe she knew exactly what she was doing. And she constantly wanted to be a better mother."[14] While in jail, Ethel had diligently kept up her subscription to *Parents* magazine.

Nothing in *Parents,* though, could help Ethel prepare for seeing Michael and Robby once more. She had no idea what sort of questions her sons were asking about her at the children's home in the Bronx where they had been placed after Tessie had declared she could no longer cope with them. In the same letter to Manny, written on April 16, Ethel asked him if he could arrange—an impossible request—for her to see Mrs. Epstein, a social worker at the home, to discuss how she might neutralize the possibly traumatic effect for such young children of visiting a mother in her circumstances. Ethel was particularly worried about "Michael's anxiety neurosis and the treatment he has been undergoing and Robby's sharp disturbance since our separation."[15]

The following day, April 17, Ethel wrote to Julius, "My very own dearest husband," admitting it was a letter she found extremely hard to start:

> I don't know when I've had such a time bringing myself to write to you. My brain seems to have slowed to all but a complete halt under the weight of the myriad impressions that have been stamping themselves upon it minute by minute, hour upon hour, since my removal here. I feel on the one hand a sharp need to share all that burdens my mind and heart and so bring to naught, make invalid, the bitter physical reality of our separation, yet am stabbed by the implacable and desolate knowledge that the swift spinning of time presents a never to be solved enigma.[16]

She told him about her first days at Sing Sing. Life had improved once she had the children's photographs taped onto a picture frame made of cardboard to "smile sweetly upon me whenever I so desire." And she told him about the book she was reading, Thomas Wolfe's posthumously published (1940) 700-page, largely plotless novel *You Can't Go Home Again,* about 1930s America, "from which inspired writing I am drawing deep emotional and intellectual gratification," she assured him.[17]

With Julius, Ethel had no restraint about revealing her inner torment, even as she sought to maintain her morale. "There begins to develop the profoundest kind of belief that somehow, somewhere I shall find that 'courage, confidence and perspective' I shall need to see me through days and nights of bottomless horror of tortured screams I may not utter, of frenzied longings I must deny!"[18]

Three days later, Ethel wrote to her sister-in-law Lena Cohen, Julius's older sister, asking if she could finish knitting some sweaters she had started at the Women's House of Detention. As she explained, the problem at Sing Sing was that she was no longer allowed needles of any sort.[19]

On May 5 she wrote again to Julius, telling him about a joke she planned to play on her matron Bessie Irving: "Ooh I just got a brilliant idea: to-morrow when she arrives at 6:30 a.m. I am going to panic her by way of greeting with a gay little ditty entitled Who's afraid of the Big Electric Chair / They can shove it up their 'spine' for all I care . . ."[20]

Julius soon realized the importance of saving the letters he and Ethel were exchanging in prison in case they proved helpful in attracting pub-lic sympathy for the appeal against their conviction, which Manny was preparing. Written in pencil on flimsy ruled prison paper, they now kept copies that they asked Manny Bloch to put together in an album, which might indicate Julius simply wanted a record for posterity, since "I con-sider my wife's writting [sic] a personal treasure."[21] But from May 1951 onward, it is possible to detect self-consciousness in some of the letters, revealed in part by regular crossings-out and corrections. At the end of April 1951, when the possibility of Julius also coming to Sing Sing arose, Ethel wrote to him: "In all humility I tell you, it is your love for me and mine for you (even though the expression of it must of necessity now be dammed up) that is enabling me to strive ever more [bravely was crossed out] consciously to [rise to was crossed out] reach that [another illegible word was then crossed out] height for which I seem somehow to have been singled out."[22] In the manner of a professional author, Ethel even used a dictionary to find more suitable or dramatic words, as well as a notebook for rough ideas.

A month after her transfer, Ethel appealed explicitly to the American public by releasing a brief statement that was quoted in the *National Guard-ian*, a radical left-wing but non-Communist weekly newspaper. She said that if government officials were trying to break her by moving her to Sing Sing they were "in for a sad awakening. We are victims of the grossest type of political frame-up ever known in American history. In our own way, we will try to establish our innocence. But we ask the people of America to realize the political significance of our case and come to our aid."[23]

Meanwhile, Ethel asked Manny Bloch to encourage what friends she had left to write. "Even though I know I'm not forgotten, my all too human feelings demand some tangible proof, some concrete evidence."[24]

Number 64 Sheriff Street, the tenement block on Manhattan's Lower East Side where Ethel Greenglass was born in 1915. Barney's repair shop fronted the street with the family living quarters behind.

(nynyma_rec0040_1_00333_0009; 1940s Tax Department photographs, 1939–1951; courtesy of the Municipal Archives, City of New York)

GREENBLATT, E. M.
C. C. N. Y.
  Service Squad
  I know everything, but don't ask me anything.

GRIEF, MORTIMER
Columbia
  Arista, Lab. Council, Chem. Club
  Great things are expected of him.

GRINGER, MOLLIE
C. C. N. Y.
  Sec'y., Swimming, Stunts Club
  True friends are like diamonds, precious and rare.

GREENGLASS, E.
  Can she act? And how.

To a rare charac-
er! May sye
ways be happy
Ethel

HAUPTMAN, BERNARD
School of Finance
  Bank Staff, Senior Council, G. O. Del.
  I've got five dollars.

GROSS, I.
C. C. N. Y.
  (Capt.) Service Squad, Senior Council
  Good replica of our advisor.

HACKER, FLORENCE
C. C. N. Y.
  Hai Archai, Arista, Program Committee
  Sweet, demure and charming.

HALPERN, CLARA
Hunter College
  Arista, G. O., Program Com.
  For everyone she has a line,
  "But, too modest," she says,
  "to make up mine."

HAUSFATHER, H. NATHAN
N. Y. U.
  Science Club, Senior Council
  Politics will gain a fine leader in future time.

HECHT, M.
C. C. N. Y.
  Service Squad
  The fingers trill the notes,
  The melodies thrill the hearts.

HELLMAN, S.
C. C. N. Y.
  Senior Council, Soccer Team, Folio
  He rivals the Greeks in historical knowledge.

HERTZ, R.
Hunter College
  Swimming, Basketball, Tennis
  Always good and doing what she should.

Ethel, pictured fourth on the left in this page of the 1931 Seward Park High School (SPHS) yearbook, has written to her friend Dora Stahl, "To a rare character! May she always be happy!" beneath the printed words "Can she act? And how."

(Courtesy of Arthur and Toby Engelberg and the Seward Park High School Alumni Association)

CELEBRITIES OF
THE CLASS OF JUNE '31

Most popular Boy — CARL SCHWARTZ

Most popular Girl — FREDA SHAEFFER

Boy most likely to succeed — DAVID FIDLER

Girl most likely to succeed — ROSE LEVITT

Handsomest boy — MAX FUCHS

Prettiest Girl — GOLDYE LUBLIN

Best dressed Boy — SAM E. COHEN

Best dressed Girl — MILLY GRINGER

Class Actor — NAT UNGER

Class Actress — ETHEL GREENGLASS

Boy Dancer — BEN TOLBER

Girl Dancer — YETTA RUBINSTEIN

Boy Athlete — DAVID SCHINDELHEIM

Girl Athlete — ESTHER KAPLAN

Class Scholar — PHEMIE GOLDMAN

Class Writer — RUTH GORDON

Class Musician — JULIUS ROSENFELD

Three Musketeers — LICAUSI, ZWIREN, LEHRMAN

Most Amiable — GERTRUDE LEVINE

Class Politician — HAROLD BERNSTEIN

Class Know-it-all — JACK SURE

Class Baby — JACK MARGOLIES

Class Twins — ZWIREN AND ZWIREN

Class Entrepreneur — NATHAN HAUSFATHER

Class Songstress — FRIEDA SCHAEFFER

The 1931 SPHS yearbook's "Celebrities of the Class" page describes Ethel as the "Class Actress."

(Courtesy of Arthur and Toby Engelberg and the Seward Park High School Alumni Association)

The basement swimming pool of SPHS was just one reason why the school offered children such as Ethel vast new horizons.

(Courtesy of Arthur and Toby Engelberg and
the Seward Park High School Alumni Association)

Ethel sitting with flowers in a formal high school graduation portrait.

(Meeropol family photographs reprinted with the permission of the copyright holders, Michael and Robert Meeropol)

Ethel acting in amateur dramatics, the activity she loved until she got involved in politics through work. The year after she left school, she won a scholarship to join the Clark Players, a local amateur dramatic group attached to the Clark Settlement House.

(Meeropol family photographs reprinted with the permission of the copyright holders, Michael and Robert Meeropol)

Ethel looking relaxed with her arm resting on her brother David's shoulder, together outside Sheriff Street.

(From The Brother *by Sam Roberts, Simon & Schuster, 2014)*

David in uniform with his wife, Ruth, outside the house in Albuquerque where Ruth lived while her husband worked at Los Alamos, site of the secret Manhattan Project.

(National Archives, photo no. 278758)

Ethel as a young mother looking intently at her toddler, Michael, on South Beach. Michael recalls they would often take the ferry and then the Staten Island Rapid Transit to a beach on the Lower New York Bay.

(Meeropol family photographs reprinted with the permission of the copyright holders, Michael and Robert Meeropol)

Ethel and Julius in the park in happier days, ca. 1942.

(Meeropol family photographs reprinted with the permission of the copyright holders, Michael and Robert Meeropol)

Julius and Ethel in swimming costumes, not dated but probably shortly after their marriage in 1939.

(Getty Images)

Ethel on the day of her press conference in her Knickerbocker Village apartment, shortly after Julius had been arrested. She hoped to show the world she was simply a poor 1950s American housewife and mother, more concerned with making sure her children were fed and cared for than worrying about the "crazy charges" against her husband.

(Shutterstock.com)

Manny was acutely aware of Ethel's emotional fragility from his own visits, compounded by her almost total isolation for long periods, with only Bessie Irving outside her cell door for company. He was still trying to have Ethel transferred back to the Women's House of Detention, and to that end sought expert testimony to present to a court hearing about the effect of Ethel's isolation.

Bloch found Dr. Fredric Wertham, a German-born, American-trained psychiatrist with progressive views who ran a low-cost clinic in Harlem for Black teenagers. Wertham was not permitted to visit Ethel or communicate with her in any way and was obliged to rely on discussions with Manny to assess her mental condition. On May 7, Wertham testified that he feared Ethel was in imminent danger of a serious mental breakdown through being completely alone and unable to see or confer with her husband.

On May 16 the government made a concession of sorts. Ethel was not allowed to return to the House of Detention but Julius was transferred to the men's wing of the Death House at Sing Sing. Unlike Ethel, Julius was not held in solitary confinement since there were other men facing death sentences with whom he could communicate during exercise in the yard or at other times. The day of his arrival he and Ethel met for the first time since the trial, in the Death House counsel room, with Manny present. For the first and only time at Sing Sing, Ethel and Julius were allowed to embrace; henceforth, the warden ruled they should have no physical contact. From May 25 onward they were given permission to meet every Wednesday morning, with Julius seated in a cage outside Ethel's cell. Forbidden to touch, they could at least talk to and see each other through the mesh and bars.

The meetings with Manny Bloch were arguably more civilized but were freighted with additional difficulties. Not only was Sing Sing a long drive outside the city, but the arrangements for him to see his clients there were complicated. They sat on opposite ends of a conference table, not handcuffed, with a guard at a discreet distance. But Manny's real handicap was the assumption that any conversation was being repeated. Julius had in his cell a car thief and government informer, Jerome Tartakow, who relayed information to the FBI. He would have been correct to assume that perhaps the matron was reporting on Ethel's state of mind or comments, even though this was illegal. In short, he was unable to give either of them any confidential advice that might save their lives.

By the end of May, Manny had arranged for Ethel's psychiatrist, Dr. Saul Miller, to make fortnightly appointments to see her at Sing Sing. Much later, Miller recalled to Ethel's son Michael how rapidly her mental health improved once his visits resumed after this yearlong gap. "Her self-hatred and misery had vanished," he told Robby.[25]

In June Julius's widowed mother, Sophie, finally recovered after a long illness, agreed to take Robby and Michael out of their hated children's home in the Bronx and look after them herself. Ethel was still estranged from her own mother, and Sam Greenglass was abiding by his eight-year-old vow never to see her again. But her middle brother, Bernie, refused to abandon her at Sing Sing, visiting her at the end of June.

Ethel's spirits, which had revived a little after the first few visits by Dr. Miller, collapsed again on July 2 when she heard that Bessie Irving, "the dearest friend I owned inside these walls," had died suddenly of a cerebral hemorrhage. She was "so overwhelmed with shock and grief," Ethel wrote to Julius, "that my personal problems, my sentence, everything has paled into complete insignificance."[26] It was only Bessie, a mother substitute as well as an imagined friend, who had made the last two months tolerable. "How black my world has gone. Tears blind me as I write, nor have I been able to staunch their flow," she told Julius. "Right now the sun has set and I am frightened and alone and lost in a world that is bleak and empty and strange!"[27]

Alone in her cell, Ethel gradually came to terms with Bessie's absence. Mrs. Helen Evans, who took over as prison matron in the mornings only, was as kind as she could be within the system but never established the same intense relationship with Ethel, while the afternoon and evening matron, Mrs. Jackson, took little interest in her. Ethel was thinking constantly about her boys, who were settling in with their grandmother Sophie at her Upper Manhattan apartment. It overlooked the Harlem River in the Bronx from its position next to the George Washington Bridge.

Bubbie, as they called Sophie Rosenberg, was still suffering from high blood pressure so she had a nurse who came to help, but at least she cooked food that the boys liked and did not impose strict discipline, which they liked even more. On July 23, Ethel wrote to Julius that she was "on fire with impatience" to see him and discuss Michael and Robby's forthcoming visit after a year of separation. "As you may well imagine it will be difficult until I see them, to think of much else than the children," she remarked.[28]

Julius was not allowed to share the visit with Ethel. That Ethel could not see her boys together with her husband was one more act of cruelty inflicted on her. Yet after this first visit Julius wrote to give her courage, saying he was glad she was "going to break the ice with them because I am certain you will come through with flying colors and set the stage for my visit."[29] Ingeniously, Ethel had collected an "envelope full of rare specimens . . . wild insects" to amuse the boys: beetles, cockroaches, ants, and spiders. She had also rehearsed her answers if Robby or Michael asked how she and Julius were coping with the fear of electrocution. She advised Julius that "if this lovely job" fell to him, to "explain it in terms of a highly magnified electric shock that anybody might sustain through contact. Believe me, my loved one, children are what their parents truly expect them to be. If we can face the thought of our intended execution without terror, so then will they. Certainly neither of us will seek to dwell on these matters unduly but let's not be afraid and they won't either."[30]

The visit on August 1 lasted one hour. When she returned to her cell, Ethel sat down at her metal table and wrote to Julius. "My heart is leaden within me," she lamented. "I'm afraid I was anything but calm . . . as I smiled and kissed the children I was experiencing such a bewildering assortment of emotions that I don't think I was enough in control of myself to have accomplished anything very far-reaching." And yet, "actually I doubt anyone else could have either; after all a first visit after a year's separation can hardly be expected to do much more than 'break the ice.'" All alone, she found it hard to "escape the terrible ache and longing that relentlessly pursues me now that the sweet sound of them is no more."[31] The following day she wrote again to Julius: "Oh, sweetheart, I love them so much, how shall I ever go on enduring without them."[32]

Dr Miller later said he left no notes of his many meetings with Ethel. In an interview with Ilene Philipson for her 1988 book about the Rosenbergs, Miller recalled that his visits to the Death House were hardly formal therapy sessions. He was seated in the corridor outside Ethel's cell, listening through the door grille to his "client" talk about how she was, or was not, coping with her emotionally stressed and solitary life. On his side of the grille, Miller tried to advise Ethel about how best to manage her situation.

Based on her letters, Ethel's mood swung from high excitement before a visit from Julius or Dr. Miller to extreme depression when she contemplated what had happened to their previous family life. In her bleaker moods, she only knew that she must stay true to her vow to Julius to face the electric chair "without terror."

•   •   •

Manny Bloch worked hard that summer on Ethel and Julius's appeal. Aware that the execution clock was ticking fast, Bloch focused on what he considered were Judge Kaufman's interventions, claiming in effect that the judge had behaved as if he were part of the prosecution team. Also, Bloch argued that Kaufman had not been stringent enough in preventing charges of Communism to permeate the trial so that Julius and Ethel were in effect "tainted" by being called Communists.

In parallel with the appeal, Manny Bloch also recognized the need to try to swing public opinion in their favor. At the end of the trial, the crusading columnist Dorothy Thompson had been almost alone among reporters in writing that the death sentence was too harsh. She argued:

Treason in our times has somehow escaped satisfactory legal definition. Treason has hitherto been equated to betrayal to an enemy with whom the country is in armed conflict. Only because the Rosenbergs gave secret information to a foreign power in 1944, in wartime, could Judge Kaufman impose the formidable sentence. But in 1944 we were not at war with the Soviet Union. The Soviets were not an enemy but an ally. In

1944 Julius and Ethel Rosenberg were in their twenties, for three years the Soviet Union had been glorified by the most respectable citizens. The prevailing myths, hopes and policies all contributed to create the climate in which their crime might seem to them hardly more than misdemeanor . . . Indeed, it is unlikely that had they been tried in 1944 they would have received any such sentence.[33]

Dorothy Thompson was one of the few clear-eyed journalists who, having worked in Europe during the 1930s and even secured an interview with Hitler, had understood the Fascist threat. Yet, since the verdict, Thompson's sophisticated political criticism of the sentence had failed to resonate with an American public now transfixed by the Soviet threat. Manny decided to take a different tack. He approached several mainstream and left-wing US newspapers, offering information for a story about Ethel and Julius's private lives that focused on their basic humanity and decency. Even the *Daily Worker*, the Communist Party newspaper, turned him down. "We didn't want to be associated in any way, shape or form with espionage," its former editor John Gates recalled in a 1991 interview. "In the public mind the words 'spy' and 'communist' were synonymous."[34]

Eventually Bloch contacted James Aronson, a prominent left-wing journalist and co-founder of the radical weekly newspaper *National Guardian*. Over a long lunch Manny poured out his insider's account of the Rosenberg story, which he hoped would win sympathy for his clients. "Manny remained to haunt me," Aronson recalled, "his urgent speech, heavy head thrust forward to emphasize his agony, intense eyes under thick brows fixed on my face. The way he took the case to his own heart was startlingly un-lawyer like."[35] Aronson went back to his office and called William Reuben, a well-known investigative reporter. Reuben agreed to look into Ethel and Julius's background, research the trial, and check out any witnesses whose testimony seemed contradictory.

On August 8, as a trailer for Reuben's seven-part series, *National Guardian* published pictures of eight-year-old Michael and four-year-old Robby, who had just been allowed an hour with their parents, separately again, in Sing Sing. On August 15 the first article appeared beneath the headline, "The Rosenberg Conviction: Is This the Dreyfus Case of Cold-War America?" referring to the notorious French miscarriage of justice in 1894 when Captain Alfred Dreyfus, a wholly innocent Jewish army officer, was falsely convicted of treason for communicating military secrets to the Germans.

The *National Guardian* series represented the first real press opposition to the guilty verdict in the United States since Dorothy Thompson's column. Reuben used the word "hoax" to describe key elements of the prosecution case, and as the succeeding articles were published each week, a tide of sympathy for Ethel and Julius among liberal East Coast Americans slowly began to gather momentum. Within this group there was also a difference among those who thought the Rosenbergs were guilty, but shouldn't be executed, and those who thought the case against them was, if not "a hoax," at least suspect.

Readers of the *National Guardian* spontaneously sent small contributions of cash to the newspaper and inquired how they could help, on the mistaken assumption that an organization already existed to fight for the couple.

One of those readers was Emily Alman, thirty, a resident of Knickerbocker Village who had once met Ethel and chatted briefly with her at a nearby children's park shortly before her arrest. Emily later said she could not get Ethel's voice and story out of her mind. Both she and Ethel had grown up in poverty, graduated from Seward Park, and had two young children. Emily was left-wing, although she had never been a Communist, while David, her husband, had left the Communist Party after the Nazi-Soviet pact of 1939. The Almans believed that Reuben's articles were truthful and decided to contact Manny Bloch. A clumsily named "Committee to Secure Justice in the Rosenberg Case" was set up in September and in late October, with Reuben as acting chairman, the committee placed a request for donations in the *National Guardian* to fund legal appeals. From the start there was a conviction that both Rosenbergs had been framed and so both must be cleared; there was never an attempt to separate Ethel from Julius (which in any event would have been impossible while Julius's mother was involved: she would never have sanctioned a fight that implicitly accepted Julius's guilt). The campaign might have stood more chance of success if it had focused its efforts solely on Ethel, a mother. It never explored that route.

Throughout the late summer and autumn, as Manny was launching the campaign, Ethel was also peppering him with requests about Robby and Michael. She recalled how the boys had always woken before their parents and worried that Julius's frail mother Sophie might now have her own sleep broken. On August 22 Ethel explained in a letter to Manny how she used to leave a variety of toys and drawing materials for Robby and Michael overnight so they did not disturb her and Julius in the morning:

> Materials like plasticene [*sic*], a couple of particularly attractive books . . . a magic slate for each of them to scribble on . . . you might even say that their mommy had made the suggestion for them to so behave in the morning and would be happy if they would try to remember to undertake this kind of play . . . a new portion of (plasticene) for each child with a set of plastic colored cookie cutters for each will keep them happy for a long time.[36]

From her prison cell, Ethel fretted that Sophie Rosenberg's health was not robust enough to withstand two lively young boys without adequate help. She set out in a long letter to Manny not only what she believed to be the correct routine and schedule for Michael and Robby, going into detail as to whether or not they should be showered or bathed, but also her basic ideas as to how she believed children should be cared for. She distilled what she had learned over the years from professionals as well as her own experience into this letter in six installments—she had to stop whenever "mail call" interrupted her flow.

"One cannot behave inconsistently with children," she wrote, "gaining their confidence and respect in one area, and exposing our lack of will and love . . . on other fronts. The good mother (or mother-substitute) wisely recognizes that 'integration' is the key to proper childrearing." She was unhappy about the nurse who had been enlisted to help Sophie and was clearly not up to the task. She asked that future helpers be screened in advance to ascertain "their knowledge and experience in the field of child psychology and their sympathy for us."[37]

She confessed at the end of the letter that the thought she put into "all these letters stems from a torment of anxiety about the future of the children"[38] and her attempt to mother them from a distance. Yet perhaps they were more resilient than she realized and the anxiety was more hers than theirs. Both sons remember the visits to Sing Sing as happy and pleasant. "They tried to make us feel calm and ordinary. They didn't like a fuss." Robert recalled that his mother appeared shorter than he had remembered her. "She would have worn heels previously but now had to make do with prison-issue slippers. And Michael played word games with Julius, including hangman."[39]

In October, the *National Guardian* started to publish some of Ethel and Julius's letters to each other. "I get so hopeful. I also get scared and yet I just can't bring myself to think in terms other than victory and our eventual release," Ethel wrote on October 19, in prose that was clearly intended for a public audience.[40] Two days later she prepared to see Michael and Robby, having added a dragonfly and locust to her insect collection to amuse them. Ethel was alarmed to have heard from Bernie that her difficult mother Tessie was planning to meet Michael. How could she prevent that, Ethel wondered?

The boys' visit was a "complete fiasco," Ethel reported to Julius on October 22: "It was in a kind of resigned stupor that I awaited the children's arrival . . . and now, no matter how sensibly I try to reason with myself that Robby's truculence and Michael's anxiety were the necessarily logical outcome of a set of circumstances over which I had no control, I am rife with a sense of personal failure."[41]

Ethel signed off, "Sweetheart, I love you, tummy and all!"—probably a humorous reference to Julius's teasing about her own weight. Ethel was getting plump, due to stodgy prison food—which she tried to improve by adding cream cheese bought from the commissary—and lack of exercise. Her extreme anxiety was causing her to bite her nails. And, like Julius, she was in agonies of sexual frustration, more than a year after she had last slept with him. She had an "implacable hunger for it [l'amour]."[42]

Two months later she wrote again of how she longed to "twine my arms seductively about your neck and lift my willing lips to yours!"[43] Soon she would have to be more circumspect as her most intimate thoughts might now be shared with the readers of the *National Guardian*.

Nine

Facing Death

In the autumn of 1951, the mainstream US press was still saturated with apocalyptic warnings about the Soviet atomic threat, drowning out the few left-wing journalists such as Aronson and Reuben who were trying to win sympathy for the Rosenbergs. On October 27 the entire issue of *Collier's* magazine was devoted to "Preview of the War We Do Not Want," a graphic, hypothetical account of a third world war between the "United Nations" (free world) and the Soviet Union. Journalists of the caliber of Marguerite Higgins, Edward Murrow, Arthur Koestler, and Walter Winchell all conveyed the bleak horror that a war involving extensive use of nuclear weapons would entail.

On December 23, the *Louisville Courier-Journal,* summing up the achievements of women in the previous twelve months, concluded that the year marked an uneven battle for news attention between those with serious accomplishments to their name and others who made sensational headlines. In the latter category, "who could feel the slightest twinge of sympathy for Ethel Rosenberg, who assisted her husband Julius in giving atomic secrets to the Russians?" it asked.[1]

At first, most of the support for the campaign to save the Rosenbergs was drawn from liberal and left-wing circles and was numbered in hundreds rather than thousands. In the United States, both the government and most of the press were quick to brand the Committee to Secure Justice as a "Communist-front organization." This was untrue: the CPUSA, under the leadership of William Z. Foster since 1945, was fearful of further arrests in the prevailing Cold War atmosphere, and in its weakened state steered clear of offering any help—financial, legal, or even moral—to the Rosenbergs, which in any case would have been counterproductive.

On February 25, 1952, Ethel and Julius's conviction was unanimously upheld by the US Circuit Court of Appeals. This was an especially bitter blow because the verdict had been a unanimous decision written by the liberal Judge Jerome N. Frank, who denied that emphasis during the trial on the Rosenbergs' Communist preferences had been prejudicial since, he argued, Judge Kaufman had repeatedly warned the jury that they were not to use such information as proof of guilt. The court argued that there was a reason to permit such testimony as it was useful for the jury in creating a motive for Julius and Ethel's spying. The Court of Appeals, however, could rule only on whether the defendant had been accorded a legally fair trial but was not able to comment on the credibility of witnesses nor the reliability of testimony.

Ethel heard the news on the prison radio and told Julius not only of her shock but how "my heart aches for the children; unfortunately they are old enough to have heard for themselves and no matter what amount of control I am able to exercise, my brain reels picturing their terror. It is for them I am most concerned and it is of their reaction I am anxiously awaiting some word."[2]

Finding a suitable home for the children was proving a challenge. After a number of experimental weekend visits with various well-wishers, Michael and Robby "wound up"[3] in the spring of 1952 being looked after by Sonia and Ben Bach, the radical couple who in the summer of 1945 had let the Rosenbergs stay at a cottage on their property in Toms River, New Jersey. The boys had become too much for Sophie Rosenberg, who was still in poor health. Ben Bach, a chicken-feed salesman, and Sonia, who was a homemaker like most women at the time, were personal friends of Ethel and Julius and parents of two children, one of whom was close in age to the Rosenberg boys: Leo, a year younger than Robby. Maxine, their daughter, was a college student, largely living away from home. "Generally we were happy at the Bachs," wrote Michael. "We had space to run, playmates and the security of attention from adults obviously stronger than Grandma."[4]

Ben and Sonia did everything they could to make the boys happy in impossible circumstances during the summer of 1952. But eventually the pressure of events were to overwhelm even this happy home.

Manny Bloch now petitioned for the US Supreme Court to review the case—in effect, Ethel and Julius's last chance of escaping the electric chair other than a pardon or mitigation of the sentence by the US president. On October 13 the Supreme Court refused to review the case or consider the merits of the appeal, with one dissenting voice, Justice Hugo Black. Black was a complicated, clever, and entirely self-made man, an Alabama-born lawyer and senator, a keen supporter of Roosevelt's New Deal who had fought against the unfair treatment of African Americans and the poor by the local criminal justice system. Nonetheless his appointment to the Supreme Court in 1937 had been controversial when it became known that he had once been a Ku Klux Klan member, even though he said he disapproved of its activities. Later that month, the Supreme Court once again refused to reconsider its original ruling, Black again disagreeing. On November 21, Kaufman set the execution date once more for the week of January 12, 1953.

Against this fraught background, the progressive but politically mainstream American Civil Liberties Union (ACLU) dealt a serious blow to the campaign when it decided not to support the Rosenbergs, in spite of some dissenting voices. The ACLU's official view that Ethel and Julius's civil rights had not been breached was partly due to the beliefs of one of its general counsels, Morris Ernst.

Also born in Alabama, two years after Black in 1888, Ernst was the son of self-made German Jewish immigrants who, after attending night classes at New York Law School, became a partner in the distinguished New York law firm of Greenbaum, Wolff and Ernst. Ernst was a clever and complicated man, an "erudite, polished, and well-connected New York hustler,"[5] well known for championing cases that expanded Americans' rights to privacy and freedom from censorship. By the 1930s this successful lawyer had a wife and three children, a fine house in Greenwich Village, and a second home in Nantucket, the exclusive Massachusetts beach resort that, for a Jewish family like the Ernsts, signaled arrival into the highest echelons of New York WASP society.

From the start he had taken a keen interest in the Rosenberg case, while remaining a fervent anti-Communist and—in his own view—an expert on the subject of homegrown "Red" subversives. In 1952 Ernst published his *Report on the American Communist,* for which he had interviewed around three hundred ex-Communists. He believed that as a result of these extensive interviews, he had "a new approach as to how to handle, in American fashion, this real enemy of freedom in our land."[6]

In the case of the Rosenbergs, the well-connected Ernst's approach was to lobby his contacts in the US government in the hope that he would be the one called upon to help unlock this case. If he could elicit a confession from one or both Rosenbergs, which would then lead to the arrest of others, it might prove possible to avoid executing the pair. Ernst started with his friend J. Edgar Hoover, the FBI's obsessively anti-Communist director. Hoover was convinced that Ethel and Julius were both guilty as charged and had no personal problem with executing them. However, Hoover also realized that killing Ethel would bring negative publicity for the US government—certainly in Europe, where "Save the Rosenbergs" campaigns were well under way in many countries, and probably in the US too, where he feared a "psychological reaction" by the public to the execution of a mother with two small children. According to Hoover's biographer Curt Gentry, he predicted that "the backlash . . . would be an avalanche of adverse criticism, reflecting badly on the FBI, the Justice Department, and the entire government."[7] Regardless of Hoover's concerns, nothing came of Ernst's discussions with the FBI director. But he did not give up.

In the presidential election on November 4, 1952, the Republican candidate and former Supreme Allied Commander Dwight D. Eisenhower won a landslide victory over his Democratic opponent, Adlai Stevenson. In characteristic style, Ernst wrote on November 10 to Eisenhower's aide, Major General Wilton B. Persons, offering his services to the new president. Ernst reminded Persons that "during the administrations of [Herbert] Hoover, Roosevelt and Truman I have with great joy performed innumerable anonymous chores always declining a title, a salary or a job."[8]

One of the "anonymous chores" the tenacious Ernst had in mind was to press his view of the Rosenberg case with Eisenhower. In doing so, he was acting on his own, without the support of the ACLU. Ernst had never even met Bloch, who, either because he was too busy or because he saw Ernst as a meddler whom he did not trust, turned down repeated requests to see him. Nor would Ernst ever meet Ethel or Julius.

•   •   •

In her cell at Sing Sing, Ethel had another focus in her isolated life. She and Julius still "met" every Wednesday morning under severe constraints, with no physical contact and no chance to be in the same room alone together, but after November 1952 they were also allowed a Friday meeting. Yet Ethel sank further into a depression, and Julius, in spite of his constant praise of her and her writing ability, appeared unable to help her. Her stream of impassioned letters to him gradually slowed to a trickle during 1952. She reserved her emotional energy for letters to Bloch and worries about the children, while at the same time her more or less fortnightly visits from her psychiatrist, Dr. Saul Miller, prompted a torrent of emotionally charged correspondence after their meetings.

"Dearest," Ethel wrote to Miller on November 15, on a torn scrap of paper now housed in the archives at Boston University. It is possible that this penciled note, with rubbing-out at the top and along the sides, was never sent and was preparation for another that, like most of Ethel's letters to Miller, appears not to have survived.*[9]

---

*   Miller gave an interview to the author Ilene Philipson in 1985 and Philipson says the letters Ethel wrote to Miller "could easily be characterized as love letters" (Philipson, *Ethel Rosenberg Beyond the Myths*, 338). However, she does not quote these in full.

It was a sure delight to be with you today; and how reluctant I was to part from you. You know I am often so overwhelmed by the intensity of my need for you that I am unable to articulate it thus I merely said "goodbye" instead of "Dearest." I hate to see you go; please come back soon . . . there is still so much we have to say to each other and we have such a tiny amount of time left in which to help me find the kind of emotional balance the difficult future (sic!) will demand. You've given me so much understanding today [that] the thought of our threatened separation at this crucial stage in my development is simply intolerable to me. When I back-slide I am terrified and consider that I'm hopeless.

Love you, Ethel

·　　·　　·

Eleanor Roosevelt, the sixty-eight-year-old former First Lady and champion of women's rights, was a long-standing opponent of the death penalty. In less feverish political times, the Committee to Secure Justice might have hoped to enlist Mrs. Roosevelt's support for the Rosenbergs. On December 11 she could hold back no longer: "I am getting a considerable number of letters, all Communist-inspired so far as I can see, from people urging me to do something to prevent the execution of Julius and Ethel Rosenberg," she wrote irritably in her syndicated and widely read "My Day" column. "This Communist-inspired campaign is certainly going to do the Rosenbergs more harm than good."

Mrs. Roosevelt described as "utter nonsense" the idea put forward by some of her correspondents that Ethel and Julius had been sentenced to death because they were Jews. She could not accept that anti-Semitism had played any role that might have interfered in the American judicial system she so prized. After all (although of course she did not spell this out), the judge and the prosecutor were Jewish. But it was more nuanced than that. The underlying fear constantly stoked during the trial was how people like the Rosenbergs (i.e., Jews and Bolshevik supporters) could be patriotic Americans if they also praised a Communist system as practiced in the Soviet Union.

"I don't believe in capital punishment," she continued, "but we do have capital punishment in our country. I don't know if putting the Rosenbergs to death will do us more good than if they were under a sentence of life imprisonment, but this country operates under law and as long as we have laws we must live up to them." Perhaps for her own reassurance, she added another strand to her case for doing nothing on the Rosenbergs' behalf: "Without question, the authorities in our country have given careful consideration as to whether the security of the United States would be benefitted by death or life imprisonment. Punishment of this kind is used as a deterrent for others who might be tempted to do likewise and that also must have been given careful consideration."[10]

Six days later Mrs. Roosevelt's friend Morris Ernst—who seemed to be unaware of her position—wrote to Eisenhower's incoming secretary of state, the aggressively anti-Communist John Foster Dulles. "If you have a moment's time," Ernst wheedled self-importantly, "it might be worth your while to see me in regard to the Rosenberg case . . . I have some information and angles on this case where I might act as a bridge for you and thus for the welfare of our nation."[11] Dulles declined owing to "a crowded schedule."

Nonetheless, the groundswell of unease about Ethel and Julius's imminent execution had now erupted into increasingly widespread protests that, even if the outgoing Democratic president Harry S. Truman chose to ignore, his successor, Eisenhower, could not possibly do so. In mid-December a vigil for the Rosenbergs began in front of the main entrance to the White House. During the day, around five hundred demonstrators gathered on Pennsylvania Avenue, with the numbers falling overnight to about two hundred as temperatures dropped. On December 21, a thousand supporters came to Ossining, led by the film actress Karen Morley, to bring flowers and messages of support to the Rosenbergs. When the police refused to let them leave the station they stood in the rain, belting out songs to Ethel and Julius way up on the hill.

On December 29, the ever-busy Morris Ernst updated Eleanor

Roosevelt about his efforts to prevent the Rosenbergs' execution, still seemingly ignorant of her view about the case. He was "quite persuaded because of several very interesting psychological factors that the lives can be saved by penance and confession," Ernst wrote to her. "In a way," Ernst speculated obscurely, "the couple are sadists, that is people of action, since a masochist never kills himself but merely asks permission to do so."[12] Ernst explained:

> I have done a lot of work on the case and I am quite clear that . . . these two people . . . on my checkup [sic] represent the real hard core. It may even be that the Communist Party does not want to save them. There is some slight evidence which might tend in that direction. Since perchance I might be helpful in saving their lives by getting a confession, I trust you will in no way ever quote me to anyone. The real payoff will come if the lawyer would ever allow me to see the defendants alone, in his absence.[13]

Mrs. Roosevelt, having stated her position, was unmoved by Ernst's latest letter.

On December 30 Manny Bloch appeared in person before Kaufman to make a desperately emotional plea for the lives of Ethel and Julius, whose scheduled execution was now just two weeks away. Bloch asked the judge to commute the death sentences to prison terms, reminding Kaufman that "in your hands, your honor, you have the fate of two human beings . . . who continued to insist on their innocence." Kaufman replied that he was at a loss to understand what stopped them from confessing and thereby saving themselves. He admitted, "I don't know the answer to that," almost turning the plea on its head and urging Manny to be the one who had the power to save their lives. But Bloch responded: "The reason they act in this way is because they believe most deeply in their hearts that they are innocent."[14]

Meanwhile time was running out, as many people in Western Europe seemed to appreciate. By the end of 1952 there were pro-Rosenberg committees in Austria, Belgium, Denmark, Italy, Sweden, Switzerland, Germany, Ireland, and Israel as well as a small but not especially vocal one in London. There was regular picketing in front of some US consulates and embassies, and even in Catholic Italy 180 postcards were sent to the American consulate in Milan from women protesting the death sentences and emphasizing that two children would be orphaned if they went ahead. The concern for Ethel and Julius was especially acute, however, in France, which had a strong anti-American tradition and powerful socialist and Communist parties, and where sympathy for the Rosenbergs had risen steadily since the trial. The red-smocked painter Pablo Picasso wrote in a message on the front cover of Paris's Communist paper *L'Humanité*, beneath a drawing of the couple sitting hand in hand in electric chairs, "The hours count. The minutes count. Do not let this crime against humanity take place."[15] Picasso's countdown clock was no artist's conceit.

On January 5, 1953, with more than a thousand protesters now camped daily outside the White House, the Nobel Prize–winning scientist Harold Urey, who had been involved in developing the atomic bomb, wrote to *The New York Times*. Urey had been shocked to discover that his name had been on the list of witnesses whom the prosecution intended to call at the Rosenbergs' trial and now felt bound to voice his opposition to their execution: "We are engaged in a cold war with the tyrannical Government of the USSR," Urey wrote. "We wish to win the approval and loyalty of the good people of the world. Would it not be embarrassing if after the execution of the Rosenbergs it could be shown that the US had executed two innocent people and let a guilty one [Ruth Greenglass] go completely free?"[16]

The day *The New York Times* published Urey's letter, Ethel, incensed, fired off one of her own to Manny Bloch. She had just learned of criticism of Bloch's handling of the case, following the publication by the same newspaper on New Year's Day of excerpts from the written opinion of one of the US Circuit Court of Appeals judges who had rejected the latest appeal. In particular, Bloch had been attacked for failing to object to Saypol's conduct at the time of the trial and moving for a mistrial. "My Very Dearest Manny," Ethel wrote, "I am sick for the unconscionable sneering attitude, the snide insinuations you have had to suffer on our behalf."[17]

On January 2, Judge Kaufman refused Manny Bloch's personal appeal to him to reduce the sentence. Three days later the Appeals Court denied a stay of execution, still set for the week of January 12. This meant that only Bloch's request to allow the couple time to apply to the president for executive clemency could delay the scheduled executions.

On January 9, Ethel signed a long and detailed letter appealing in her own name to the outgoing president, Harry S. Truman. Julius submitted a substantially similar appeal. Both petitions were clearly drafted as legal documents on Manny's advice. Truman had obviously found the whole issue of the Rosenberg case difficult and something to be avoided. Now it looked as if he would be able to duck it entirely as his tenure drew to a close.

In her address to Truman, Ethel first set out her own role. "Upon the birth of our two sons, I ceased my outside employment and discharged the responsibility of mother and housewife."[18] Then she took direct aim at her brother David. "The modesty of our standard of living," she wrote, "bordering often on poverty, discredits David's depiction of my husband as the pivot and pay-off man of a widespread criminal combination, fed by a seemingly limitless supply of 'Moscow gold.'" She continued: "Our relationship with the Greenglasses, both during and after the war, was on a purely familial and social level, the cordiality becoming strained to the breaking, however, with the advent of bitter quarrels which arose in the course of our postwar business ties."

Ethel's use of the plural "we" meant, at the very least, that she was allowing a lie to be written in her name. Regardless of her case, Julius certainly did have a relationship with David that extended beyond normal family and social ties into a conspiracy to commit espionage. There followed an extended denial of all the charges, placed in the context of Cold War hysteria, and then Ethel returned again to her despicable brother and sister-in-law:

We have never been able to comprehend that civilized and compassionate consciences could accept a smiling "Cain" like David Greenglass—or the "serpent," Ruth, his wife—who would slay not only his sister, but his sister's husband, and orphan two small children of his own blood.

We have always said that David, our brother, knowing well the consequences of his acts, bargained our lives away for his life and his wife's. Ruth goes free, as all the world now knows; David's freedom, too, is not so far off that he will not have many years to live a life—if we should die—that, perhaps, only a David Greenglass could suffer to live.[19]

Toward the end of this long legal document rebutting the charges she then made an appeal to the heart. "We do not want to die," Ethel wrote. "We are young, too young, for death. We long to see our two young sons, Michael and Robert, grown to full manhood. We desire with every fiber to be restored sometime to our children and to resume the harmonious family life we enjoyed before the nightmare of our arrests and convictions. We desire someday to be restored to society, where we can contribute our energies toward building a world where all shall have peace, bread and roses."[20]

The petitions were formally submitted on January 10, prompting an immediate stay of execution until five days after a decision. In effect, the petitions had bought Ethel and Julius at least another fortnight, and almost certainly longer, as Truman vacated the presidency on January 20 without responding to these petitions, thereby passing the problem to his successor, Eisenhower.

On January 12, *The New York Times* printed a letter from Albert Einstein stating: "my conscience compels me to urge you [Eisenhower] to commute the death sentence of Julius and Ethel Rosenberg . . . this appeal to you is prompted by the same reasons which were set forth so convincingly by my distinguished colleague, Harold C. Urey." Only Reuters among the wire services carried reports of the scientist's intervention, prompting *Le Monde* to ask: "Can it be that there is a conspiracy of silence?"[21] By this time dozens of representatives of US trade unions, including the San Francisco Building Trades Council, the all-Black International Longshoremen's Association Local 968, and the International

Longshoremen and Warehousemen's Union in Los Angeles, New Orleans, and San Francisco signed an appeal for clemency.

On Monday, January 19, the day before Eisenhower's inauguration, Ethel received a nasty shock: a visit from her estranged mother, Tessie, who had not come to Sing Sing throughout either of the past two years. She told Manny to "brace yourself for a shock; fact is I am still in a state of stupefaction over its bold-faced immorality." Ethel went on:

> At one point, while verbalizing the emotional factors she could employ in speaking with Davy, I pointed out to her that what-ever unfounded fear of reprisal he might be harboring it was my life that was in peril not his—and further, if I while awaiting electrocution was not afraid to continue to assert my innocence and give the lie to his story, why couldn't he, in a far more advantageous position, be man enough to own up at long last to this lie and help to save my life, instead of letting it to be forfeited to save his face!

Ethel carried on quoting the conversation almost verbatim to Manny. "Said she, 'So what would have been so terrible if you had backed up his story?'—I guess my mouth kind of fell open. 'What,' I replied, 'and take the blame for a crime I never committed and allow my name, and my husband's and children's to be blackened to protect him?'"

When Ethel, as she reported to Manny, continued to protest and finally asked her mother, "But, Ma, would you have had me willingly com-mit perjury?" Tessie shrugged her shoulders indifferently and maintained doggedly, "You wouldn't be here!"[22]

. . .

By the time President Truman left office on January 20, without respond-ing to Ethel's clemency appeal, the number of letters and telegrams sent to the White House from around the world in support of the campaign to save the Rosenbergs had reached three million. What mattered most to Ethel at this moment was how to arrange the next, and possibly last visit from her two young sons. "Julie and I are both agreed we must see them, even if clemency is denied us," she wrote courageously to Manny on January 21. "So bend every effort you can dear to get them here Saturday morning." She advised Manny not to tell them until a day in advance because "Mike will get all tensed up otherwise."[23]

Meanwhile, the indefatigable Morris Ernst had read both petitions carefully and reached his own conclusion about the best "strategy" to prevent the couple's execution. On January 23, Ernst wrote again to Eleanor Roosevelt to share his thoughts on the matter: "The basis of any such strategy, I think, might soundly rest on the thesis that Mrs. Rosenberg is the master and Mr. Rosenberg the servant in the relationship. As a matter of fact the dominance of Mrs. Rosenberg seems so clear to me that my mind went back to the tragic Leopold and Loeb story."[24] This was the notorious 1924 child murder case when two wealthy Chicago teenagers had kidnapped and killed a fourteen-year-old boy to "prove" they were Nietzschean "supermen," not bound by ordinary morality.

A garbled version of Ernst's pop-psychological notion that Ethel was the master to Julius's slave somehow filtered through to senior figures in Eisenhower's incoming administration. It fitted neatly into the general belief in 1950s America that a woman who refused, like Ethel allegedly had, to confine herself to the domestic sphere was in some way deviant, especially one who was three years older than her husband. "The way I see it she's worse than Julius," the assistant prosecutor Roy Cohn claimed he had told a possibly wavering Kaufman, when suggesting that Ethel should also be sentenced to death. "The way I see it, she's the older one, she's the one with the brains, she recruited her younger brother into the Young Communist League and into the spy ring . . . she engineered this whole thing. She was the mastermind of this conspiracy. So unless you're willing to say that a woman is immune from the death penalty, I don't see how you can justify sparing her."[25]

Henri Pierre, Le Monde's Washington correspondent, entirely disagreed with this view of Ethel. On January 23, The Washington Post published a long letter from Pierre about the case in which he argued that "from the point of view of justice it is inadmissible that Mrs. Greenglass should never have been bothered [*sic*] while Mrs. Rosenberg was sentenced to death for having been the moral support of her husband."[26]

For her part, as the petitions clearly demonstrated, Ethel was adamant that her fate could not be separated from Julius's: either both of them would be spared, or both would go to the electric chair. "A cold fury possesses me and I could retch with horror and revulsion for these unctuous saviors, these odious swine [who] are actually proposing to erect a terrifying sepulcher in which I shall live without living and die without dying," she wrote to Manny on February 9. Ethel had learned that she might be saved "out of a humanitarian consideration for me as a woman and as a mother while my husband is to be electrocuted," an idea that appalled her.[27] The irony was that Ethel did not want to be spared simply out of pity for being a wife, nor could she accept that she was the mastermind. Both stereotypes of her as either a dutiful or domineering wife failed to take account of how she had struggled all her life to forge her own identity as a wife and mother but above all as herself, Ethel.

Ethel concluded by asking Bloch to make sure that Dr. Miller received a copy of a book of their letters that was about to be published, if it was ready before he left New York City for a two-week vacation: "He told me yesterday he would phone you on Friday but I'd appreciate it if you got in touch with him upon receipt of this letter and made arrangements to get the stuff to him before he departs!"[28] Ethel was preparing herself to die and Miller presumably felt there was nothing further he could do.

Two days later, Eisenhower formally rejected both clemency petitions. The new president deliberately framed his February 11 decision in the context of the Cold War, rather than address the legal and humanitarian arguments put forward in Ethel's petition. "The nature of the crime for which they have been found guilty and sentenced far exceeds that of the taking of the life of another citizen," Eisenhower declared. "It involves the deliberate betrayal of the entire nation and could very well result in the death of many, many thousands of innocent citizens. By their act these two individuals have in fact betrayed the cause of freedom for which free men are fighting and dying at this very hour [in Korea]."[29]

Next day, Eisenhower repeated this argument to his cabinet, adding for their benefit, but not the public's, that he was also worried about the "unfavorable psychological effect of an Executive reversal of Justice in a case that seemed so clean [*sic*] cut."[30]

In New York, Judge Kaufman now set the executions for the week of March 9.

Eisenhower's rejection immediately swelled the crowds of protesters on the street outside the White House demanding a reversal of the death sentences. Emily and David Alman, who often joined the Washington vigil for hours at a time, reckoned the daily turnout more than doubled to at least ten thousand people following Eisenhower's statement, although the figure is impossible to verify. In Rome, Pope Pius XII, a virulent anti-Communist, made a second appeal for the Rosenbergs' lives to be spared, after a previous appeal to President Truman in December.

On February 17 the Court of Appeals stayed the executions yet again so the Supreme Court could consider once again a petition from Manny for a review of the case. But at Sing Sing this latest reprieve did little to convince Ethel that freedom was at hand. She told Bloch:

> Am terribly restive, but one of these days some writing's bound
> to pour out of me onto paper. In the meantime patience, just
> remember that I have to struggle bitterly to function with any
> degree of ease or comfort at all. Talent, without the emotional
> ability to release it, humiliates and mocks one, until one is ready
> to shriek aloud in pain and in desperation—so please don't ex-
> pect too much, too fast . . . the loneliness is impossible.[31]

In her extreme isolation, desperately seeking human warmth and re-assurance of her self-worth, Ethel may have lost her emotional bearings as she tried desperately to hang on to her sanity. She was allowing herself to fall in love with Dr. Miller, or an idealized version of him at least. "Darling awful," began one of her letters to Miller in early March:[32]

> I very heartily added "awful nice" do you remember? (after all, it
> was St. Valentine's day only 3 weeks ago). "You're awful" meant

you're dear—and you are, Saul, so very dear, and always dearer as time passes. To me it is something in the nature of a revelation every time I sit facing you.

To feel the heart in me welling with the depth and the sweetness of my love. I want so terribly for you to know how much happiness you have given me, how much I miss you and want to be with you—granted I am a voice crying in the wilderness! Seriously is not every decent voice today just that?

Love, Ethel[33]

These tragic notes show a different, raw version of Ethel, not always true of the bulk of the letters, some clearly intended for publication, others concerned with practical matters in which overall Ethel's love and concern for her sons, in spite of any feelings of inadequacy, shines brightly. When Ethel had so little to give her hope, they did. But this is a one-sided correspondence reflecting the one-sided love affair that it inevitably was. There was always a guard sitting not far away at these unorthodox therapy sessions and Ethel could never truly "know" Miller nor even ask him questions about his own home life, let alone touch him. She simply had to imagine all that. Seeing Miller only through the narrow prism of Ethel's desperation, it is tempting to criticize him for allowing her to indulge such fantasies, and then for abandoning her by going on holiday knowing he might never see her again. But perhaps the intensity of the relationship and the looming tragedy was too much even for him to deal with.

In between these fortnightly visits by Miller, and her now twice-weekly meetings with Julius, Ethel waited for the Supreme Court to complete its second review of the case. On April 13 the *National Guardian* published a story that seemed to offer a sliver of hope that the Supreme Court justices might rule in favor of the defense. One of its reporters, Leon Summit, had uncovered conclusive evidence that the Rosenbergs' console table, which the Greenglasses had claimed was a present from Julius's Russian friends, had in fact been bought at Macy's department store, exactly as Julius had testified. In this convoluted tale, the table had been taken to Julius's mother's home by his sister after his and Ethel's arrest.

Since Sophie Rosenberg did not read English, she had not followed the story in the papers and failed to recognize the table's importance.

The *National Guardian* was convinced that its article could form the basis of a new appeal that revealed the trial as a staged event with props. Bloch was not persuaded: In this race against time, what was a console table when set against the prevailing paranoia about Communist subversives? The story withered, along with good relations between Bloch and the Almans, who were sure that Manny had missed a potentially critical opportunity to save Ethel and Julius.

By now, the tide of political and public opinion that still moved so powerfully against the Rosenbergs in the United States—notwithstanding the vigil outside the White House—was flowing just as strongly in the opposite direction across Europe and also in Australia, where a number of local campaigns were doing what they could to apply pressure as well.[34] On April 16, the official Vatican newspaper *L'Osservatore Romano* published a lengthy elaboration of the pope's plea for the Rosenbergs' lives to be spared. A month later, on May 16, the US Ambassador to France, C. Douglas Dillon, sent a telegram to the newly appointed secretary of state, John Foster Dulles, to warn him about the diplomatic consequences of executing the Rosenbergs: "The great majority of French people of all political leanings feel that death sentence is completely unjustified from moral standpoint and is due only to political climate peculiar to United States now . . . If death sentence is carried out, this will have a most harmful long term effect on the opinion and attitudes of the French people toward the United States."[35] Dillon also predicted that the Rosenbergs would be seen as "victims of what the European press freely terms 'McCarthyism,'" adding that other American diplomats in Europe shared his analysis.[36] Dillon wrote to Washington in May 1953 to explain why he thought the president should reconsider clemency. In France most people opposed the executions, which they saw as "unjustifiable punishment," whether the Rosenbergs were guilty or not. The ambassador tried to explain why a "substantial segment of French opinion" distinguished between Julius's guilt as the principal spy and the guilt of "his wife as an accessory."[37]

On May 25 the Supreme Court rejected the petition for review; in New York, Kaufman reset the execution date for the week of June 15. But the government was still hoping to get the Rosenbergs to talk as it continued to play a "war of nerves"[38] with them right until the end. Two weeks before the deadline, on June 2, the director of the Federal Bureau of Prisons, James V. Bennett, visited Sing Sing to offer Ethel and Julius a final chance to "disclose information which would be helpful in solving some as yet unanswered questions." According to the government's account of the visit, Bennett saw Julius first. Bennett found that Julius "lacked the detached calmness and self-assurance that characterized my former conversations with him. He no longer seems to have the attitude of the martyr . . . was quite belligerent, excitable and made some statements that on questioning he was willing to modify." Above all, Bennett noted, Julius asked: "How could it be possible under any circumstances that a death sentence be meted out to him and his wife in the face of the sentence of thirty years given to Harry Gold and fifteen years to David Greenglass, who were admittedly arch-conspirators in an espionage plot?"[39]

Bennett went next to see Ethel. He reported that she "wasn't quite as verbose or excited as he [Julius] was." However, Ethel, robust once again, now firmly insisted that the government obviously could not prove whatever suspicions it had against her and Julius, or it "would not be turning to her for cooperation and that she had no intention of putting her finger on somebody else or giving false or misleading information even though it might have the effect of staying her own execution." She said that if the government wanted her testimony on any matter she would have to be brought into open court.[40]

After the meeting, Ethel and Julius issued a joint statement shedding a different light on what had transpired:

Yesterday, we were offered a deal by the Attorney General of the United States. We were told that if we cooperated with the government, our lives would be spared. By asking us to repudiate the truth of our innocence, the Government admits its own doubts concerning our guilt. We will not help to purify the foul record of a fraudulent conviction and a barbaric sentence. We solemnly declare, now and forever more, that we will not be coerced, even under pain of death, to bear false witness and to yield up to tyranny our rights as free Americans. Our respect for truth, conscience and human dignity is not for sale. Justice is not some bauble to be sold to the highest bidder. If we are executed it will be the murder of innocent people and the shame will be upon the Government of the United States.[41]

The focus now turned back to President Eisenhower, who alone could save Ethel and Julius from the electric chair. On June 10, Eisenhower explained his thinking on the case in reply to a letter he had received from Clyde Miller, a professor of education at Columbia University, where Eisenhower had been president from 1948 to 1953. Eisenhower told Miller that he had been "studying" the case from the moment of his inauguration in 1953 and in his first few months in office had had "innumerable conferences" about the Rosenbergs. He maintained that "the record has been reviewed and re-reviewed by every appropriate court in the land," and that "in no single instance has there been any suggestion that it was improperly tried, that the rights of the accused were violated, that the evidence was insufficient or that there was any factor in the case which justified intervention."[42]

After this defensive preamble, the president explained more candidly why he was under such intense pressure. He knew that he had to appear strong in the face of Communist attacks since "free governments—and especially the American government—are notoriously weak and fearful and that consequently subversive and other kinds of activity can be conducted against them with no real fear of dire punishment on the part of the perpetrator."[43]

Eisenhower finally turned to the sensitive matter of putting a young mother of two small boys to death. "Another factor that appeals, quite naturally, to Americans is that one of these criminals—indeed the more strong-minded and the apparent leader of the two—is a woman," he wrote in a phrase that would not have sounded jarring to most Americans who expected a woman merely to follow. "But the question presents itself if the Executive should interfere because of this fact, would we be justified in encouraging the Communists to use only women in their spying process?"[44]

Only Eisenhower, the great military commander, had the power to spare Ethel and show the world he was frightened neither of Communism nor McCarthy. His conscience was clearly troubled, but not troubled enough to resist what he understood was realpolitik. In the end he clung to his views that the couple had had the benefit of justice and that Ethel was the dominant partner. This was what most Americans who voted for him also believed. Women should be homemakers and nothing more. In the midst of the final demands for clemency, Eisenhower's popularity ratings rose. According to Gallup polls taken at this time, 70 percent of Americans agreed with Eisenhower that both Rosenbergs should be killed.[45]

The day after Eisenhower's letter to Miller, the Appeals Court upheld Kaufman's decision to schedule the execution for the following week; once again, a petition for review was submitted to the Supreme Court. On June 14 Michael and Robby got up early to board a chartered bus to Washington, DC, filled with their adult friends. In the capital they joined their grandmother Sophie and the Almans and thousands of Clemency Campaign supporters who watched as they walked to the West Wing of the White House and gave the guard a letter, in Michael's handwriting, to be forwarded to Eisenhower. In it Michael asked the president to "not let anything happen to my mommy and daddy."[46] Michael said later he had been given the text to copy. "I think this tactic was a mistake . . . my own formulation of a letter to Eisenhower would have been more effective."[47]

On June 15, at noon, the Supreme Court announced that the pending Rosenberg petition for a stay of execution had been denied by a narrow 5–4 majority. Immediately another request was made by Bloch's team for permission to file a habeas corpus petition. Later that day that too was denied. The court then adjourned until October and most of the judges prepared to go on holiday. However, even though the summer recess had officially begun, the defense team had one last shot at a reprieve as they made an approach to the dissenting judge, Justice William O. Douglas.

Douglas, the same as any member of the Supreme Court, had the power to grant a stay on grounds he deemed substantial, which would provide time for a litigant to present important legal issues to a lower court.

At the end of the day, however, Bloch left Douglas's chambers telling journalists: "He did not deny it. He did not grant it."[48]

But at this point, two newcomers stepped in: Fyke Farmer, a former corporate lawyer from Nashville, and Daniel G. Marshall, an associate lawyer from Los Angeles, neither of whom knew the Rosenbergs. Farmer and Marshall, insisting they were acting solely for humanitarian reasons, spoke with Justice Douglas promoting their argument that the Rosenbergs had been tried under the wrong law. At issue was whether the 1917 Espionage Act, under which the couple had been indicted and sentenced, had been superseded by the penalty provisions of the 1946 Atomic Energy Act, which covered how the United States could control and manage secret information. Under the latter act, the death sentence may be imposed only when recommended by the jury and the offense was committed with intent to injure the United States. Neither of these requisite conditions, they argued, was fulfilled in the Rosenberg conviction.

As Douglas studied the new arguments, the boys were driven to Sing Sing to visit Ethel and Julius and, in all likelihood, say goodbye to their parents for the last time. On that occasion, a rule was broken and the children were permitted to see both parents together, albeit with Ethel and Julius seated at opposite ends of the table so still unable to touch. Michael left the room wailing "one more day to live, one more day to live,"[49] a desperate appeal to his parents not to be so brave and apparently nonchalant in the face of their imminent death. With great insight, Ethel immediately wrote to both boys, one of her most powerful messages that Michael understood only years later and insists became a comfort as he was growing up:

> *My dearest darlings*
> *This is the process known as "sweating it out" and it's tough, that's for*
> *sure. At the same time, we can't let a lot of chickens that go about their*

business without panic, even when something's frightening them—we can't let them put us to shame, can we!*

. . . Maybe you thought that I didn't feel like crying too when we were hugging and kissing goodbye, huh, even though I'm slightly older than 10 . . . Darlings, that would have been so easy, far too easy on myself; and I had to resist a very real temptation to follow your lead and break down with you . . . because I love you more than myself and because I knew you needed that love far more than I needed the relief of crying.[50]

She went on:

I know, sweethearts, an explanation of this kind cannot ever substitute for what we have been missing and for what we hope to be able to return to, nor do I intend it as any such thing. Only, as I say, we need to try to remain calm and free from panic, so that we can do all we can to help one another to see this thing through! . . .

All my love and all my kisses—
Mommy

Meanwhile, in Washington, Eisenhower with ghastly symmetry was also writing a letter to his son John, then serving in Korea, in which he tried again to justify his position on not granting clemency. "I must say that it goes against the grain to avoid interfering . . . where a woman is to receive capital punishment," he explained. However, he had overcome his distaste, because "in this instance it is the woman who is the strong and recalcitrant character, the man is the weak one. She has obviously been the leader in everything they did in the spy ring. The second thing is that if there would be any commuting of the woman's sentence without

---

* Michael said that he concluded years later this was a particularly thoughtful metaphor used by his mother as there were chickens where Michael and Robby were living so she knew they would understand the reference.

the man's then from here on the Soviets would simply recruit their spies from among women."[51]

The day before Manny's final visit with the boys to Sing Sing, Ethel had written a deeply personal appeal to Eisenhower, which she dated June 15 and mailed to Bloch for him to hand-deliver to the White House. Ethel wrote that she had been prevented from writing to the president before through "a certain innate shyness, an embarrassment almost . . . in the presence of the great and famous." She described Eisenhower as "liberator" to millions before he was ever "president." In this light, she argued, "what single action could more effectively demonstrate this nation's fealty to religious and democratic ideals than the granting of clemency to my husband and myself!"

She implored him to "Take counsel with your good wife; of statesmen there are enough and to spare! . . . take counsel with the mother of your only son; her heart which understands my grief so well and my longing to see my sons grow to manhood like her own with loving husband at my side even as you are at hers—her heart must plead my cause with grace and with felicity!"[52]

Meanwhile, another last-minute legal development was unfolding in Washington. Justice William Douglas had remained in his chambers until almost midnight studying the Farmer-Marshall brief and also meeting with government lawyers. On Wednesday morning, June 17, he announced that he had before him two applications for a stay of execution made to him after the adjournment of the court. He believed that one of these raised a completely new point regarding the power of a district court judge to impose the death sentence in the Rosenbergs' case. Douglas accepted the importance "that the country be protected against the nefarious plans of spies who would destroy us." However, he continued, "it is also important that before we allow lives to be snuffed out we be sure— emphatically sure—that we act within the law."[53]

Having made his pronouncement, Justice Douglas then resumed his vacation, confident that his stay of execution would be effective at least until the Supreme Court reconvened in early October so that it could

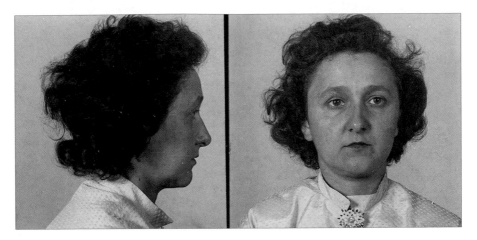

Prison mug shots of Ethel taken immediately after her second grand jury appearance in August 1950. She had dressed carefully for the occasion, wearing white gloves and a pretty brooch at her neck, but had hoped to be going to another appointment afterward.

(Alamy)

Ethel and Julius were arrested three weeks apart but were inextricably linked immediately after Ethel's arrest.

(Alamy)

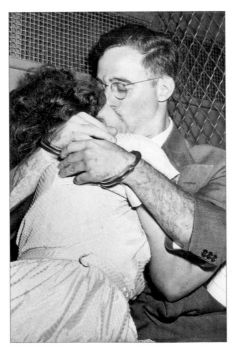

Ethel and Julius, handcuffed, kissing in the prison van after they had been first arraigned.

(Getty Images)

Ethel and Julius now firmly separated in the prison van as they were taken to court. Fellow prisoners allowed Julius to occupy the seat on the other side of the grate so they could at least be close to each other on these occasions. *(Alamy)*

The side of the Jell-O box that played such a devastating role in the trial. David accused Julius of cutting it in a specific way in order to be used as a recognition signal. By referencing something in almost every American kitchen, the prosecution made it appear as if the Rosenbergs were attacking the heart of the home. For Rosenberg supporters, the Jello-O box was one more example of why the trial was a staged event with props. *(Alamy)*

Ethel leaving the courtroom after she and Julius had been sentenced to death, managing not to betray her emotions.
(Alamy)

Ethel in 1951 being taken from the Women's House of Detention to Sing Sing Prison, after she had been sentenced to death. She made a heroic effort to smile and wave to the friends she had left behind.

(Shutterstock.com)

Emanuel Bloch with Michael and Robby outside the main entrance of Sing Sing just after a visit to see Ethel and Julius.

(Meeropol family photographs reprinted with the permission of the copyright holders, Michael and Robert Meeropol)

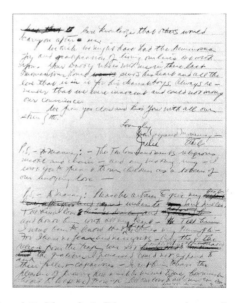

The Rosenbergs' last letter to Michael and Robby, their "dearest sweethearts" and "most precious children," written by Ethel on the flimsy prison notepaper and with several crossings-out, hours before they died. It was delivered via Manny Bloch.

(Meeropol family photographs reprinted with the permission of the copyright holders, Michael and Robert Meeropol)

Grandma Sophie Rosenberg with Michael and Robby in their smartest clothes and Brooklyn Dodgers caps, protesting outside the White House in June 1953 to spare their parents' lives.

(Meeropol family photographs reprinted with the permission of the copyright holders, Michael and Robert Meeropol)

Walking mourners followed the hearse bearing the bodies of Julius and Ethel Rosenberg en route to Wellwood Jewish Cemetery on Long Island after funeral services in Brooklyn. Mounted police kept order as crowds of people lined the streets. *(Getty Images)*

The Rosenbergs were interred side by side on June 23. Several Jewish cemeteries had refused to allow the couple to be buried in their grounds.   *(Getty Images)*

Tessie Greenglass, Ethel's mother, who denounced her daughter to the FBI as "a soldier of Stalin," talking to newsmen. She did not go into mourning for her daughter, who she claimed had never loved her.
(Shutterstock.com)

Anne Meeropol, a former actress and teacher who became Michael's and Robby's adoptive mother, providing some musical entertainment for the boys in the living room of their apartment at 149th Street in 1954.
(Meeropol family photographs reprinted with the permission of the copyright holders, Michael and Robert Meeropol)

Michael and Robby playing trains on the floor with songwriter Abel Meeropol, who became the boys' adoptive father. This and the above photo were taken to show the court how happy the boys were in their new home.
(Meeropol family photographs reprinted with the permission of the copyright holders, Michael and Robert Meeropol)

Irving Kaufman, the judge at the Rosenberg trial, who told Ethel that her crime was "worse than murder."
(Getty Images)

Irving Saypol was forty-five and already dubbed the nation's chief legal hunter of Communists when he acted as chief prosecutor at the Rosenberg trail.

(Shutterstock.com)

Roy Cohn, only twenty-three when he made his name as Saypol's thrusting assistant prosecutor at the Rosenberg trial.

(Alamy)

Ruth Greenglass, Ethel's sister-in-law who came to the trial, according to the prosecution, looking "dolled up, arrogant, smart, cute, eager-beaver like a phonograph record."

(Shutterstock.com)

Morton Sobell, Julius's close friend from the City College of New York, sentenced to thirty years for his part in the Rosenberg conspiracy. *(Alamy)*

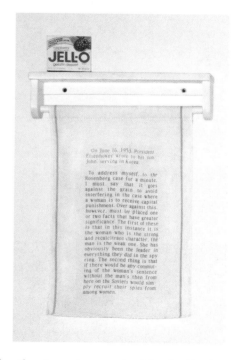

On June 16, 1953, President Eisenhower wrote to his son John, serving in Korea.

To address myself to the Rosenberg case for a minute. I must say that it goes against the grain to avoid interfering in the case where a woman is to receive capital punishment. Over against this, however, must be placed one or two facts that have greater significance. The first of these is that in this instance it is the woman who is the strong and recalcitrant character, the man is the weak one. She has obviously been the leader in everything they did in the spy ring. The second thing is that if there would be any commuting of the woman's sentence without the man's then from here on the Soviets would simply recruit their spies from among women.

Unknown Secrets, a 1988 installation by the American artist Martha Rosler that has a screen-print photograph of Ethel washing dishes at its heart, bordered by magazine clippings featuring politicians and fashion items of the era. The accompanying image of a tea towel reinforces Ethel's central domestic pose. In the years since her death, Ethel has become a cultural icon.

(Copyright © Martha Rosler, detail from Unknown Secrets:
The Secret of the Rosenbergs, *1988)*

His Famous Smile, a vicious caricature of President Eisenhower with teeth made out of electric chairs, was created by the Polish-born French artist Louis Mittelberg in 1952 and became a popular protest poster in Paris.

(Wisconsin Historical Society, WHS 3504)

The final resting place of Ethel and Julius Rosenberg as it looks today.

(Mike Rogers)

be discussed. He was wrong. On June 18, the Supreme Court was summoned to consider Douglas's opinion. On June 19, by a majority of 6–3, with Justices Douglas, Black, and Frankfurter dissenting, the court ruled that the 1946 law could not be applicable because the primary overt acts in the case were committed in 1944 and 1945. By the time Manny Bloch handed in a typed version of Ethel's appeal on the afternoon of June 19, the Supreme Court had vacated the Douglas stay and Eisenhower had, for the second time, denied clemency. The final obstacles to Ethel and Julius's execution had, in a matter of hours, been removed.

•   •   •

Ethel had long since assumed that she and Julius would eventually be electrocuted. Julius had managed to remain optimistic for longer, perhaps helped by the fact that he at least could have some interaction with other male prisoners in the Death House, even if it was only playing chess through the cell wall or talking to other inmates, one of whom at least he naively failed to realize was then passing on his comments to the FBI. Ethel, by contrast, was alone with her thoughts.

Three months after her incarceration at Sing Sing, she had written to Julius that one way to face her impending death was to try not to focus on it. After all, people about to be killed in car crashes, unaware that this is to be their fate, carry on as normal until their deaths, she had suggested. Yet as each of their appeals was turned down, and each appeal for clemency rejected, it became increasingly hard for her to maintain this attitude. Getting through the day and not breaking down in public required all the energy she could muster.

In her final months in Sing Sing, when Ethel had grown resigned to being killed and never seeing her beloved sons again, she admitted privately to Manny Bloch that sometimes "she shivered from head to foot"[54] when she thought of getting into the electric chair and having a powerful current run through her. Yet she had also repeatedly promised to those she loved that she would do her best "to die with honor and with dignity."[55]

Ethel and Julius were allowed to spend most of their final day together, separated as they always had been by a wire mesh, offering each other words of comfort and hope for the future of their boys. One of Ethel's last acts was to scribble notes to Manny. In one she asked him to make sure he gave the children her Ten Commandments religious medal and chain and wedding ring. In the other she asked him: "Please be certain to give my [deepest love affection and regard all crossed out] best wishes to Saul Miller. Tell him I love and honor him with all my heart. Tell him I want him to know that I feel he shares my triumph—for I have no fear and no regrets . . . I want him to have the pleasure of knowing how much he meant to me, how much he did to help me grow up."[56]

At 7:20 p.m. she and Julius said goodbye for the last time. They were taken to separate holding cells, each one with a heavy door leading down a cement path to the execution chamber.

At 7:32 p.m. the White House announced that President Eisenhower had read the "mercy" letter from Mrs. Rosenberg, hand-delivered by Bloch, but felt that it added nothing to his opinion on the case expressed earlier in the day.

At 8:02 p.m. it was time for Julius, his mustache shaven off, to walk to his death. He did so following Rabbi Koslowe, who was constantly praying aloud, intoning psalms, and kissing the prayer book from which he was reading them. At 8:06, following three charges of electricity, Julius Rosenberg was pronounced dead. His body was immediately placed on a trolley and wheeled out.

Then it was Ethel's turn. Rabbi Koslowe came back down the path to fetch her, told her that her husband was dead, and asked her one more time "if she had any information she wanted to give . . . did she have any names to give . . . She said she was innocent."[57] "After that she followed me down the corridor right to the chair," Koslowe later told a journalist.

Ethel's black hair had been close-cropped. She was wearing a prison-issue dress and slippers, and walked with "firm steps and stony face," according to one reporter allowed into the execution chamber to witness the death sentences being carried out.[58] Ethel paused only to embrace the short, white-haired matron, Mrs. Evans, and then turned to sit in the chair as the black helmet, straps, and leg contacts were fixed. "Mrs. Rosenberg closed her eyes. She winced slightly as the electrode was fixed on her head." Five minutes later, after five massive charges of electricity, Ethel Rosenberg was finally pronounced dead.

Neither the government nor the FBI had wanted it to end this way. They wanted names of other spies, not the brutal death of young parents. But as William Rogers, deputy attorney general, commented, "She called our bluff."[59]

Ten

Redemption

A handful of shirtsleeved reporters, cigarettes dangling, ran out of the prison in a race to grab one of the public phones and file their accounts of what had happened. It was the well-known Hearst reporter Bob Considine who announced to the world in a shaky, uncertain voice, frequently not looking directly at the camera, that "Ethel Rosenberg who had wanted to be an opera singer . . . had everything to live for . . . had died a lot harder . . . When she meets her maker she'll have a lot of explaining to do."[1]

Unlike Ethel, Julius had thought they would escape the electric chair until almost the end. "I think we're just going to make it, Sis," Julius had told his sister on one of her last visits. His optimism was misplaced. On the day of the executions, Supreme Court Justice Felix Frankfurter had complained in a dissenting opinion about the haste with which the final legal points had been dispatched. Admitting how "unfortunate it may be that that issue did not emerge earlier than it did," he maintained now that more time should have been given to discussing it. "To be writing an opinion in a case affecting two lives after the curtain has been rung down upon them has the appearance of pathetic futility," Frankfurter wrote, apparently enraged that he could not slow the judicial process that would send

Ethel and Julius to their deaths a few hours later. "But history also has its claims, "[2] he wrote in a comment that did little for Ethel or her legal team.

Michael learned of his parents' death on the day it happened, Friday, June 19, from Sonia and Ben Bach, the couple who had been looking after him and his brother for the past year at their home in Toms River. Having just endured the most appalling summer imaginable, the boys were fractious and not easy to handle. Initially the *National Guardian* and the Committee to Secure Justice had wanted to keep the Rosenberg boys out of their campaign, but in the end that was not possible. The Bachs had been watching television with Robby and Michael, waiting for the news, when a bulletin announcing that the executions would go ahead flashed across the screen. So, with few options, they decided to go to a different house and encouraged the boys to play baseball in the garden. But when it grew too dark to continue, ten-year-old Michael came inside and immediately understood what had happened. "I just sat on the couch and stared at my hands. I couldn't react. I was not to cry emotionally for six years,"[3] Michael said later. Sonia cried and hugged him, but they decided not to tell six-year-old Robby immediately that his parents were dead.

The funeral took place in Brooklyn on Wednesday, June 21. Emily Alman did most of the organizing. She had immediately claimed the bodies from Sing Sing Prison, telling the warden that the Rosenbergs would be buried in a Jewish cemetery in accordance with Jewish ritual and rabbinic law. Emily arranged a day and night vigil at a funeral chapel in Brooklyn, where the bodies were dressed for viewing in open coffins, Julius wearing a tallit (a Jewish prayer shawl), Ethel with a white head bandage covering the injury inflicted on her. Almost five hundred mourners were allowed inside while at least ten thousand people filled the adjoining streets, according to *The New York Times*. An exhausted and disappointed Bloch made an angry speech describing the execution of the Rosenbergs as "murder." But Rabbi Abraham Chronbach, a leading figure in the Save the Rosenbergs campaign, who a week earlier had personally pleaded with Eisenhower at the White House to spare their lives, called for calm and told the mourners to avoid hatred, rancor, and retaliation. "Let us give our detractors not a scintilla of an excuse for impugning the caliber of our citizenship. Let us make it clear that we cannot possibly gain by anything through which America is injured," Cronbach declared.[4]

After the eulogies, the bodies were driven to Wellwood Jewish Cemetery in Farmingdale, Suffolk County, about an hour's drive from New York City on Long Island, for interment side by side. It was not the first choice, but several Jewish cemeteries had refused to allow the couple to be buried in their grounds. Hundreds more attended this service on June 23, some of whom arrived by bus. A distraught Sophie Rosenberg, now seventy-one, was supported at the graveside by Manny Bloch. As the two caskets were lowered into the ground, the rabbi intoned a solemn Kaddish, the most sacred Jewish prayer recited by mourners for the merit of the departed soul.

Amid this throng, a conspicuous absentee was Tessie, who five days after her daughter's death decided to call the FBI and denounced her dead daughter as "a soldier of Stalin." She spoke to FBI agent John Harrington, chief field officer in the Rosenberg investigation. Tessie said she could not understand how her daughter could hurt the United States of America in the manner that she did. From her perspective, Ethel had committed suicide and the only person who should have her death on his conscience was Manny Bloch. "Mr. Harrington," she concluded, "you should know that I do not attend political rallies."[5] Nor did Tessie go into mourning for the daughter who she said did not love her.

The executions triggered widespread protests all over Europe, especially in France. The day after the Rosenbergs died, the anti-American political philosopher Jean-Paul Sartre wrote in the left-wing daily *Libération*:

> Now that we have been made your allies, the fate of the Rosenbergs could be a preview of our own future. You, who claim to be masters of the world, had the opportunity to prove that you were first of all masters of yourselves. But you gave in to your criminal folly and this very folly might tomorrow throw us headlong into a war of extermination . . .

By killing the Rosenbergs you have quite simply tried to halt the progress of science by human sacrifice. Magic, witch hunts, autos-da-fé, sacrifices—we are here getting to the point: your country is sick with fear . . . you are afraid of the shadow of your own bomb.[6]

The French feminist writer Simone de Beauvoir wrote to Sartre to praise him, even though the two were no longer lovers. In a letter to another former lover, the American writer Nelson Algren, a vocal Rosenberg supporter, de Beauvoir wrote how nobody felt like swimming or looking at paintings anymore: "In France and Italy even right-wing people agree on one point: this is the biggest mistake made by the USA in the Cold War. Nobody could have done such a propaganda against them as they did themselves, all pro-American French people are terribly embarrassed with this scandal." The leading French publisher Gallimard had already produced some of the Rosenbergs' prison letters in French and de Beauvoir commented on how moving they were—"chiefly the woman's."[7]

Sartre's and de Beauvoir's response may have been expected. That of the French biochemist Jacques Monod, who wrote a long, reasoned letter to the editor of the international *Bulletin of the Atomic Scientists,* less so. Monod was especially exercised by Ethel's execution:

We could not understand that Ethel Rosenberg should have been sentenced to death when the specific acts of which she was accused were only two conversations; and we were unable to accept the death sentence as being justified by the "moral support" she was supposed to have given her husband. In fact the severity of the sentence, even if one provisionally accepted the validity of the Greenglass testimony, appeared out of all measure and reason to such an extent as to cast doubt on the whole affair, and to suggest that nationalistic passions and pressure from an inflamed public opinion had been strong enough to distort the proper administration of justice.[8]

Meanwhile, back in Moscow, Alexander Feklisov later claimed that he followed the unfolding drama in despair. All Feklisov's recollections of the Rosenbergs have to be treated with extreme caution, given that he was a Soviet intelligence officer operating at the height of the Cold War whose only interest in making "friends" with Julius was to obtain US military secrets. Yet Feklisov's memoirs, published in 2001, at least provide an insight into the version of the Rosenberg case that the KGB wished to record for posterity. Feklisov said he believed "one should pull out all the stops to help friends in danger"[9] while realizing that he was powerless to help. Unable to sleep on the night of the execution, full of remorse, he had gone to KGB headquarters in Lubyanka Square before dawn to listen on a shortwave radio to the latest news on the BBC World Service. Even then, Feklisov wrote, he was hoping against hope for a reprieve.

In his memoir, Feklisov portrayed Julius as an anti-Fascist soldier rather than a Communist spy and revealed his frustration that the Rosenbergs did not have a better defense lawyer. "Emanuel Bloch, as devoted as he may have been, didn't have the experience or the caliber required to take on the American judicial system," Feklisov wrote. He also blamed the Soviet Union, saying he was "convinced that my country should have taken a bold step, unprecedented but honest, which offered the only possibility of improving the chances of the accused."[10] Feklisov maintained that Julius Rosenberg and Morton Sobell would have been able to confess their espionage and save their lives if the Soviet Union had unilaterally declared that they had passed on secrets. "Despite the damage . . . it would have become impossible to say that Rosenberg and Sobell were the main culprits in America's loss of the atomic monopoly."[11]

However, it was not that simple.

•   •   •

By the time of the executions, US intelligence had cracked the codes and deciphered thousands of intercepted cables sent to the Soviet Union by American agents. Julius, under a code name, was mentioned in these intercepts, which became known as the Venona Transcripts, a randomly chosen name.

The Venona Project, based near Washington in Arlington, Virginia, had started on a small scale in 1943, due to American suspicion that the Soviet Union and Germany might be conducting secret peace negotiations. American code-breakers discovered that the Soviet Union was using a complex two-part ciphering system involving a "one-time pad" code that in theory was unbreakable. However, the Russians made a mistake due to wartime shortages, which forced them to duplicate several pads. In 1946 Meredith Gardner, the chief decrypter at the inchoate project, broke into a Soviet intelligence message sent to Moscow Center two years previously, which contained a list of the leading scientists working at Los Alamos during the Manhattan Project. But it took till 1948 for the first messages to be translated into coherent, readable text that contained more than simply the scientists' names. The teams working on this were headed by Gardner and FBI agent Robert Lamphere and included some British cryptanalysts. The decoded intercepts revealed widespread wartime espionage by Soviet intelligence officers and pro-Soviet US sympathizers in New York. Most alarmingly, the translated messages proved that the Soviet Union had infiltrated the atomic bomb project at Los Alamos—Operation Enormoz.

In 1949 the British double agent Kim Philby informed Moscow about the Venona Project. While Philby's alert enabled Soviet intelligence to change its current encryption regime, the United States continued its slow, painstaking decipherment of wartime Soviet cables in the hope that they would reveal people who were still active as spies. Among thousands of transcripts, the names of Julius and Ethel Rosenberg, David and Ruth Greenglass, Harry Gold, and Klaus Fuchs surfaced in 1949 and 1950.

Only nineteen of the three thousand transcripts that were eventually declassified and published in 1995 mention Julius or Ethel. Julius was given the code name "Antenna" or, as already seen, "Liberal" in the messages. David was code-named "Kalibr" (Caliber) and Ruth was called "Osa" (Wasp). However, Ethel had no code name and was mentioned only once, and then by her given name. This message read:

Information on Liberal's wife. Surname that of her husband, first name Ethel, 29 years old. Married five years. Finished secondary school. A FELLOWCOUNTRYMAN since 1938. Sufficiently well developed politically. Knows about her husband's work and the role of METR [references to the spy Joel Barr or Al Sarant] and NIL [another spy, called Nathan Sussman]. In view of delicate health does not work. Is characterized positively and as a devoted person.[12]

The precise nature of the work that Ethel did not do "in view of her delicate health" was not specified. It could have referred to espionage work or, equally, to earning a living in a paid job. Meredith Gardner explained his interpretation in 1948: "The work that Ethel cannot do in view of her delicate health may not be the earning of her bread and butter, but conspiratorial work."[13]

However, another intercept stated: "LIBERAL [Julius] and his wife recommend her [Ruth Greenglass] as an intelligent and clever girl." This message is open to different interpretations, depending on the reader's preexisting attitude to the Cold War, Communism, and McCarthyism generally. In 1999 the historians John Earl Haynes and Harvey Klehr took it to mean that Ethel was fully aware of her husband's espionage work and "assisted in recruiting her brother and sister-in-law."[14] In 2002 the Canadian academic Bernice Schrank argued that the cable might simply have meant "that Julius met with the Russians and told them that he (and, by the way, his wife) agreed that his sister-in-law was 'an intelligent and clever girl,' presumably code for his sister-in-law's usefulness in some unspecified espionage activity." According to Schrank, the cable "does not prove that Ethel recruited Ruth"; it is "vague and suggestive."[15]

Amid this ambiguity about Ethel, it is not even certain that Venona was decisive in uncovering Julius as an active Soviet agent. In the published transcripts, the earliest positive identification of Julius as Antenna and later Liberal was in a memorandum dated June 27, 1950. This was almost two weeks after the signed confession of David Greenglass on June 15 and the first FBI questioning of Julius the following day. Morton Sobell was among those who believed that it was David who led the FBI to conclude that Antenna/Liberal had to be Julius Rosenberg.

Whatever the truth about how the FBI reached Julius, it became impossible in the wake of the publication of the Venona messages to maintain that Julius had not been a Soviet agent; just as before 1995, the absence of hard evidence about his espionage had allowed campaigners to believe that Julius had been framed as well as Ethel. Their sons, Michael and Robert, who spent much of their adult lives trying to prove their parents' innocence, came to the painful conclusion—in Michael's words—that Venona was "the beginning of a process that changes our point of view . . . It's now clear that there was a spy ring."

"My father was not an atomic scientist. He was a recruiter," Robert explained in a 2011 interview. "The government wanted him because he knew names."[16]

However, the Venona revelations did not end the debate about Ethel's precise role—or lack of one—in Julius's spy ring. Under US law, Ethel was not obliged to report Julius's illegal activities to the authorities. On the other hand, it was (and is) against the law to take affirmative actions to conceal a crime. Between these two legal principles, it is clear that Ethel and Julius's relationship was so close that it is inconceivable she did not know and encourage his espionage for the Russians, which in the legal terms of 1951 made her complicit to a conspiracy. But was that a crime— let alone a crime punishable by death?

One of the key ironies of the case is that the two co-heads of the Venona team hoped that Ethel would be spared. Meredith Gardner was a quiet, scholarly man with a wife and two children, who after Ethel's arrest suffered pangs of guilt at the prospect of her execution and the orphaning of her sons. When he died in 2002, his wife recalled that, despite his pride in his work, he was sorry it had led to the Rosenbergs' execution because "those people at least believed in what they were doing."[17] Both Gardner and Lamphere, based on their insights from Venona, believed that executing Ethel was wrong, but were powerless. They had been ordered to keep their knowledge secret. No one could know about the existence of Venona.

However, Bob Lamphere felt so strongly that he wrote a blunt memo to Hoover, "stating that the facts of the case were clear; at the very least the wife did not deserve her sentence. She should not be executed."[18]

Lamphere's memo prompted Hoover to write to Irving Kaufman, who refused to change his mind. Later, Kaufman let it be known to the media that before imposing sentence he had gone to the synagogue to pray for guidance. Shortly before his death in 1986, Roy Cohn remarked of this story: "Judge Kaufman has said that he sought divine guidance in his synagogue before deciding on the sentences. I can't confirm or deny this. So far as I know, the closest he [Kaufman] got to prayer was the phone booth next to the Park Avenue Synagogue. He called from that booth to a phone I used, behind the bench in the courtroom to ask my advice on whether he ought to give the death penalty to Ethel Rosenberg."[19]

Cohn was a thoroughly unreliable source, so his account of regular phone booth conversations with Kaufman during the trial cannot be assumed to be true, although Cohn's overweening arrogance makes such revelations that he, at twenty-three, felt in a position to advise the judge perfectly likely. As for Kaufman, the synagogue story appalled Supreme Court Justice Felix Frankfurter: "I despise a judge who feels God told him to impose a death sentence," Frankfurter told Judge Learned Hand, one of America's most senior jurists.

*   *   *

Michael and Robert, ten and six when their parents were executed, faced an uncertain future as orphans. Robby, three when his parents were arrested, had few memories of home life before the catastrophe.

Looking back, Michael acknowledged that he made life difficult for the adults looking after him and started doing badly at school. "No one was sufficiently strong and skilled to deal with me consistently, calm me down and at the same time communicate the sense of warmth and love they obviously felt," he recalled.[20] By contrast, Robby became quiet and withdrawn.

In the immediate aftermath of the execution, the question of where the boys should live became a major concern for Manny Bloch, who was also now fighting for his professional life: Manny's funeral accusation of murder against the US attorney general and President Eisenhower had prompted a formal disbarment procedure against him. He now had to prepare his own defense case at the same time as he was organizing multiple publications of a limited edition of *The Rosenberg Letters*. He hoped the proceeds from the latter would be enough to set up a trust fund for the boys. He wanted Michael and Robby to have "a fighting break in the world"[21] by giving them the chance of a good education and the opportunity to go to college. But first he had to find them a home and stability.

Manny received various offers to adopt the boys, including one from a kibbutz in Israel and another from a family in France. He and Gloria Agrin, now his fiancée, even considered taking them in themselves. The problem was urgent because during the weeks and months after the execution Michael felt as if his life was "sliding downhill." None of the boys' three aunts and uncles on the Rosenberg side, however supportive they had been, felt up to the task, fearing the risk to their own livelihoods of looking after the children of convicted Soviet spies. On the Greenglass side, the family was deeply divided over David and Ruth's behavior.[22] Yet a gesture of this magnitude by those who sympathized with Michael and Robby's plight was out of the question, given the irreparable family breach that David and Ruth had caused.

And so the issue of settling Michael and Robby continued to drift as the end of 1953 approached. The Bachs had hoped that the boys could live in relative obscurity in suburban New Jersey. But news of their temporary home in Toms River leaked out and they began receiving anonymous hate mail, including a postcard to Michael saying: "Of course you feel for the loss of your parents but when you think of all the boys they killed in Korea you should realize that they deserved to die. Why don't you change your names and become Christians?"[23]

On another occasion a school bus driver, having recognized the boys from press photographs, reported them to school officials. This led to a ban on them attending school in New Jersey on the grounds that they lived in New York. Even an enraged Bloch could not prevent their being taken out of school.

But in December 1953, just as the situation was becoming critical, the boys were taken by Ben Bach and Manny Bloch to a Christmas party in New York at the home of W. E. B. Du Bois, the Black author and social rights activist. It was a fun evening, full of music and magicians, unlike anything they had experienced in their short lives, and here they were introduced to the inspirational couple who eventually turned their lives around.

Anne and Abel Meeropol were both teachers, admirers more than friends of Du Bois, who had never known Ethel or Julius but had first offered the Rosenberg boys a home in 1952. With no children of their own, they now renewed their offer. Anne, forty-five, had been the director of a nursery school and a highly effective teacher of the neglected "latchkey" children of Harlem. This made her "strong enough and sure enough in her understanding of children to deal successfully with me," Michael later recalled. Abel, aged fifty in 1953, was the son of Russian Jewish immigrants, a former high-school English teacher, songwriter, and member of the CPUSA until around 1947, according to his biographer David Newstead. He left partly in disillusionment, but mostly in an attempt to save his career. However, they remained friendly with several party members. In 1941, Meeropol had been brought before the Rapp-Coudert Committee, which had been set up by the New York State legislature to investigate alleged Communist influence in the public school system. He was asked by the committee if the CPUSA had paid him to write the song that made his name, "Strange Fruit." He survived the investigation, but it was a narrow escape. Meeropol had initially written "Strange Fruit" as a poem, possibly in response to a photograph that haunted him for days, of an especially gruesome lynching of two teenage African American boys in Alabama in 1930. Later, he set it to music and his wife Anne sang it informally to friends. But early in 1939 a young and unknown Billie Holiday performed it in a New York nightclub, transforming both her career and Abel Meeropol's fame. The song's message was considered so controversial that it was banned from several radio stations, including Britain's BBC.[24]

The Meeropols had lost two babies at birth and were ideally qualified to give these two boys the love and security they craved. Soon the brothers moved into the Meeropols' Upper West Side apartment on Riverside Drive and 149th Street. They shared a bedroom while Anne and Abel slept on a sofa bed in the living room and, from the start, a life of music, games, and a sense of feeling welcome meant they quickly settled in. A formal adoption process was set in motion, including a protective change of name.

"One of the most remarkable things was how quickly we adapted," Robby recalled in an interview about his adoptive father. "First of all, Abel, what I remember about him as a six-year-old, was that he was a real jokester. He liked to tell silly jokes and play word games and he would put on these comedy shows that would leave me rolling."[25]

Yet no sooner had Michael and Robby moved in with the Meeropols than a completely unexpected tragedy threatened their newfound security. In January 1954 Manny Bloch died suddenly of a heart attack at the age of only fifty-one. This meant that the boys now had no legal guardian, prompting the city's social services to take both of them away from the Meeropols and place them in a children's shelter in Pleasantville, New York, thirty miles north of Manhattan.

In this bureaucratic nightmare, the New York Society for the Prevention for Cruelty to Children filed a petition, charging the Meeropols with "retaining the children without legal right and contrary to law." The petition further alleged neglect, claiming that Michael and Robby were being exploited for propaganda by people seeking to raise funds "using the names of the children publicly for this purpose."[26] A court case ensued, in which the Meeropols were aided in their effort win back the boys by Manny's father, Alexander, and his bereaved fiancée, Gloria Agrin. Evelyn Williams, a young Black probation officer chosen to investigate the case, found herself "pressured from the beginning of my investigation to recommend institutionalization."[27] Williams was shocked to be summoned to the chambers of Judge Jacob Panken, who "threatened to fire me if I did not follow [his] recommendation." Fortunately for Michael and Robby she stood her ground, choosing to base her decision concerning the children's future solely on her own findings "and the hell with the job."

Williams visited both Sophie Rosenberg and the Meeropols at their homes and was convinced that "their only concern was what was best for the children." She knew that a future with the Meeropols probably offered both boys the best long-term chance in life. On the other hand, Williams understood the system well enough to recognize that, in the short term, the most likely route to avoiding institutional placement was to recommend that they remain with a loving relative. She therefore advised that Michael and Robby should live with their grandmother Sophie.

Even now, the State of New York refused to relinquish its determination to institutionalize the Rosenberg children, a punishment beyond death for Ethel. Three separate courts became involved in this battle, each with its own probation officers. "I imagined all kinds of behind-the-scenes deals being made to implement the state's plans," recalled Williams, worried about "frightening and well-structured political maneuvers"[28] to ensure that the boys did not grow up in a family where they would be encouraged to see their parents as wrongfully convicted political martyrs.

Finally, in April 1954, the New York Surrogate's Court awarded custody to Sophie Rosenberg, appointing the dean of the New York School of Social Work, Kenneth Johnson, as co-guardian. Michael and Robby felt they had won "the first victory our family had ever won in the courts." Dean Johnson "turned out to be a wonderful man," Michael explained. "He and Grandma became good friends and he also established an immediate rapport with the Meeropols."[29] The court also recommended formal adoption, a legal change of name, avoidance of all publicity, and admission to special private schools. The royalties from "Strange Fruit," "The House I Live In" (1945), and other songs provided the earnings from which most of the family's income derived over the next decade. Anne also worked running teenage drama workshops and, in the summer, as a camp counselor, and the fund that Manny Bloch had set up brought in some income too.

Thus began a long redemptive journey that just a few months previously had seemed impossible to all concerned. Although the boys stayed with Grandma Sophie, assisted by a governess and teams of friends, for the next few months they spent afternoons with Anne and Abel until they could go and live with them full-time in the summer of 1954. In February 1957 Michael and Robby were asked if they wished to be formally adopted by the Meeropols, which they did, changed their names to theirs, and were sheltered from the outside world. "In fact, considering our experiences, Michael and I were in remarkably good shape," wrote Robby, "our relative sanity reflects the strong base they provided for us. The [Meero-pols] did not continually refer to our parents though they did reinforce our great love and respect for Ethel and Julius by portraying them as courageous people who died for their beliefs."[30]

This period of peace and security allowed both boys to complete their education and come of age. In the turbulent 1960s, this was not without complications. Both were to varying degrees radical activists and constantly questioned themselves as to how they should display their loyalty to Julius and Ethel without compromising their gratitude to the Meeropols. Should they try to forget their past, or should they claim their birth identity?

In 1960 Michael, a guitar-playing top student, began studying for his first degree at Swarthmore College, a liberal arts college in Pennsylvania. On graduating, he won a place at King's College Cambridge for two years of further studies, gaining a BA (later an MA) in economics, and, in 1973, received his PhD in economics from the University of Wisconsin–Madison. In 1965 he married Ann Karusaitis, a teacher, writer, and his longtime girlfriend. Three years later their first child, Ivy, now a documentary film maker, was born and soon after they adopted a second child, Gregory, who became an executive with a variety of nonprofit and governmental agencies in Washington, DC.

Robby followed a similarly academic route, studying social anthropology and earning both his BA and MA at the University of Michigan, followed by a candidate in arts degree in 1972. In April 1968, not yet twenty-one, he married Ellen Diamond, a feminist social activist who became a pediatric nurse practitioner. Ellen Meeropol left nursing to write full-time in 2009 and has published four novels. Robert and Ellen have two daughters, Jennifer and Rachel. Rachel became a senior constitutional lawyer, while Jennifer now runs the Rosenberg Fund for Children, a public foundation founded and directed by her father from 1990 until 2013. In 1985, after several years as a college instructor in anthropology followed by work for the National Committee to Reopen the Rosenberg Case, Robert became an attorney. These careers were exactly what Manny Bloch had hoped for them.

Reflecting recently on the need for the Rosenberg Fund, Robert commented that he did not accept "the idea that parents should not work to change the world because their struggles could adversely affect their children. But we are keenly aware of the terrible price children may pay for their parents' actions, even if that activism is motivated by a desire to make a better world for their children."[31]

•   •   •

As Michael and Robby grew up, the unresolved controversy about Ethel and Julius's guilt or innocence continued, always colored or distorted by an individual's attitude toward the Soviet nuclear threat. It was possible, for instance, to argue that in "stealing secrets" from Los Alamos, Julius's "spy ring" was only doing illegally what the director of Los Alamos, J. Robert Oppenheimer, would soon be advocating publicly, but described as sharing information.

Often called the "father" of the atomic bomb, Oppenheimer's radical politics had made him suspect for years in the view of the US government. Both his ex-lover, Jean Tatlock, and his brother Frank had had close links with the Communist Party and he had flirted in his youth with Communist ideals. Oppenheimer was also tormented by the destructive power of the terrible weapon he had been responsible for creating, telling Truman after the bombs were dropped on Hiroshima and Nagasaki: "Mr. President, I feel I have blood on my hands,"[32] a comment that ensured a permanently difficult relationship between the two men.

Oppenheimer then threw himself into the effort to create an international authority to control nuclear weapons. In early 1946 he was largely responsible for drafting the Acheson-Lilienthal Report, an ambitious plan for international control through the creation of an Atomic Development Authority that would own all uranium mines, atomic power plants, and laboratories. Oppenheimer went even further in his frequent public lectures, in which he called for a dramatic "renunciation of national sovereignty" to safeguard the world from nuclear war through the exchange of information.[33] The government concluded that Oppenheimer must be a member of a Communist front organization, "engaged in treasonable activity to transfer our military secret to our greatest enemy, the Soviet government."[34]

In late 1953, Oppenheimer visited London to deliver the BBC's prestigious Reith Lectures. Although the lectures received lukewarm reviews, Oppenheimer's support for sharing nuclear information with the Russians was widely praised. "In public and private he has constantly opposed the US policy of extreme secrecy in atomic matters," *The Observer* noted in an admiring profile.[35]

Back in Washington, the suspicions that Oppenheimer was a Soviet agent hardened. In early December, shortly after a blistering speech by Senator McCarthy accusing Eisenhower of "whining, whimpering appeasement" toward Communists, Oppenheimer's national security clearance was revoked.[36]

It was in this paranoid atmosphere, immediately following the executions, that the radical journalist Virginia Gardner was commissioned by a small publisher called Masses & Mainstream to write a book about the Rosenbergs. Gardner contacted Manny Bloch, who told her to see Ethel's psychiatrist Saul Miller, who gave her what she called "a valuable tip" in her quest to understand Ethel. According to Miller, Ethel had said that her prewar participation in a strike had completely changed her viewpoint, so that she no longer primarily wanted to pursue a singing career. Instead, Miller said, she had looked from then on to involvement in political activities with others.[37]

Gardner tried to meet everyone who had ever known or worked with Ethel. In the prevailing climate of fear after the execution several declined, while others agreed to talk only if she gave them false names. One former school friend from Seward Park High School, nom de plume "Gertrude," had subsequently dated "Sam," an unemployed musician, who had also known Ethel. Together with Julius, they had gone out as a foursome several times after the strike. Sam recalled how he had introduced Ethel at a small meeting to support Republican Spain where she had sung "most movingly."

"We talked for hours and I felt the interview had produced riches," Virginia commented. However, an argument eventually broke out between the couple as Sam berated Gertrude for being "crazy enough to burn all those programs and things in your memory book just because Ethel's name and yours were on them." Gertrude retorted: "You're just as responsible as I am. I would give anything in the world to have those things back."[38] Other former friends and acquaintances of Ethel and Julius were in a similar state of panic about their past association with Soviet spies. One man even cut out Julius from his school group photo.

Gardner nonetheless caught some immediate memories and her book, while verging on hagiography in places, has a strong contemporary authenticity. This was also true of *The Judgment of Julius and Ethel Rosenberg*, published in 1955, by John Wexley, a Hollywood screenwriter who had worked with Fritz Lang and Bertolt Brecht before he was blacklisted as a suspected Communist. The apocalyptic cover image of a barefoot woman kneeling, seemingly praying, suggested that bleak times lay ahead for a nation that could kill its own citizens in this way. "There was a great unease throughout America that night following the execution of the Rosenbergs," wrote Wexley in his preface. "Even though [people] were constantly assured that the 'A-spies' had been fairly tried and justly sentenced, two perplexing questions continued to gnaw at mind and heart: if the Rosenbergs were really guilty, if no doubt whatsoever existed that they had received their full measure of justice, then why had the conscience of the world been so deeply aroused?

And if the Rosenbergs were truly innocent, why had they been put to death?"[39]

Yet for every writer who saw the Rosenbergs as innocent or at worst naive, there were others in the 1950s who regarded them as beneath contempt—none more so than the literary critic and anti-Communist Leslie Fiedler, who published his *Afterthoughts on the Rosenbergs* in the same year as Wexley's book. Fiedler mounted an explicit vindication of the government case and attacked the Rosenbergs' defenders as naive and sentimental. He was especially harsh on Ethel, seeing the labored nature of her writing in her letters as evidence of a narrow, petit bourgeois mentality. In Fiedler's acid view, Ethel was "hopelessly the victim not only of her politics but of the painfully pretentious style that is its literary equivalent."[40]

For the next twenty years, the pro- and anti-Rosenberg camps maintained these entrenched positions while lacking any access to the original record of the case. The situation changed in 1975, when Michael and Robert successfully petitioned under the Freedom of Information Act for the release of thousands of pages of FBI documents that related to the investigation of Julius and Ethel.

What prompted Michael and Robby to take this action was the publication in February 1973 of a book about Ethel and Julius by Louis Nizer called *The Implosion Conspiracy*. They were especially irked by Nizer's "characterization of our parents as political fanatics who neglected us for political causes."[41] "We were further horrified by the book's ending in which he labeled us as 'normal, decent citizens . . .' the implication being that we were leading normal happy lives because we rejected everything our parents represented. This was a vicious characterization," they concluded.[42]

By this time both sons had families of their own as well as careers, but were still known as Meeropol. So, before taking any action, they discussed the matter thoroughly with their wives as well as with Anne and Abel Meeropol, then decided they had to proceed to sue Nizer for copyright infringement, invasion of privacy, and libel. The case was eventually settled out of court but, as a result, the privacy that living as Meeropols had given them for the last two decades vanished overnight as their identities now became widely known. Then, in February 1974, when a group called the National Committee to Reopen the Rosenberg Case was set up, Michael and Robert decided to cooperate with them. From then on, as both men were determined to vindicate their parents, the search for FBI documents was key. This meant there was plenty of material for the American Bar Association to enact a mock trial in August 1993 to mark the fortieth anniversary of the Rosenbergs' death. There were real lawyers and a judge, with Ethel played by Tovah Feldshuh and Julius by Lonny Price. Of the original lawyers, only James Kilsheimer played a role; he participated in the post–mock trial panel discussion.

A key difference from the original trial was that the actors who played the Rosenbergs admitted immediately to being members of the Communist Party, while emphatically denying they were spies. Ethel's legitimate, constant use of the Fifth Amendment was not therefore mocked as it had been in the highly charged atmosphere of 1953, even though it was not actually illegal to be a card-carrying member of the Communist Party until August 1954. In that year Senator McCarthy had been thoroughly discredited after accusing the US Army of being infiltrated with Communists, a charge that was flatly refuted. Furthermore, by 1993, with the Cold War over, American Communists could be seen as misguided or foolish idealists without automatically being regarded as evil. The historian Ronald Radosh, author of *The Rosenberg File,* who believed Ethel and Julius were Soviet, not American, "patriots," accepted on the panel after the event that it was clear the original trial had been flawed.

In 1993, forty years on, the actor-Rosenbergs were acquitted.

•   •   •

Many of the protagonists in the real trial had not flourished in the intervening years. When Irving Saypol died from cancer in 1977 aged seventy-one it was not with an unblemished career. The year beforehand he had been indicted on bribery and perjury charges by a grand jury investigating how to root out corruption in the city's criminal justice system. Although the charges were dismissed, his former junior and friend, Roy Cohn, commented: "He was never the same after that happened . . . He was in a state of disbelief that something like that could have happened. He was a very, very proud person."[43]

Cohn himself lived another nine years after that, dying in 1986 following complications from AIDS. Shortly before his death, Cohn was finally disbarred for unethical and unprofessional conduct, including misappropriation of clients' funds, lying on a bar application, and pressuring a client to amend his will. Cohn had learned early to lie easily, whether hiding his homosexuality or defending Mafia clients who he argued were good Americans, unlike upstart Communist women like Ethel.

What motivated Cohn to see Ethel executed was mostly naked personal ambition, the result of being reared by a possessive mother who saw her only child as a genius Jewish prince who had to win against the establishment, but also a desire to show that Jews like him were the patriotic kind, partly in order to hide his shame over his own uncle, who had been sent to Sing Sing Prison for fraud.

Yet would it have made any difference to Ethel had he not been on the prosecution team? Probably not, although Cohn's conduct during the Rosenberg trial was, if not illegal, highly unethical, and his forceful views were delivered with such conviction that, however much they lacked evidence, they somehow gained credence among otherwise rational thinkers and particularly among those in government.

Today Roy Cohn has come to personify the wickedness at the heart of McCarthyism and remains an irresistible character for anyone wishing to explore a link between the McCarthy and Trump eras. More than twenty years after his death, Cohn's willingness to abandon legal safeguards, especially his readiness to discuss the case privately with the judge, which by any standards represented a gross abuse of judicial independence, and his depravity, deployed at full force against Ethel, are of such dramatic magnitude that in 2019 alone there were two excellently reviewed documentaries about him. One is by Ivy Meeropol, called *Bully. Coward. Victim.* and the other is Matt Tyrnauer's *Where's My Roy Cohn?* The latter takes its title from a comment made by President Trump, who as a young property developer had known and used Cohn's services, and asked in frustration and fury in 2017: "Where's my Roy Cohn?"

Judge Kaufman himself, who lived until 1992, hoped that some of his landmark rulings establishing important legal precedents in constitutional, antitrust, and civil rights cases would be his crowning glory. But he could not escape always being described as the judge who had sentenced the Rosenbergs to death.

David Greenglass, whose weakness and malleability gave Cohn his early fame, was released from prison in 1960, having served ten years of his fifteen-year sentence. He and Ruth, who was never charged, lived out the rest of their long lives quietly under an assumed name in the New York City borough of Queens.* In 2001 he finally broke his silence to appear

---

* Out of respect for the privacy of David and Ruth's children, the Meeropols and I have made a decision not to reveal the name.

on a CBS *60 Minutes* documentary, heavily disguised, to talk about the case. David finally admitted that he had lied in court about having seen Ethel type up his spying notes on her portable Remington typewriter before sending them to Moscow. Aged seventy-nine, Greenglass said that his 1951 trial testimony was based on the recollection of his wife Ruth, rather than his own firsthand knowledge.

"I don't know who typed it, frankly, and to this day I can't remember that the typing took place," he said. "I had no memory of that at all—none whatsoever." It was Ethel's stupidity, David claimed, that made his sister responsible for her own death in the electric chair. He said that he was still haunted by the case but added: "I sleep very well. I would not sacrifice my wife and my children for my sister. I had no idea they would give them the death sentence."

David gave a slightly different version of the same story to the journalist Sam Roberts, whose bestselling biography of Greenglass was published the same year. Roberts finally got to interview David after reluctantly agreeing to pay him an undisclosed sum for his cooperation. (For his part, David insisted he had barely enough money to live on.) David admitted to Roberts that he had been a spy and, crucially, that his wife Ruth had helped him with his notes, not Ethel. He also suggested that Ruth had been the crux of the whole plan to accuse Ethel of typing and that it was she who had made him change his testimony. "I told them [the FBI] the story and left her [Ethel] out of it, right?" David explained. "But my wife put her in it. So what am I gonna do, call my wife a liar? My wife is more important to me than my sister. And she was the mother of my children."[44]

Ruth died in 2008, having never again given her side of the story following her lethal testimony at the trial. David died in 2014 in a care home. The following year, his 1950 grand jury testimony was finally released, confirming that David had told them under oath that Ethel was not involved in espionage activities. "I never spoke to my sister at all about this," David had told the grand jury in August 1950 before his trial. And then he repeated to his inquisitor: "I said before, and say it again, honestly, this is a fact: I never spoke to my sister about this at all."

The dramatic contrast between David's grand jury testimony and what he ultimately said at the trial led legal scholars with no ax to grind to state that the final release of documentation revealed prosecutorial misbehavior of an unforgivable kind since the chief prosecutors, Saypol and Cohn, were guilty either of "having suborned false testimony, or presenting testimony they had reason to know was false."[45]

Morton Sobell was the last of the protagonists to die, on December 26, 2018, aged 101. He had served nineteen years of his thirty-year sentence, some of them in Alcatraz, and in 2008 had grudgingly admitted to Sam Roberts that he had been a spy. "Yeah, yeah, yeah, call it that," Sobell replied. "I never thought of it as that in those terms."[46] Sobell added that while Ethel was aware of Julius's espionage, she had not actively participated. "She knew what he was doing, but what was she guilty of? Of being Julius's wife."[47]

Epilogue

The Many Ways of Imagining and Seeing Ethel

"It was a queer, sultry summer, the summer they executed the Rosenbergs . . ." So begins one of the great works of American twentieth-century feminist literature. *The Bell Jar* was published just ten years after the execution of the Rosenbergs by a woman who called herself Victoria Lucas because she did not think highly enough of her novel's literary merit. Sylvia Plath, relatively unknown at the time, had in fact written a novel powerfully re-creating an era: a period of time that sentenced the Rosenbergs, when women were subjugated to a life of domesticity and not expected to stray into male spheres.

Above all, *The Bell Jar* symbolized a feeling of imprisonment, of being confined to a place in life from which there is no hope of escape. It was a semi-autobiographical rather than a political novel, for Plath had suffered her own mental breakdown that she was retelling through her heroine Esther Greenwood's account of a year within the "Bell Jar." Esther, whose very name is a variation of Esther Ethel Greenglass, feels the Bell Jar has at this moment lifted for her and she is returning to a healthy life after undergoing electroshock therapy at a mental asylum. Nonetheless, she fears the return of her symptoms so that "wherever I sat—on the deck of a ship or a street café in Paris or Bangkok—I would be sitting under the same glass bell jar, stewing in my own sour air."[1]

Ostensibly, *The Bell Jar* was not a book about Ethel Rosenberg, or at least it was not marketed as such when first published. But Sylvia Plath had spent the summer of 1953 in New York City, having won a writing competition that gave her a chance to sample an editorship at *Mademoiselle* magazine. The one event she remembered clearly that month was the electrocution of the Rosenbergs.

After Plath's compelling opening, Ethel appears only once again in the narrative as an explicit presence. This is when Esther's friend Hilda reacts to Esther's constant ruminations about the horror of Ethel's impending execution that night: "'Yes!' Hilda said, and at last I felt I had touched a human string in the cat's cradle of her heart. It was only as the two of us waited for the others in the tomb-like morning gloom of the conference room that Hilda amplified that 'Yes' of hers. 'It's awful such people should be alive.'"[2]

The Bell Jar illustrates the degree to which Ethel's fate continued to grip the American imagination in the long aftermath of her execution, even when she hovered offstage. It was as if different visions of Ethel, and more broadly the whole Rosenberg case, could be invested with a wider meaning to sum up an era defined by political paranoia and repression. Indirectly in *The Bell Jar,* Ethel's imagined spirit infuses every fiber of what Esther Greenwood is suffering—not simply her imprisonment, but the madness of an America that incarcerated so many women in different ways during the early 1950s. In this patriarchal society any clever woman was bound to feel repressed or a failure unless she aspired to the traditional ideals of being a homemaker and mother, and nothing more. Seen in this context, it is easy to imagine why Sylvia Plath, via her semi-autobiographical heroine Esther, could fixate on the brutal electrocution of Ethel and the ill-fitting pads attached to her head, having had her own dose of ECT a month after Ethel's killing. In 1953 this was still a relatively new treatment with a horrifically similar procedure, involving electrodes placed on her head and chest and a small amount of electric current passed through her brain intended to relieve her depression.

"It had nothing to do with me," comments Esther in the novel, talking about the Rosenberg story, "but I couldn't help wondering what it would be like, being burned alive all along your nerves."

More than three decades after *The Bell Jar* was published, the Irish American writer Mary Cantwell borrowed its evocative first words for the start of her 1995 memoir, *Manhattan, When I Was Young*: "because that's the way I remember my first summer in New York too." In those hot, overbearing months, Cantwell recalled in particular a newsstand near her subway stop, "and every day the headlines screamed the Rosenbergs' impending death. The headlines terrified me because my boyfriend [later her husband] was Jewish." Cantwell described how, when her mother was introduced to him, she asked his religion and he replied "atheist." "She paused and said in her nicest voice, 'Does that mean you're a Communist?'" Cantwell's boyfriend said no, but she knew that his aunt and uncle had been Communists: "the weekend we spent at their cabin in the Catskills, smearing cream cheese on toast, was torture because they reminded me of the Rosenbergs and I thought we would all be arrested and I, too, would die in the chair."[3]

Cantwell's story distills the way many Americans in the 1950s reflexively assumed that Jews were Communists. "There was an evident quota of anti-Semitism in the McCarthy wave of hysteria. Jews in that period were automatically suspect. Our evaluation of the general mood was that the people felt if you scratch a Jew you can find a Communist," recalled Arnold Forster of the American Jewish Committee, a strongly anti-Communist organization.[4] In reality the Rosenberg case split the Jewish community during the Truman and Eisenhower years as profoundly as it divided the entire country, right up to the Supreme Court.

After all, 1953 was only eight or so years after the revelation of the Holocaust, "the discovery of the mounds of dead in Dachau, Bergen-Belsen, Auschwitz and other marks of Cain on the forehead of our century," wrote Arthur Miller. "They could not merely be two spies being executed but two Jews. It was not possible to avoid this in the second half of the 20th century; not even with the best will in the world could the prejudicial stain be totally avoided—no, not even if it were undeserved. Such were the times."[5]

Miriam Moskowitz, Ethel's Jewish friend in the Women's House of Detention whom I met one snowy December morning in December 2017 at her home in New Jersey, believed that anti-Semitism "hovered over the trial . . . with an unmistakable presence":

> It was not for nothing that the prosecution leaders and the judge (the same in both trials) were conspicuously Jewish, as of course were the defendants . . . But the Jewish establishment, perhaps fearing that an association with Jewish radicalism would revive latent anti-Semitism in the country, expediently avoided asking questions about the overzealous prosecution, never demurred about the use of tainted evidence from problem witnesses, and never voiced doubts about the judges' obvious bias or the prejudicial atmosphere generated by the FBI and exploited by the media blitz. Rather it maintained a detached and profound silence. Some leaders in the Jewish community . . . were especially vitriolic about the Rosenbergs, as though to reinforce public perception of their own patriotism. For those of us nurtured on the ancient sanctity of Jewish brotherhood it was the ultimate coup de grâce and I have never been able to forgive them.[6]

When Miriam made those comments she did not know that Judge Jerome Frank, and other Jewish justices on the Appeals Court who considered the Rosenberg case, had been "inundated" with anti-Semitic hate mail threatening any "Jew judge" who might let the "Jew-Commie Rosenbergs" off.[7] Yet even anti-Semitic hate mail was not the real reason why the Supreme Court justices repeatedly refused to reexamine the Rosenberg case. Only in their final hours did the court hold a hastily scheduled oral argument on their statutory claim, which was rejected.

There is a telling vignette that illustrates how hard it was for the justices to reverse Kaufman's decision: on June 19, 1953, the day scheduled for the execution, Manny Bloch and a colleague drove to the Alexandria home of Justice Black, about seven miles south of downtown Washington. Black sent his daughter Josephine to answer the door and say he could not and would not see him. "Why can't you see them?" Josephine asked her father. "They're going to be killed?" Black replied: "It has been decided by the Court." As Josephine recalled to an interviewer in 2008, "The pain of the ordeal lingered . . . And it still brings tears to my eyes, because tears were streaming down his face." She maintained: "That was the most drama I ever had in terms of my father . . . it just broke his heart."

"Black's respect for the Court as an institution outweighed his outrage at its mishandling of *Rosenberg*—even if it cost two people their lives," commented Brad Snyder, assistant professor at the University of Wisconsin Law School reviewing the case in 2010.[8] Yet by the early 1950s the Supreme Court "was in chaos, racked by long-simmering divisions . . . The personal squabbles among the four intellectually towering figures—Felix Frankfurter, Robert Jackson, Hugo Black and William O. Douglas—sometimes seemed more serious than the political ones."[9] Petty squabbles among grown men who should have represented the highest attributes of American justice, both to the rest of the world and to their own compatriots, were one more reason why Ethel could not be saved.

•   •   •

In 1971, when Edgar Lawrence Doctorow published *The Book of Daniel,* the prevailing view among American left-wingers was that Ethel and Julius were innocent Communists who had been framed. Doctorow—like Ethel, of Russian Jewish ancestry—was too good a writer to fall into this trap. In what he described as an "explicitly political novel," Doctorow imagined the impact on Ethel and Julius's sons of their parents' execution, while leaving open the question of the Rosenbergs' guilt or innocence. Doctorow said his main interest in using the Rosenbergs (renamed as Paul and Rochelle Isaacson) was "in terms of what happens when all the antagonistic force of a society is brought to bear and focused on one or possibly two individuals. What kind of anthropological ritual is that?"[10]

According to Doctorow, he did not know at first how he was going to tell this story. Once he found the narrator's voice, through the Isaacsons' son Daniel, "I sat down and put a piece of paper in the typewriter and started to write with a certain freedom and irresponsibility, and it turned out Daniel was talking, and he was sitting in the library at Columbia [University], and I had my book." Daniel, the classic unreliable narrator, is telling a story that at one level is predicated on his parents' appalling death. However, the catalyst for the story is not their electrocution but the attempted suicide of his younger sister, Susan. It is a complicated tale in which violence is never far from the surface. Yet, for all its brilliance, *The Book of Daniel* shines less light on Ethel than on her persecutors.

While Michael Meeropol admires the book, Robert is less enamored. He stated that his difficulties with the book do not arise from Doctorow's characterizations of him and Michael, which he accepts involved a degree of fictionalizing. His objection concerns how Doctorow distorted his and Michael's positive memories of the generosity shown by leftist friends who cared for them after the execution. "Doctorow is entitled to his artistic creation," Robert wrote. "But it is difficult for me, given the obvious parallels between the story he tells and my own, not to bristle at what I perceive as his undeserved attack on people who did everything in their power to protect us."[11]

Six years after *The Book of Daniel* the American novelist Robert Coover published *The Public Burning,* an exuberant, brutal fantasy woven around the last three days of Ethel and Julius Rosenberg. In this satire in extremis, Coover captured the lurid razzmatazz of the 1951 trial: the theatrical production of the Jell-O box, cut to order, with the flavors and packaging questioned; the console table that had to be identified from store catalogues; the polished lens mold diagram re-created years after the alleged original had been drawn by Ethel's brother David. In Coover's fantasy trial, everybody was playing a part, including Ethel. Coover noted on the first page that Ethel had once hoped to be an actress and had even played the role of the sister of a condemned man.

The Public Burning was in grotesquely bad taste, at its most nauseating when the dominant narrator, Eisenhower's vice president, Richard Nixon, is aroused by the idea of having sex with Ethel. Yet Coover's obscenely disturbing narrative succeeds in showing how everyone in Cold War America was implicated directly or indirectly in the ruthless public burning of the Rosenbergs, especially the dark and complex Nixon. Had Nixon, then a very junior member of the House Un-American Activities Committee who was being fed information by the FBI, not doggedly insisted on continuing to pursue Alger Hiss when the case looked as if it might otherwise wither, a whole chain of events culminating in the Rosenberg execution might not have unfolded in the way they did. Coover's satire culminates in a carnivalesque auto-da-fé in Manhattan's Times Square, recalling the ritual festivals of penance and public execution held by the sixteenth-century Spanish Inquisition. References to burning—what Coover calls a "lot of goddam fire in this case"—are inescapable throughout the story: Ruth's burning night dress, newspaper headlines referring to Ethel and Julius as "flaming Reds," and constant references to the "infernal conspiracy."[12] Hovering over the action is the recent memory of the incineration of Jews in the Nazi Holocaust and the fear of a future atomic war that will reduce the planet to ashes.

For the American playwright Tony Kushner, the full horror embedded in the Rosenberg story extended beyond the gruesome electrocution and the fact that Ethel and Julius had been found guilty of betraying their country. Far more shocking for Kushner was the notion that a brother, David Greenglass, could betray his own sister and send her to the electric chair. In *Angels in America,* a two-part "gay fantasia on national themes" that premiered in 1991 and 1992, Kushner sees David as the embodiment of "Reaganist tribalism:" the idea that if you take care of your own first the rest will be fine.

In 2004 Ethel's granddaughter Ivy Meeropol interviewed Kushner for her documentary film *Heir to an Execution.* She asked him: "What does this case teach us about how to live our lives as political people?"[13] According to Kushner, the Rosenberg case is an intensely Jewish story that requires careful handling. "Just as the rabbis approached complicated stories with humility, not arrogance and proprietorial attitudes, you spend time interpreting the Talmud [the holy books] by careful textual study, or Midrash [commentary upon these] as if you are approaching something sacred . . . because it is written in blood."

Kushner suggested that through studying the Rosenbergs' story, "we will come to understand a lot about what our next move ought to be, a lot about how to conduct ourselves and what kind of sacrifice political work requires and the dangers of falling in love with the notion of sacrifice."[14] With this in mind, Kushner's Ethel, or to be accurate, her ghost, appears to forgive Roy Cohn, the lawyer who ensured her death by persuading David to commit perjury. Standing over Cohn's graveside, she even intones the Kaddish. But she also calls him a "son of a bitch." "I would have pulled the switch if they let me," Cohn snarls. "Why? Because I hate traitors. I HATE Communists. Was it legal? FUCK legal. Not nice? Fuck nice. The nation says I'm not nice? FUCK THE NATION. Do you wanna be NICE? Or you wanna be EFFECTIVE?"

As Robert Meeropol commented, "My mother utters no lines in *Angels in America* that indicate her desire to forgive Roy Cohn. I see my mother's [words] as Tony Kushner's final tribute to Ethel Rosenberg. It is his statement that she was a better person than her tormentors."[15]

Kushner's play, like the novels of Coover, Doctorow, and Plath, were all factually untrue to a greater or lesser extent in their representations of Ethel. Yet although the story of the Rosenbergs' trial and execution has proved fertile ground for many other artists, composers, and playwrights,* it is the conflicting images of Ethel herself that have made her so irresistible as a tragic figure. The way she continues to defy labeling as mother, wife, sister, daughter, Communist, or would-be opera singer has penetrated the American consciousness deeply. It is this complexity that has encouraged audiences to project her, more often than the dramatically less interesting, more predictable Julius, into works of fiction, even where she was originally absent from the script.

On January 22, 1953, Arthur Miller's play *The Crucible*, about the witchcraft trials in 1692–3 in the town of Salem, Massachusetts, opened at the Martin Beck Theater on Broadway. Miller recalled in his 1987 autobiography *Timebends* how he had made his initial research visit to the Salem

---

* Among others *The Rubenstein Kiss,* recently revived, was the 2005 debut play of the British playwright James Phillips, while in Ottawa the Canadian composer Kelly-Marie Murphy wrote a song cycle in 2019 called *All My Love, Ethel* based on the prison letters between the couple.

Historical Society in April 1952, almost two years after the Rosenbergs' arrest and a year after their trial. Yet Miller insisted in 1988 that the play was not specifically about the Rosenbergs, and indeed that he had written it "two and half years before their names were even in the papers."[16] From Miller's perspective, the play was written as a more general response to "the Red scare" that had "paralyzed a whole generation and in a short time dried up the habits of trust and toleration."[17]

New York's theatergoing public made the direct parallel with Ethel and Julius anyway. On June 19, the night of their execution, the audience stood up and observed a minute's silence at the end of the play. *The Crucible,* with its witch hunts, lethal repetition of wild rumors, and barbaric executions, has since become the quintessential Rosenberg drama.

Only for Ethel and Julius it was not a drama. It was true.

•   •   •

In 2018, on a research visit to Los Alamos, where the wartime Manhattan Project was based, I received a telephone call in my Santa Fe hotel suggesting that if I wanted a "story" about Ethel I should speak to a man whose elderly aunt had run a dress shop in the town and who remembered Ethel as a customer. I knew immediately that this was a most unlikely lead. Ethel never went to Santa Fe, and buying clothes was something she rarely indulged in. I realized the extent to which Ethel had taken on mythical status as I listened to the tale of the shop owner supplying Ethel with dresses, and further details about how a yellow box from the shop with Ethel's name on it had been dropped under a bridge and then miraculously discovered years later with papers in readable condition. During her short life, and her much longer afterlife, she had been given so many different identities that it was difficult to strip back all the accretions and find the essence of the woman who was arrested on August 11, 1950.

Who exactly was Ethel Rosenberg? Her sons Michael and Robert, ten and six, respectively, when their mother was killed, still have distinct memories of her. Robert remembers his mother singing him to sleep and Michael remembers her cooking. "She loved bacon and she always saved the bacon fat 'for the war effort!'" long after the war was over. Both remember their parents being very physical, touching them a lot, carrying them around, and generally indulging in horseplay. The child psychotherapist Elizabeth Phillips told me when I flew to California to meet her why she believed Michael and Robert had flourished as adults, despite seeing their parents publicly vilified and then executed. "Three things saved those boys," she said: "wonderful adoptive parents [the Meeropols], their innate intelligence, and good mothering by Ethel in the early years."[18]

My starting point for discovering Ethel was to assume that she was a far more complex person in real life than any of the myths that enveloped her.

"The Rosenbergs," commented historian of the press John Neville, "appeared too average, too unremarkable for visual news-pegging. No bald heads, jutting jaws, monocles, scars, disfigurements, cosmopolitan soignée or striking good looks . . . they might have been chosen at random from the telephone directory. They were stubbornly mundane even after being condemned to death."[19]

This perception of ordinariness was certainly shared by many of the journalists who observed Ethel during the trial and could not see past her dowdy clothes and unsmiling expression to anything more singular beneath the surface. Yet Ethel was far from typical or mundane, despite the impoverished obscurity of her Lower East Side childhood and her superficial resemblance to an aspiring, upwardly mobile first-generation immigrant. As she resolved to break free from a family that did not cherish learning for women—a mother who resented her daughter's intelligence and a father who was too weak to argue Ethel's corner against this—Ethel honed her determination to make something valuable of her life according to her own moral standards. In the process she displayed an extraordinary single-mindedness, a source of both strength and of her eventual destruction. Ethel was defined by her dogged persistence, from the moment when she discovered that studying alone, in her dismal room on Sheriff Street, brought her academic rewards at school, to the time when she bought a cheap secondhand piano, taught herself sight-singing, and at the second attempt won a place in the Schola Cantorum choir. When she joined the payroll of the National New York Packing and Shipping Company, this deceptively quiet young woman went further than merely fighting for better working conditions and the right to have a union. Ethel helped organize the strike, held meetings in her bedroom in Sheriff Street, and lay down in the street to prevent the delivery trucks getting through. Later, when she had children, she did not turn to the other mothers at Knickerbocker Village to ask for advice on how to be a good mother; she enrolled in an avant-garde course on childcare theory at the New School for Social Research run by the intellectual émigré Edith Buxbaum.

This was the "Ethelness" of Ethel. And her "Ethelness" was still a project in development when in the autumn of 1940, just before the United States joined in the war, she gave up her relatively well-paid job in Washington to return to New York because Julius had landed a job with the Army Signal Corps after his poor health meant that he would not be called up and sent abroad to fight. The mores of the time demanded that she make way for her husband's career, but personally she wanted Julius to succeed to prove that she had married the right man. They soon moved into better accommodations and started a family. Yet Ethel did not make friends easily with the other mothers at Knickerbocker Village because she was not like them. She was exceptional. And this exceptionalism was mistaken by other mothers for being "peculiar."

●   ●   ●

This seemed a very masculine story when I started work. The subject matter—spying and atomic weapons—is usually considered of interest primarily to men. And apart from Ethel, the leading actors all appeared to be men: diplomats, politicians, and lawyers who saw they had a woman in their toils and were intent on her destruction.

Yet the longer I have sat with this story, the more I have seen a different picture emerging. At its heart is a tale of three women and the man they all loved: Tessie, Ethel, Ruth—and David. The story is, in fact, all about women; wives, mothers, and sisters. Ruth, Ethel, and Tessie were women for whom life was intensely hard, yet in the end they did not

support each other, as jealousy overrode sisterhood and even motherhood. Why did Ruth, a clever girl who, like Ethel, had graduated young
from Seward Park with a gold seal diploma and ambitions for college,
sink these ambitions into early marriage and domesticity? Ruth was only
twelve when she met David, two years older but still a boy with over-
inflated confidence thanks to his doting mother, Tessie, and at that point
still doting elder sister, Ethel. David was "cute, even cuddly . . . [with]
a mild-mannered good nature that proclaimed itself in his easy smile."[20]

Ruth fell for him, mesmerized by his easy banter about science and
politics, believing he was bound to "invent something or discover something or do something one day."[21] Ruth and David saw themselves as teenage sweethearts who were as much buffeted by circumstances as anyone
else in this story; clever Ruth who, like Ethel, had to learn how to type
instead of going to college; less clever David, who had flunked his education and who during the war was not sent abroad to fight like his older
brother Bernie but to Los Alamos as a lowly machinist. Rather than be
separated, they married when David was only twenty and Ruth eighteen.
But when they became parents in May 1946, they swiftly discovered that
the left-wing politics of their youth did not measure up to the realities
of parenthood. As Ruth's superior intellect quickly dominated David's
natural laziness and weak will, admiration and respect for Ethel and Julius swiftly turned to disappointment, envy, and jealousy. When the FBI
came calling in 1950, Ruth and David did not have far to look as they cast
around for people to blame for their own failure to succeed in embracing
the American Dream. It was all too easy for one lie to follow another,
especially as they assumed that if Ethel and Julius were so smart, all they
had to do to save their own skins was to confess as well.

But they did not, which is what no one from Kaufman to Hoover,
Tessie, or Ruth had imagined possible. This stubborn refusal made it easier
for David to believe, as he declared in a 2003 interview, that his clever big
sister must therefore be more stupid than he was. He said in the same interview that he did not realize the importance of the evidence that he gave
under oath about Ethel typing up his notes on the Remington portable.

Asked why he thought Ethel maintained her silence to the end, David responded: "One word: stupidity."[22]

.   .   .

Another word David used to describe his sister was "fanatical." Ethel was, he said, "a very fanatical lady. There's a fanaticism that runs through the Greenglass family. Fanatics can kill."[23] Miriam Moskowitz hinted at something similar when she described Ethel as "doctrinaire" in her uncritical support for the Communist Party at a time when the party was not helping them at all. "She was not a rebel," Moskowitz told Ilene Philipson, "she was a good soldier. She followed the party line uncritically, unquestionably and aggressively. It wasn't only that she followed the line, but she argued for it and justified it with a lot of voluminous verbosity. She was totally uncritical . . . if I had met her outside of prison I probably would not have liked her because I never liked doctrinaire people and she was doctrinaire."[24]

There is no evidence that Ethel abandoned her belief in Communism while in prison nor that she blamed the Communist Party for not rallying round to throw money into their defense. However, by 1950 Communism was merely one aspect of Ethel's ambiguous, many-sided life and it was not her principal focus. While it is inconceivable that she and Julius had not discussed, and agreed on, the need to support Soviet Russia, America's wartime ally, when Ethel finally consulted a psychiatrist in 1950, it was not because of any postwar stress or anxiety about working for an ally that had turned swiftly into America's mortal enemy, nor from any fear of being exposed as a Communist. Ethel sought psychiatric counseling for deeply personal reasons: to help correct her view of herself within the family orbit, where her value and talent had never been appreciated, and because she wanted to be a better mother to her sons than Tessie had been to her.

Ethel's underconfidence in herself as a mother is heartbreaking. She aspired to be not only the best mother possible but also a progressive mother, especially in relation to Tessie. Yet, judged by the impossibly high

standards that society set for women like Ethel—and which, according to
Elizabeth Phillips, she was so close to achieving—she felt she had failed.
Misogyny ran deep in 1950s America, despite the gains made by women
during the war when they had proved their mettle in both military and
nonmilitary capacities. Judge Kaufman's harsh emphasis on Ethel's age
in his summing-up reflected the prevailing attitudes of the era. In 1951
a woman who married a man who was three years younger was sending
a clear signal that she might not simply be a stay-at-home wife. Kaufman
gave this chauvinist stereotype a further twist by insinuating to the jury
that Ethel might well be a spy, even though espionage was seen by the
public as an overwhelmingly male activity. The judge then drove his point
home by criticizing Ethel's shortcomings as a mother. J. Edgar Hoover's
initial desire to charge Ethel was not predicated only on the belief that "no
mother would willingly desert her two children"; since she subsequently
failed to conform to Hoover's cultural norms, Ethel's behavior then reduced her to the stereotype of wicked witch or evil mother.[25]

It is ironic that for a quite different reason Ethel saw herself as a de-
ficient mother. In her self-perception, she believed she had much to learn
about the new, progressive childcare and motherhood theories championed
after the war by specialists such as her favorite *Parents* magazine columnist,
Dr. Dorothy Whipple. Communism could not help her cope with this
profound sense of personal failure. Only her therapists were helping her
to see that she was not a failure at all, just as time, which she was denied,
would have reinforced.

Similarly, Ethel's Jewishness had no influence on her behavior as she
inched day by day at Sing Sing closer to the electric chair. Being Jewish
was simply a fact of her life, although, as Michael's happy memories of
Ethel cooking bacon indicate, she was a secular Jew for whom ritual was
of no importance. In this secularized world, it was still a given that she
and Julius married in a local synagogue, that their union was blessed by a
rabbi, and that little Michael and Robby were circumcised. In Sing Sing
she and Julius both attended religious services, partly in Ethel's case as an
activity to relieve the daily tedium, and because she enjoyed singing the
hymns of all religions. At the very end, she was accompanied by Rabbi

Koslowe on her final walk to her execution, yet there is no evidence that the spiritual side of Judaism had given her any comfort or insight into her life while in prison.

Her only published thoughts about Judaism appear in a September 1951 letter to Julius that was plainly written for a public audience:

> I am thinking now of the darkened streets of the Lower East Side . . . early tomorrow morning throngs of people will be hurrying to the synagogues to pray. I earnestly hope their prayers are answered, yet life has taught me that theory without practice can be a pretty empty, meaningless gesture, lip service simply does not bring about the peace and goodwill and security all decent humanity so bitterly craves; we must not use prayer to an Omnipotent Being as a pretext for evading our responsibility to our fellow beings in the daily struggle for the establishment of social justice. Jew and Gentile, black and white all must stand together in their might to win the right![26]

These words provide little guidance about her true beliefs beyond revealing that religion had never been a useful prop for her. In writing the letter, Ethel was perhaps even reminded of the backwardness and prejudice of the Lower East Side ghetto where she had grown up and that she had wanted to escape.

•   •   •

If religion did not help her get through her solitary days in prison, what did? Ethel's loneliness is almost impossible to contemplate as she lay on her three-inch-thick mattress with hours and hours stretching ahead each day in which to think, determined not to ask for painkillers or other medicines in case this was interpreted as showing weakness. She longed to see her children but slumped into deep melancholy after each visit from them. Her active attempts at mothering from prison in the early days soon diminished, as she recognized her impotence in alleviating her children's needs and inability to share their joys. In this light it is all the more remarkable that, for Robert and Michael, the memory of cheerfulness and laughter during these visits remained long into adulthood, an indication of how much effort Ethel put into them.

For a brief time in Sing Sing the Irish American matron Bessie Irving had been a companion of sorts. When Bessie died suddenly in July 1951, Ethel's isolation increased, a form of emotional torture that the FBI hoped would eventually make her buckle and talk. But it did not.

Another way to describe "Ethelness" is perfectionism. As Ethel's long-term project for self-improvement was blown off course by her incarceration, she turned to her psychiatrist, Saul Miller, for help simply to survive. Ethel came to depend increasingly on her unusual relationship with Miller. Even more than Julius, Miller appears to have been crucial in helping Ethel to try to invest her life with meaning and face her impending electrocution with dignity. Yet even Miller could not ultimately prevent his patient from sinking into a deep depression where she could no longer think clearly about her situation.

Miller later told Michael that their mother was preoccupied by her journey away from her roots, from her dominant mother, to becoming her own person. "She felt she had been short-changed in the family relationships encountered since childhood," he said.[27]

In June 1951, Ethel wrote an angrily impassioned letter to Julius in which she described how Tessie's dismissive attitude toward her had always caused her deep pain. According to Ethel, this feeling of rejection was exacerbated by the situation in which she now found herself where almost her entire family had turned against her. She felt guilty, she told Julius,

> or so terribly so achingly regretful for the wound you are suffering through my seeming inability to render the sting of a certain group of poisonous snakes of my sorry acquaintance [the Greenglasses] powerless against me. Love of my heart, in all humility I ask your forgiveness and solemnly promise you that I shall take the necessary steps to break loose once [and] for all from the emotional trap that has held me a prisoner, far more than the bars behind which I have been living some eleven months.[28]

More than ever, Ethel grew to despise David and Ruth and the entire family that had rounded on her; in Ethel's view, this was the reason she was in prison, not Julius giving information to the Russians. When she wrote to President Truman in January 1953 begging for her life, she highlighted the perfidy of David and Ruth. An unwanted visit from Tessie in January 1953 prompted an enraged letter to Manny Bloch. As Ethel saw it, the most important aspect of her legacy, which she now clung to single-mindedly, was that no one could ever say she was like the contemptible Greenglasses. Her determination to be morally and intellectually superior to them obscured almost every other consideration.

Yet it is impossible to imagine that in the long, lonely hours alone in her cell she did not sometimes think about whether, for the sake of the sons she adored, she should try to separate her fate from Julius's. Michael and Robert believe Ethel could not have lived with herself if she had repudiated her marriage to Julius or betrayed any of her friends. She could not admit failure in this way, which may explain why she continued to idealize Julius. When Ethel enthused about Julius's many attributes to Miriam Moskowitz, Miriam wondered if any man could be that perfect.

There is no way of knowing the extent to which Ethel knew what her husband was doing as a spy-ring recruiter sending information to the Soviet Union because no one was party to their pillow talk. Yet whatever the truth about Ethel's complicity, it was not a crime under US law to approve spousal wrongdoing, either during the war or at the time of the trial. Ethel's overarching motivation throughout her life was trying to overcome where she came from. Julius had appeared as her savior, helping her escape from her family, and she remained determined to support him, even as their options narrowed at Sing Sing to a straightforward choice between confession or death.

Yet anyone who examines this story must consider: if it was impossible for Ethel to free herself from Julius, might Julius, or indeed *should* Julius, have separated himself from Ethel, the woman he loved and constantly praised, and thus given her a chance to live and his sons a chance to have a parent?

Julius was naive, optimistic, easygoing, and occasionally lazy, as when he needed Ethel to coach him through his college exams. He also sincerely believed he was not guilty of treason, either legally or morally, and he did not want to confess and be forced to give names of others who had passed information to the Soviet Union during the war. Furthermore, he did not know about the Venona intercepts, and so had good reason to believe that there was no direct evidence to prove he had been engaged in espionage. Last, the mounting national and international campaign Save the Rosenbergs gave Julius's naturally optimistic nature another reason to believe that he and Ethel would be spared to return to their children if they continued to protest their total innocence.

Julius's unbending stance placed Manny Bloch in an impossible position, because the one slim chance of saving at least Ethel's life probably depended on a confession by Julius. As Julius and Ethel's lawyer, Manny could not in any event give them candid, confidential advice that would remain between him and his clients; everything he said or wrote to Julius or Ethel was monitored by the authorities. Yet, as a lawyer, Manny must have realized that the circumstantial evidence against Julius was extremely strong, in contrast to Ethel: Cohn had needed to get David and Ruth to concoct their typewriter story to build a case against her. Such a legal opinion would not have been inconsistent with Manny's passionate belief that the entire trial was a travesty of justice and that the executions amounted to judicial murder.

Julius, no less than Ethel, was subjected to sustained psychological torture, which he resisted no less doggedly. The problem created for Manny was having two clients, deeply in love, who never wavered in their insistence that they were totally innocent and who had been systematically deprived of all means to assess their predicament in any other light.

•   •   •

Ethel Rosenberg was driven first by singing, and when that did not work out she was driven by politics. Once she married and had children she was driven by child-rearing, and when her children were taken from her she was driven by a sense of ethics and loyalty. Toward the end of her life Communism was no longer her predominant interest; her main concern was how to be a good person and specifically how to be a good mother. Love for her two boys was quite possibly her only solace. One of Ethel's closest school friends was asked by her daughter years later whether or not she thought Ethel was guilty. She replied: "Whatever she did, she would have done with the highest of ideals."[29]

At least one person, Harry Steingart, a cousin of the Bach family who had looked after Michael and Robby, acknowledged that he owed his life and freedom to their courage. At the age of 103, living out his final days in a retirement home, he told Ethel's granddaughter Ivy that he was convinced his name had been on a list shown to Ethel and Julius hours before they died. They refused to identify him as someone they knew or who had been involved in espionage.

Seen from this perspective, it is possible to understand why Ethel believed she was dying to make sure that she left her sons with not simply the memory of a mother they loved but a human role model of how to live a good life. Showing her sons dignity, confidence, and courage in the face of adversity was Ethel's mantra and the source of what little strength she retained by the end.

For Ethel, this also represented the core of what it meant to be a Communist.

"I knew they were both devoted Communists, but we didn't discuss it. I just knew that they really believed in the cause and she really believed in him," Elizabeth Phillips told me sadly as we discussed Ethel and Julius. "I knew he was the love of her life, but I cannot say more because we did not discuss it. Yes, she died for the cause," Elizabeth reflected, "but the cause was that they were not going to give other names. She died for her ideals and her ideals included not ratting on others and supporting her husband."[30]

In that light it is possible to understand Ethel's final words, "Always remember we were innocent." By cleaving to her belief that she was innocent of the charges leveled against her Ethel could maintain that "This is the whole truth." As she explained in her letter to President Truman, "To forsake this truth is to pay too high a price even for the priceless gift of life—for life thus purchased we could not live out in dignity and self-respect."[31]

My own conclusion is that ultimately Ethel saw her death as inevitable. She could not confess to something that she had not done and so, in a topsy-turvy world where logic and rationalism no longer played a role, she believed she was dying for truth and justice and for her personal legacy. For one brief moment in time, hysteria overtook common sense and, in order to appear strong in the face of a credible Communist threat, the American government allowed this profoundly moral woman to be executed, and in the most brutally incompetent manner. It is hard to imagine any other country, in Western Europe or the wider free world, where this terrible fate would have been inflicted on Ethel.

In the end Ethel's story is, for me, not about a narrow definition of what is meant by innocence or guilt. It is about the multiple meanings of betrayal. Few would deny today that David and Ruth betrayed Ethel when they lied about the typewriter. Many would also argue that Julius and David betrayed their country when they spied for the Soviet Union. Tessie betrayed Ethel by failing to love or cherish her only daughter. Saypol, Cohn, and Judge Kaufman betrayed the high ideals of American justice. Truman and Eisenhower betrayed their better selves by refusing to grant Ethel clemency.

Only Ethel betrayed no one, thus sealing her own fate.

Acknowledgments

It is hard to remember when the story of Ethel Rosenberg first invaded my conscious thoughts as something I wanted to write about. I now realize it was lurking for many years before it took over. Once it did, I have thought of Ethel constantly over the last five years and am grateful to many people who have helped me shape these thoughts into a book.

My gratitude extends first of all to Ethel's two sons, Michael and Robert Meeropol, who, while never imposing on me their own interpretation of their mother's story, were, in addition to being witnesses as well as experts on the story, always ready to answer my questions and accept that there was not always only one way to interpret character.

Critically, they were able to put me in touch with some of those still living who had known Ethel and could share their memories with me. Chief among these was the insightful Dr. Elizabeth Phillips, who had been Michael's therapist before Ethel's arrest. Meeting Elizabeth in her midnineties, living an active life in California, was inspiring. I am most grateful to her for our stimulating one-to-one conversations, which we continued by email. I also had the great privilege of meeting Miriam Moskowitz, who had been in prison with Ethel during her trial. In addition I have benefited from meeting other members of the Meeropol family, including Ann and Ellen Meeropol and Michael and Ann's daughter, Ivy Meeropol.

I would also like to thank the following:

David Aaronovitch, Nelson Aspen, Martin Bartle, Nicholas Belfrage, Sir Rodric Braithwaite, Piers Brendon, Kate Bucknell, Charles Chadwyck-Healey, Stephen Dubner, Toby and Arthur Engelberg, Barbara Epstein, Boris Fishman, Sue Fox, Gino Francesconi (Carnegie Hall), Sarah Glazer and the late Nathan Glazer, Professor Lawrence Goldman, Lyndall Gordon (for an invaluable conversation about 1950s political women), James Harmon, Emily Harrold, Vincent Houghton (Director, Washington Spy Museum), Anthony Julius, Peter Kleban, Rachel Levy, Bill Lucey, Tobias Mostel, Frederick Mostert, Ilene Philipson, James Phillips, Roland Phillips, Ronald Radosh, Sam Roberts, Saul Roskes, Eric Schlosser, Professor Martin Sherwin, David Sklansky, Sam Tanenhaus, and Professor Stephen Zipperstein. For an extended tour of Sing Sing Prison I am grateful to Officer Wolpinsky and Dr. Lesley Malin of the Department of Corrections and Community Supervision; for a fascinating tour of Ethel's school, Seward Park High School, and subsequent help I must thank Marty Kane. For deepening my understanding of Anne and Abel Meeropol, I thank David Newstead; for guiding me around Belarus and Minsk, Artur Livshits and Debra Brunner of the Together Plan; and for sharing her understanding of the damage done to mothers in prison, I thank Daphne Muse.

For generous hospitality while in California, I thank warmly my friends Carol and Rand Selig. For editorial help at an early stage, I owe a huge debt to Richard Tomlinson, my first reader, who brought a clear eye as well as a critically useful depth of knowledge about the period and was unafraid both to cut and shape.

I have been helped by several institutions. Most of the Rosenberg and Meeropol documents are housed in the Howard Gotlieb Archival Research Center of Boston University, which was both a delight to work in and a treasure trove, and where I must thank Vita Paladino and her team, as was the Tamiment Library and Robert F. Wagner Archives at New York University, where I should like to thank Danielle Marie Nista.

The British Library has rich treasures too, and in particular I was grateful for the help I received from Dr. Mercedes Aguirre, Lead Curator, American Collections, who suggested useful areas for me to research just as I began this project. In particular, the Newspaper Library, now housed at the BL, is always a joy for historians, providing unrivaled excitement by revealing unvarnished contemporary sources.

At the University of Texas at Austin, which houses the Morris Ernst Papers, I was most fortunate to have insightful help from Jennifer Hecker in locating documents as well as a useful exchange of thoughts on Ernst himself. Mark Dunton was, as ever, a valuable source of information on Cold War material at the National Archives in Kew. I should also like to thank Rebecca Collinsworth and Heather McClenahan for enabling me to visit the Los Alamos Historical Society Archives and walk in the footsteps of some of those I am writing about.

My home from home, the London Library, never fails to inspire and stimulate with unexpected discoveries on its open stacks and helpful librarians who locate books you did not realize you needed and then allow you to work with them for long periods at home.

It is hard to know how to express my thanks to my late husband, Mark Sebba. He was the first person with whom I shared the initial idea for a book about Ethel and his encouragement and support were immediate. We had lived as twentysomethings, the age that Julius and Ethel were for much of this story, in Brooklyn, when we both discovered and discussed Doctorow's fictional interpretation of this story. We would often spend Sunday mornings on the Lower East Side, wondering about life there had our own ancestors stopped in New York rather than Dublin or London, respectively. Forty years later, in 2018, we went together to New York again on one of my research trips and discussed emerging details of this story. A few weeks later, Mark suddenly died. I was, of course, overwhelmed with grief but fortunately, "How about getting back to work," Mark's favorite maxim, prevailed.

All my family, especially my children, Adam Sebba, Amy Dullage, and Imogen Sebba, have been an enormous support in multiple ways during the writing, research, and editing phases for this book, providing a sounding board as well as technical help. Imogen Sebba, in addition to being a passionate supporter of the project before she had read a word, accompanied me to Minsk and then brought her own sharp intellect into the editorial process, for which I am hugely grateful.

Publicly thanking one's agent and publishers may be commonplace but in this most difficult of years, 2020, never more necessary and, in my case, I do feel extraordinarily lucky to have such an enthusiastic, energetic, and effective three-part team. Charles Spicer, although based in New York, makes himself unfailingly available for his authors, not only when he is in London, to discuss the progress of their books. He is ably assisted by Sarah Grill and the whole team at St. Martin's Press. I am fortunate to have an equally helpful and nurturing crew in London: Alan Samson, Lucinda McNeile, Linden Lawson, Natalie Dawkins, and Maura Wilding are a dream ticket. Clare Alexander has been not only a steady friend, an inspiring source of advice, enthusiasm, and creative ideas but the best sort of agent who does not encroach during the writing process but becomes an immediate and fierce advocate of the finished book. She is brilliantly assisted by Lesley Thorne, Lisa Baker, and the team at Aitken Alexander. Heartfelt thanks to you all.

I alone must take responsibility for the final manuscript, which has been a privilege to work on for the last five years. I have learned much about ways to behave in extremis but recognize I have much still to learn.

Anne Sebba
Richmond, 2020

Notes

INTRODUCTION

1   Julius to Manny Bloch, *The Rosenberg Letters*, June 18, 1953, 701. See also Meeropol and Meeropol, *We Are Your Sons*, 230.

2   Ibid.

3   Ethel to Michael and Robby via Manny Bloch, *The Rosenberg Letters*, June 19, 1953, 703.

4   Ibid.

5   Ethel to Manny Bloch, *The Rosenberg Letters*, 704.

6   Various newspapers.

7   Gentry, *J. Edgar Hoover*, 427.

8   *The Rosenberg Letters*, xiii.

9   Meeropol and Meeropol, *We Are Your Sons*, 237.

ONE

1   Dubner, *Turbulent Souls*, 74.

2   Howe, *World of Our Fathers*, 26.

3   Letter to author B. Epstein, April 24, 2018.

4   Gardner, *The Rosenberg Story*, 23.

5   "The Old Days of Sheriff Street."

6   Ibid.

7   Edward Steiner, cited in Kessner, *The Golden Door*, 130.

8   Gardner, *The Rosenberg Story*, 23.

9   Ibid., 14.

10   Stephen Dubner, conversation with author, June 11, 2018.

11   Gardner, *The Rosenberg Story*, 14.

12   Philipson, *Ethel Rosenberg Beyond the Myths*, 28, citing anonymous interviewee.

13   Thanks to Toby and Arthur Engelberg, children of Dora Stahl, for emails and phone conversations with information about their mother's friendship with Ethel.

14   Gardner, *The Rosenberg Story*, 3.

15   Ibid., 16.

16   Ibid.

17   US District Court, Southern District of New York, Trial of Julius Rosenberg, Ethel Rosenberg, and others. New York, March 6, 1951, stenographer's minutes. Hereafter Trial Transcript, 1972.

18   The SPHS 1931 Yearbook; thanks to Toby and Arthur Engelberg and Marty Kane.

19   Tam 100 box 1 folder 37. Notes from Virginia Gardner Tamiment Library, New York University.

20   Howe, *World of Our Fathers*, 387.

21   Ibid.

22   Gardner, *The Rosenberg Story*, 20–21.

23   Ibid.

24   Ibid., 19.

25   Dubner, *Turbulent Souls*, 77.

26   Stephen Dubner conversation with author, June 11, 2018.

27   Gardner, *The Rosenberg Story*, 31, citing "Jeff."

28   Miriam Moskowitz conversation with author, December 16, 2017.

29   Gornick, *The Romance of American Communism*, 13.

30   Ibid.

31   Ibid., 113.

32   Braunstein, "Anti-Semitism Is America's Concern."

33   Gardner, *The Rosenberg Story*, 62.

TWO

1 Goldfield, *Practices and Experiences of the Lavanburg Homes.*

2 Email to author, October 13, 2018, facilitated thanks to his daughter, Sarah Glazer.

3 All of above thanks to SG for conversations with NG relayed to me until his death in January 2019.

4 Sobell, *On Doing Time*, 24.

5 Ibid., 115.

6 Ibid., 27.

7 Gardner, *The Rosenberg Story*, 38.

8 Roberts, *The Brother*, 42.

9 Ibid., 43.

10 Ibid.

11 Interview with Ivy Meeropol, *Heir to an Execution.*

12 Philipson, *Ethel Rosenberg Beyond the Myths*, 131.

13 Radosh and Milton, *The Rosenberg File*, 53.

14 Trial Transcript, 1944.

15 "Testimony of Max Elitcher in the Rosenberg Trial," 9.

16 Arnow-Alman and Alman, *Exoneration*, 28.

17 Philipson, *Ethel Rosenberg*, 124.

18 Aaronovitch, *Party Animals*, 268, and interview with author, November 13, 2017.

19 Sobell, *On Doing Time*, 31.

20 Koestler, Introduction to *The God That Failed*, 11.

21 FBI files JR-HQ 450X 8/2/50.

22 Radosh and Milton, *The Rosenberg File*, citing US Official Hearing Records, 55, 504.

23 Ibid.

24 Philipson, *Ethel Rosenberg*, 132.

25 Cited in Radosh and Milton, *The Rosenberg File*, 55, 504.

26 Gardner, *The Rosenberg Story*, 63.

27 Ibid.

28 Interview for *The Unquiet Death of Julius and Ethel Rosenberg*, DVD.

29 Philipson, *Ethel Rosenberg*, 139.

30   Gardner, *The Rosenberg Story*, 63.

31   Ibid.

32   "Des Moines Speech."

33   Gardner, *The Rosenberg Story*, 67.

34   Trial Transcript, 1975.

35   Gardner, *The Rosenberg Story*, 68–69.

36   Philipson, *Ethel Rosenberg*, citing interview with Annette Kardon, 155.

37   Ibid., 161.

38   Ibid., 152.

39   Stout, "Dorothy Whipple, 94."

40   Trial Transcript, 1972.

41   Ibid., 1973.

42   Roberts, *The Brother*, 50.

43   Ibid., 67.

44   Arnow-Alman and Alman, *Exoneration*, 35.

45   Ibid.

46   Howard Gotlieb Archival Research Center (HGARC), Boston University, The Rosenberg Papers, Box 5, May 11, 1944.

47   HGARC, Ruth to David, January 2, 1944.

48   HGARC, David to Ruth, May 21, 1944.

49   HGARC, Ruth to David, May 11, 1944.

50   HGARC, Ruth to David, n.d.

51   Ibid.

52   HGARC, Ruth to David, May 11, 1944.

53   Trial Transcript, 349–50.

54   Feklisov, *The Man Behind the Rosenbergs*, 109.

55   Schneir, *Final Verdict*, 80–81.

56   Ibid., 81.

57   Ibid., 121.

58   Cited in Blum, *In the Enemy's House*, 142.

59   Feklisov, *The Man Behind the Rosenbergs*, 109.

60   Cited in West, *Venona*, 160.

61   Feklisov, *The Man Behind the Rosenbergs*, 149.

62   Ibid., 120–27.

63   HGARC, Box 5, Rosenberg Papers.

64   Ibid., citing March 28, 1945, memorandum of charges against Julius Rosen-
     berg.

65   Trial Transcript, 344.

66   "Testimony of Helene Elitcher."

THREE

1   Sobell, *On Doing Time*, 42.

2   David to Ruth, June 3, 1943. Extracts of letters taken by FBI in June 1950,
     cited in Radosh and Milton, *The Rosenberg File*, 59, 505.

3   Radosh and Milton, *The Rosenberg File*, 71.

4   Philipson, *Ethel Rosenberg*, 181.

5   Roberts, *The Brother*, 163.

6   Philipson, *Ethel Rosenberg*, 180.

7   Ibid.

8   Roberts, *The Brother*, 118.

9   Olmsted, *Red Spy Queen, a Biography of Elizabeth Bentley*, 50–51.

10   Roberts, *The Brother*, 118.

11   Ibid.

12   Feklisov, *The Man Behind the Rosenbergs*, 157.

13   Ibid., 157.

14   Ibid., 122.

15   All the above from "Testimony of Helene Elitcher."

16   Sobell, *On Doing Time*, 4.

17   Spock, *The Common Sense Book of Baby and Child Care*.

18   Halberstam, *The Fifties*, 10.

19   Sobell, *On Doing Time*, 42.

20   Ibid.

21   Interview with author, *The Times*, July 1, 2004.

22   Ibid.

23   Philipson, *Ethel Rosenberg*, 157.

24   Meeropol and Meeropol, *We Are Your Sons*, 94, citing Dr. Elizabeth Phillips.

25   Gardner, *The Rosenberg Story*.

26   Roberts, *The Brother*, 159.

27 Ethel to Julius, *The Rosenberg Letters*, August 29, 1950, 22.

28 All the above from conversation with author, February 17–18, 2018, Marin County.

29 Meeropol and Meeropol, *We Are Your Sons*, 20.

30 Ibid., 95.

31 Ibid.

32 Ibid., 38.

33 Philipson, *Ethel Rosenberg*, 193.

34 Ibid., 194.

35 Roberts, *The Brother*, 189.

FOUR

1 Monk, *Robert Oppenheimer*, 503.

2 FBI file, quoted in Philipson, *Ethel Rosenberg*, 217.

3 Roberts, *The Brother*, 210.

4 Greenglass, "Grand Jury Statement," 38–39.

5 HGARC, Box 5 f 12.

6 https://www.senate.gov/about/powers-procedures/investigations/mccarthy-hearings/communists-in-government-service.htm.

7 "60 Minutes: The Traitor," CBS, December 5, 2011, https://www.cbsnews.com/news/the-traitor.

8 HGARC, Box 5 f 12, memo, June 19, 1950.

9 Roberts, *The Brother*, 261.

10 Ibid., 228.

11 Bloch, "Office Memorandum."

12 Gardner, *The Rosenberg Story*, 95.

13 Cited in Halberstam, *The Fifties*, 69.

14 Gary R. Hess, citing Memoirs of President Truman, *Presidential Decisions for War*, 9.

15 Trial Transcript, 1994.

16 Ibid., 1992.

17 Ibid., 1994–96.

18 Ibid., 1997.

19 Roberts, *The Brother*, 267–68.

20 Cited in Radosh and Milton, *The Rosenberg File*, 97.

21 Ibid., 98.

22 Roberts, *The Brother*, 277.

23 Ibid., 278.

24 Bederson, "SEDS at Los Alamos," 52–75.

25 Philipson, *Ethel Rosenberg*, 234.

26 Meeropol and Meeropol, *We Are Your Sons*, 8.

27 Roberts, *The Brother*, 273.

28 US Government Office Memorandum, A. M. Belmont to D. Ladd Boston, July 17, 1950, University Archives JR HQ 188.

29 JEH/doj: AN 151 g, cited in Arnow-Alman and Alman, *Exoneration*, 160.

30 Arnow-Alman and Alman, *Exoneration*, 92, facsimile.

31 Greenglass, "Testimony," 3191.

32 Interview between Ethel Appel (nee Rosenberg) and Ilene Philipson, January 13, 1985, cited in Philipson, *Ethel Rosenberg*, 248.

33 "Testimony of Ethel Rosenberg."

34 Ibid.

35 Various sources. See Trial Transcript.

FIVE

1 Julius to Ethel, *The Rosenberg Letters*, July 24, 1950, 8.

2 *New York Times*, August 12, 1950, cited in Ellen Meeropol, *The Ethel Rosenberg Story*, privately printed.

3 Gurley Flynn, *The Alderson Story*, 12.

4 Ibid., 16–17.

5 Ibid.

6 Ethel to Julius, *The Rosenberg Letters*, August 12, 1950, 18.

7 Meeropol and Meeropol, *We Are Your Sons*, 18.

8 Ibid., 5.

9 Ethel to Julius, *The Rosenberg Letters*, August 20, 1950, 21.

10 Ibid.

11 Ibid.

12 Meeropol and Meeropol, *We Are Your Sons*, 22.

13 Ibid.

14   Roberts, *The Brother*, 280.

15   Cited in Meeropol and Meeropol, *We Are Your Sons*, 23.

16   Ibid., 24.

17   Ethel to Michael, *The Rosenberg Letters*, November 4, 1950, 36.

18   Ibid.

19   Ibid., 50.

20   Ethel to Michael and Robby, *The Rosenberg Letters*, December 11, 1950, 51.

21   Ethel to Michael and Robby, *The Rosenberg Letters*, January 22, 1951, 56.

22   Ibid.

23   Ethel to Michael, *The Rosenberg Letters*, March 2, 1951, 60.

24   Meeropol and Meeropol, *We Are Your Sons*, Ethel to Julius, August 20, 1950, 21.

25   Ibid.

26   EP to author, February 21, 2018.

27   Meeropol and Meeropol, *We Are Your Sons*, 5, and interview with Dr. E. Phillips, February 18, 2018.

28   Interview as above.

29   EP email to author, April 26, 2020.

30   HGARC, November 9, 1950, quoted in *WAYS*, 26.

31   Quoted in Moskowitz, *Phantom Spies*, 123.

32   Gardner, *The Rosenberg Story*, quoting MM as Martha, 83.

33   Interview with author, December 16, 2017.

34   Ibid.

35   Ethel to Julius, *The Rosenberg Letters*, August 29, 1950, 22.

36   Moskowitz, *Phantom Spies*, 120.

37   Law and Social Conscience Online Archive of UCLA Library Department of Special Collections, Ben Margolis interview, 1984.

38   Arnow-Alman and Alman, *Exoneration*, 15.

39   Ethel to Manny Bloch, *The Rosenberg Letters*, n.d., 30.

SIX

1   Gardner, *The Rosenberg Story*, 77.

2   *New York Times*, March 7, 1951.

3   Sobell, *On Doing Time*, 105.

4   Julius to Ethel, *The Rosenberg Letters*, July 22, 1951, 171.

5   Philipson, *Ethel Rosenberg*, 275.

6   Gentry, *J. Edgar Hoover*, 24.

7   Philipson, *Ethel Rosenberg*, 275.

8   Morgan, "The Rosenberg Jury," quoting Vincent Lebonitte, 127.

9   Garber and Walkowitz, *Secret Agents*, 186, lists multiple sources for this quote. Also Arnow-Alman and Alman, *Exoneration*, 74.

10   Ruth Greenglass grand jury testimony, August 3, 1950, https://catalog.archives.gov/id/2364087.

11   Schneir, *Final Verdict*, citing newly released KGB files argues that this meeting could not have taken place in this way as JR had been relieved of his duties by the KGB at this time.

12   Morgan, "The Rosenberg Jury," 108.

13   *New York Times,* April 3, 1988.

14   Cited in Arnow-Alman and Alman, *Exoneration*, 74.

15   Wexley, *The Judgment of Julius and Ethel Rosenberg*, 243.

16   von Hoffman, *Citizen Cohn*, 89.

17   Deborah Dash Moore, "Reconsidering the Rosenbergs: Symbol and Substance in Second Generation American Jewish Consciousness," *Journal of American Ethnic History*, Fall 1988, 1–37.

18   William Zukerman, "Spy Trials Pose a Sore Question," *Jewish Advocate*, April 12, 1951.

19   Trial Transcript, 38.

20   Morgan, "The Rosenberg Jury."

21   Trial Transcript, 181.

22   Ibid., 223.

23   Ibid., 224.

24   Ibid., 226.

25   Ibid., 228.

26   *New York Times*, March 8, 1951.

27   Trial Transcript, 242.

28   Ibid., 243.

29   Ibid., 270.

30   Ibid., 275.

31   Ibid., 353–55.

32   Ibid., 574.

33   Ibid., 585.

34   Ibid., 589.

35   *New York Times*, March 10, 1951.

36   Ibid.

37   Trial Transcript, 621.

38   Ibid., 624.

39   Ibid., 625.

40   Ibid., 631.

41   Ibid., 632.

42   Ibid., 662.

43   Ibid., 670.

44   Ibid., 703.

45   Ibid.

46   Morgan, "The Rosenberg Jury," 127.

47   Trial Transcript, 705.

48   Ibid., 722.

49   Ibid., 768.

50   Ibid., 872.

51   Ibid., 829.

52   Ibid., 828–29.

53   Ibid., 950.

54   Ibid., 974.

55   Ibid.

56   Ibid.

57   Ibid., 1010.

58   Ibid., 1011.

59   Ibid., 1017.

60   Ibid., 1023.

61   Ibid., 1024.

62   Ibid., 1025.

63   Ibid., 1026.

64 Ibid., 1092.

65 Ibid., 1093.

66 Ibid., 1092.

67 Ibid., 1093.

68 Ibid., 1057.

69 Ibid., 1062.

70 Ibid., 1112.

SEVEN

1 *Time*, "My Friend Yakovlev," March 26, 1951.

2 Trial Transcript, 1192.

3 Roberts, *The Brother*, 357.

4 Trial Transcript, 1442.

5 Ibid., 1443.

6 Ibid., 1420.

7 Ibid., 1392.

8 Ibid., 1394.

9 Ibid., 1601.

10 Ibid.

11 Ibid., 1602.

12 Ibid., 1607.

13 Ibid., 1750.

14 Ibid., 1840.

15 Ibid., 1862.

16 Ibid., 1881.

17 Ibid., 1883.

18 Ibid., 1900.

19 Ibid., 1887.

20 Robb, *Minneapolis Star*, March 12, 1951.

21 Trial Transcript, 1927.

22 Ibid., 1936.

23 Ibid., 1937.

24 Ibid., 1939.

25 Ibid., 1975.

26 Ibid., 1996.

27 Ibid., 1997.

28 Ibid., 2015.

29 Ibid., 2042.

30 Sobell, *On Doing Time*, 181.

31 Trial Transcript, 2044.

32 Ibid., 2078.

33 Ibid., 2050.

34 Ibid., 2051.

35 Ibid., 2062.

36 Ibid., 2070.

37 Ibid., 2079.

38 Sobell, *On Doing Time*, 181–84.

39 Trial Transcript, 2063.

40 Helen Sobell, quoted in Philipson, *Ethel Rosenberg*, 294.

41 Trial Transcript, 2140.

42 Ibid.

43 Ibid., 2149.

44 Ibid., 2150.

45 Ibid., 2149.

46 Ibid., 2157.

47 Ibid., 2192.

48 Ibid., 2194.

49 Ibid., 2196.

50 Ibid., 2197.

51 Ibid.

52 Ibid., 2206.

53 Ibid., 2207.

54 Ibid., 2214.

55 Ibid., 2208.

56 Conklin, *New York Times*.

57 Trial Transcript, 2210.

58 Ibid., 2236.

59 Ibid., 2238.

60   Ibid., 2272.

61   Ibid., 2291.

62   Ibid., 2313.

63   Morgan, "The Rosenberg Jury."

64   Ibid.

65   Wexley, *The Judgment of Julius and Ethel Rosenberg*, 383.

66   Ibid., 582.

67   Ibid.

68   Morgan, "The Rosenberg Jury."

69   *New York Times*, March 30, 1951.

70   Morgan, "The Rosenberg Jury."

71   Ibid.

72   *New York Mirror*, April 6, 1951, 35, cited in Neville, *The Press, the Rosenbergs, and the Cold War*.

73   Trial Transcript, 2447.

74   *New York Times*, November 16, 1975.

75   Trial Transcript, 2449.

76   Ibid., 2454.

77   Ibid., 2451.

78   Ibid., 2453.

79   Conklin, "Atom Spy Couple Sentenced to Die," *New York Times*, April 6, 1951.

80   Neville, *The Press, the Rosenbergs, and the Cold War*, 49.

EIGHT

1   Gardner, *The Rosenberg Story*, 93.

2   Miriam Moskowitz interview with author, December 16, 2017.

3   *New York Times*, April 7, 1951.

4   Moskowitz, *Phantom Spies*, 121.

5   Ibid., 122.

6   Philipson, *Ethel Rosenberg*, 315.

7   Ibid.

8   Interview with author, December 16, 2017.

9   Gardner, *The Rosenberg Story*, 99.

10 Ethel to Manny Bloch, *The Rosenberg Letters*, April 16, 1951, 65.

11 Ibid.

12 Ibid.

13 Gardner, *The Rosenberg Story*.

14 Dr. Elizabeth Phillips, interview with author, February 18, 2018.

15 Ethel to Manny Bloch, *The Rosenberg Letters*, 66.

16 Ethel to Julius, *The Rosenberg Letters*, April 17, 1951, 67.

17 Ibid.

18 Ibid., 68.

19 Ethel to Lena (nee Rosenberg), *The Rosenberg Letters*, April 20, 1951, 76.

20 Ethel to Julius, *The Rosenberg Letters*, May 5, 1951, 93.

21 Julius to Manny Bloch, *The Rosenberg Letters*, 80.

22 Ethel to Julius, *The Rosenberg Letters*, April 29, 1951, 89.

23 Neville, *The Press, the Rosenbergs, and the Cold War*, 55.

24 Ibid.

25 Meeropol, *Rosenberg Realities*, 243.

26 Ethel to Julius, *The Rosenberg Letters*, July 2, 1951, 153.

27 Ibid., 154.

28 Ethel to Julius, *The Rosenberg Letters*, July 23, 1951, 172.

29 Julius to Ethel, *The Rosenberg Letters*, July 25, 1951, 173.

30 Ethel to Julius, *The Rosenberg Letters*, July 29, 1951, 176.

31 Ethel to Julius, *The Rosenberg Letters*, August 1, 1951, 177.

32 Ethel to Julius, *The Rosenberg Letters*, August 2, 1951, 179.

33 Dorothy Thompson, April 11, 1951, *Pittsburgh Post-Gazette* and other newspapers.

34 Neville, *The Press, the Rosenbergs, and the Cold War*, 56.

35 Belfrage and Aronson, *Something to Guard*, 172.

36 Ethel to Manny Bloch, *The Rosenberg Letters*, August 22, 1951, 193.

37 Ethel to Manny Bloch, *The Rosenberg Letters*, September 4, 1951, 205.

38 Ethel to Manny Bloch, *The Rosenberg Letters*, August 31–September 4, 201–9.

39 Robert Meeropol, conversation with author, January 5, 2020.

40 Ethel to Julius, *The Rosenberg Letters*, October 19, 1951, 244.

41 Ethel to Julius, *The Rosenberg Letters*, October 22, 1951, 245.

42 Ethel to Julius, *The Rosenberg Letters*, July 25, 1951, 174.

43 Ethel to Julius, *The Rosenberg Letters*, September 17, 1951, 220.

NINE

1 *Louisville Courier-Journal*, December 23, 1951.

2 Ethel to Julius, *The Rosenberg Letters*, February 25, 1952, 313–14.

3 Meeropol and Meeropol, *We Are Your Sons*, 136.

4 Ibid., 138.

5 Chabon, "'Ulysses' on Trial."

6 Morris Ernst to Major General Wilton Persons, November 10, 1952, Harry Ransom Center, University of Texas at Austin.

7 Gentry, *J. Edgar Hoover*, 24.

8 Morris Ernst to Major General Persons, November 10, 1952, Harry Ransom Center.

9 Ethel to Saul Miller, Boston University Archives Box 3 f 2, Saturday, November 15, 1952.

10 All the above from Roosevelt, "My Day, December 11, 1952."

11 Morris Ernst to J. Foster Dulles, December 17, 1952, Harry Ransom Center, as above.

12 Morris Ernst to Eleanor Roosevelt, December 29, 1952, Harry Ransom Center.

13 Ibid.

14 Exchange, cited in Schneir and Schneir, *Invitation to an Inquest*, 184.

15 Picasso said this in May 1951 but was quoted in *Time*, December 1, 1952.

16 January 5, 1953, cited in Arnow-Alman and Alman, *Exoneration*, 219.

17 Ethel to Manny Bloch, *The Rosenberg Letters*, January 5, 1953, 544.

18 Full text, cited in Schneir and Schneir, *Invitation to an Inquest*, 186.

19 Ibid.

20 *The Rosenberg Letters*, First Petition for Executive Clemency, cited, xlix.

21 Belfrage and Aronson, *Something to Guard*, 173.

22 Ethel to Manny Bloch, *The Rosenberg Letters*, January 21, 1953, 60.

23 Ibid., 562.

24 Morris L. Ernst to Mrs. Franklin D. Roosevelt, January 23, 1953, MLE Papers, Harry Ransom Center, University of Texas at Austin.

25 Zion, *The Autobiography of Roy Cohn*, 76–77.

26 *The Rosenberg Letters*, 583.

27 Ethel to Manny Bloch, *The Rosenberg Letters*, February 9, 1953, 591.

28 Ibid., 592.

29 Hagerty, "Press Secretary to the President."

30 "Minutes of Cabinet Meeting."

31 Ethel to Manny Bloch, *The Rosenberg Letters*, February 24, 1953.

32 Ethel to Saul Miller, n.d. but thought to be March 7, 1953, Boston University Archives.

33 Both the letters from Ethel to Miller from Box 3 f 2, Boston University, Howard Gottlieb Archival Center.

34 See *Journal of Australian Studies* for more details.

35 Clune, *Executing the Rosenbergs*, 96.

36 Piers Brendon, *Ike: His Life and Times* (Harper & Row, 1986), 266, citing AWF AS box 34, Dillon to Dulles, May 15, 1953.

37 Ibid.

38 Ibid., 98.

39 "Memorandum for the Attorney General."

40 Ibid.

41 *The Rosenberg Letters*, 674.

42 "Personal and Confidential."

43 President to Clyde Miller, June 10, 1953, DDE Library, Abilene, Kansas.

44 Ibid.

45 Cited in Clune, *Executing the Rosenbergs*, 124.

46 Meeropol and Meeropol, *We Are Your Sons*, 223.

47 Ibid., 222.

48 Schneir and Schneir, *Invitation to an Inquest*, 237.

49 *The Rosenberg Letters*, 699 notes.

50 Meeropol and Meeropol, *We Are Your Sons*, 227.

51 DDE, cited in Schneir and Schneir, *Invitation to an Inquest*, 242.

52 Ethel to Dwight D. Eisenhower, June 15, 1953, quoted in *The Rosenberg Letters*, 697.

53 Schneir and Schneir, *Invitation to an Inquest*, 243; Rosenberg v. United States (346 U.S. 273)/Dissent Douglas, https://en.wikisource.org/wiki/Rosenberg_v._United_States_(346_U.S._273)/Dissent_Douglas.

54 Ethel to Manny Bloch, *The Rosenberg Letters*, xiii.

55 Meeropol and Meeropol, *We Are Your Sons*, 237.

56 Ethel to Manny Bloch, *The Rosenberg Letters*, June 19, 1953, 703.

57 Unidentified newspaper cutting, Koslowe interview with Ken Valenti, June 19, 1995.

58 Associated Press, June 20, 1953.

59 Cited in Roberts, *The Brother*, 438.

TEN

1 Alvin Goldstein, dir., *The Unquiet Death of Julius and Ethel Rosenberg*, 2010, DVD.

2 Although Frankfurter published his dissent after the execution he made his opinion known on the day of the execution; Rosenberg v. United States (346 U.S. 273)/Dissent Frankfurter, https://en.wikisource.org/wiki/Rosenberg_v._United_States_(346_U.S._273)/Dissent_Frankfurter.

3 Meeropol and Meeropol, *We Are Your Sons*, 238.

4 Cited in Arnow-Alman and Alman, *Exoneration*, 321.

5 Philipson, *Ethel Rosenberg*, 354.

6 Cited in Schneir and Schneir, *Invitation to an Inquest*, 254.

7 Simone de Beauvoir to Nelson Algren, June 21, 1953, *Beloved Chicago Man*, 491–92.

8 Cited in Schneir and Schneir, *Invitation to an Inquest*, 256.

9 Feklisov, *The Man Behind the Rosenbergs*, 321.

10 Ibid., 319.

11 Ibid.

12 Benson and Warner, *Venona*, November 27, 1944, 381.

13 Comment on *Revised Translation of Message on Antenna-Liberal's Wife Ethel*. See also Blum, *In the Enemy's House*, 161.

14 Haynes and Klehr, *Venona: Decoding Soviet Espionage in America*, 363.

15 Shrank, "Reading the Rosenbergs After Venona," 189–210.

16 All the above quoted in interview for *Tablet*, Jacob Silverman, October 17, 2011, https://www.tabletmag.com/sections/news/articles/rosenberg-boys -appear-at-%E2%80%98daniel%E2%80%99-screening.

17 Stout, "Meredith Gardner Obituary."

18 Blum, *In the Enemy's House*, 1.

19 Zion, *Autobiography of Roy Cohn*, 76–77.

20 Meeropol and Meeropol, *We Are Your Sons*, 241.

21 Ibid., 242.

22 Stephen Dubner conversation with author, June 11, 2018.

23 Meeropol and Meeropol, *We Are Your Sons*, 240.

24 Margolick, *Strange Fruit*.

25 I am most grateful to David Newstead for allowing me to read his unpublished biography of Abel Meeropol for this information.

26 Meeropol and Meeropol, *We Are Your Sons*, 246.

27 Williams, *Inadmissible Evidence*.

28 Ibid.

29 Meeropol and Meeropol, *We Are Your Sons*, 254.

30 Ibid., 259.

31 Meeropol, "A First for Elli and Me."

32 Monk, *Robert Oppenheimer*, 476.

33 Ibid., 502.

34 Ibid., 503, citing letter to secretary of state for war Robert Patterson from Gregory Bern, June 3, 1946, in FBI file.

35 *The Observer*, November 22, 1953.

36 Conaway, "Remembering McCarthyism."

37 Tam 100 box 1 folder 37, Notes from Virginia Gardner, Tamiment Library, New York University.

38 Ibid.

39 Wexley, *The Judgment of Julius and Ethel Rosenberg*.

40 Cited in Knox, "The Genealogy of Treason," 37.

41 Meeropol and Meeropol, *We Are Your Sons*, 341.

42 Ibid., 342.

43 Saypol, "Obituary."

44 "60 Minutes II: The Traitor."

45 Blanton, "National Security Archive."

46 Roberts, "Figure in Rosenberg Case Admits to Soviet Spying."

47 Ibid.

EPILOGUE

1 Plath, *The Bell Jar*, 178.

2 Ibid., 96.

3 Cantwell, *Manhattan, When I Was Young*, 10.

4 Cited in Smith, *Something on My Own*, 134.

5 Miller, "The Crucible and the Execution: A Memoir," 88.

6 Moskowitz, *Phantom Spies*, 249.

7 Yergin, "Victims of a Desperate Age."

8 Snyder, "Taking Great Cases," 885.

9 Halberstam, *The Fifties*, 411.

10 Doctorow, *The Book of Daniel*.

11 Garber and Walkowitz, *Secret Agents*, 245.

12 Coover, *The Public Burning*, 204.

13 HBO DVD, 2004.

14 Ibid. See additional interview material.

15 Meeropol, "Angels in America."

16 Okun, *The Rosenbergs: Collected Visions*, 85–88.

17 Interview with Arthur Miller, *Guardian & Observer*, June 17, 2000.

18 Dr. Elizabeth Phillips interview with author, February 18, 2018.

19 Neville, *The Press, the Rosenbergs, and the Cold War*, 49.

20 Roberts, *The Brother*, 37.

21 Ibid.

22 "The Traitor."

23 Roberts, *The Brother*, 38.

24 Philipson, *Ethel Rosenberg*, 318.

25 Gentry, *J. Edgar Hoover*, 427.

26 Meeropol and Meeropol, *We Are Your Sons*, 69.

27 Ibid., 38.

28   Ethel to Julius, *The Rosenberg Letters*, June 27, 1951, 150.

29   Conversation with Toby Engelberg, daughter of Dora Stahl, January 16, 2020, and subsequent emails.

30   Conversation with author, February 17–18, 2018, as before.

31   *The Rosenberg Letters*, Petition for Executive Clemency, cited, xlviii.

Bibliography

Aaronovitch, David. *Party Animals: My Family and Other Communists*. London: Vintage, 2016.

Albright, Joseph, and Marcia Kunstel. *Bombshell: The Secret Story of America's Unknown Atomic Spy Conspiracy*. New York: Times Books, 1977.

Arnow-Alman, Emily, and David Alman. *Exoneration: The Trial of Julius & Ethel Rosenberg and Morton Sobell*. Seattle, WA: Green Elms Press, 2010.

Bederson, Benjamin. "SEDS at Los Alamos: A Personal Memoir." *Physics in Perspective* 3, no. 1 (2001): 52–75.

Belfrage, Cedric, and James Aronson. *Something to Guard: The Stormy Life of the National Guardian 1948–1967*. New York: Columbia University Press, 1978.

Belfrage, Sally. *Un-American Activities: A Memoir of the Fifties*. New York: HarperCollins, 1994.

Benson, Robert Louis, and Michael Warner, eds. *Venona: Soviet Espionage and the American Response, 1939–1957*. Washington, DC: National Security Agency and Central Intelligence Agency, 1996.

Berger, David, ed. *The Legacy of Jewish Migration 1881 and Its Impact*. New York: Brooklyn College Press, 1983.

Blanton, Thomas, ed. "National Security Archive." July 14, 2015.

Bloch, Emanuel. "Office Memorandum." https://archive.org/stream/EmanuelBloch/Bloch-%20Emanuel-NY-vol.01#page/n201/mode/2up/search/1901.

Blum, Howard. *In the Enemy's House*. New York: HarperCollins, 2018.

Braithwaite, Rodric. *Armageddon and Paranoia: The Nuclear Confrontation*. London: Profile Books, 2017.

Braunstein, Baruch. "Anti-Semitism Is America's Concern." December 12, 1939, Washington, DC. http://www.ibiblio.org/pha/policy/1939/1939-12-12b .html.

Brendon, Piers. *Ike: His Life and Times*. New York and Toronto: Harper & Row and Fitzhenry & Whiteside, 1986.

Cantwell, Mary. *Manhattan, When I Was Young*. New York: Penguin Books, 1996.

Carmichael, Virginia. *Framing History: The Rosenberg Story and the Cold War*. Minneapolis: University of Minnesota Press, 1993.

CBS. "60 Minutes: The Traitor." 2001.

Chabon, Michael. "'Ulysses' on Trial." *New York Review*, September 26, 2019.

Churchwell, Sarah. *Behold, America: A History of America First and the American Dream*. London: Bloomsbury, 2018.

Clune, Lori. *Executing the Rosenbergs*. Oxford: Oxford University Press, 2016.

Collier's Magazine, October 27, 1951.

Conaway, James. "Remembering McCarthyism." *Washington Post,* December 3, 1984.

Conklin, William R. *New York Times*, March 1951.

Coover, Robert. *The Public Burning*. New York: Viking, 1977.

De Beauvoir, Simone. *Beloved Chicago Man: Letters to Nelson Algren 1947–64*. London: Victor Gollancz, 1998.

"Des Moines Speech." Charles Lindbergh, September 11, 1941. http://www .charleslindbergh.com/americanfirst/speech.asp.

Doctorow, E. L. *The Book of Daniel*. New York: Signet, 1972.

Dubner, Stephen J. *Turbulent Souls: A Catholic Son's Return to His Jewish Family*. New York: William Morrow, 1998.

Evanier, David. *Red Love*. New York: Scribner's, 1991.

Feklisov, Alexander. *The Man Behind the Rosenbergs*. New York: Enigma Books, 2001.

Feynman, Richard B. *Surely You're Joking, Mr. Feynman!* New York: W. W. Norton, 1985.

Garber, Marjorie, and Rebecca L. Walkowitz, eds. *Secret Agents: The Rosenberg Case, McCarthyism and Fifties America*. New York: Routledge, 1995.

Gardner, Meredith. *Revised Translation of Message on Antenna-Liberal's Wife Ethel.* Rosenberg Fund for Children, August 12, 1948.

Gardner, Virginia. *The Rosenberg Story.* New York: Masses & Mainstream, 1954.

Gentry, Curt. *J. Edgar Hoover: The Man and the Secrets.* New York: W. W. Norton, 1991.

Goldfield, Abraham. *Practices and Experiences of the Lavanburg Homes.* New York: Fred L. Lavanburg Foundation, 1934.

Gornick, Vivian. *The Romance of American Communism.* New York: Basic Books, 1977.

Greenglass, David. "Grand Jury Statement." https://www.archives.gov/files /research/court-records/rosenberg-greenglass.pdf.

Greenglass, David. "Testimony in the Rosenberg Trial." https://www.archives.gov /files/research/court-records/rosenberg-greenglass.pdf.

Gurley Flynn, Elizabeth. *The Alderson Story: My Life as a Political Prisoner.* New York: First New World, 1963.

Hagerty, James C. "Press Secretary to the President." February 11, 1953. https:// www.eisenhowerlibrary.gov/sites/default/files/file/Rosenberg_3a.pdf.

Halberstam, David. *The Fifties.* New York: Villard Books, 1993.

Haynes, John Earl, and Harvey Klehr. *Venona: Decoding Soviet Espionage in America.* New Haven, CT: Yale University Press, 1999.

Haynes, John Earl, Harvey Klehr, and Alexander Vassiliev. *Spies: The Rise and Fall of the KGB in America.* New Haven, CT: Yale University Press, 2009.

Hess, Gary R. *Presidential Decisions for War: Korea, Vietnam, the Persian Gulf, and Iraq.* Baltimore: Johns Hopkins University Press, 1999.

Hofstadter, Richard. "The Paranoid Style in American Politics." In *The Paranoid Style in American Politics and Other Essays*, ed. R. Hofstadter. New York: Vintage, 2008.

Howe, Irving. *World of Our Fathers: The Journey of East European Jews to America and the Life They Found and Made.* London: Phoenix Press, 2000.

Katznelson, Ira. *Fear Itself: The New Deal and the Origins of Our Time.* New York: Liveright Publishing, 2013.

Kearns Goodwin, Doris. *No Ordinary Time: Franklin and Eleanor Roosevelt: The Home Front in World War II.* New York: Simon & Schuster, 1994.

Kessner, Thomas. *The Golden Door: Italian and Jewish Immigrant Mobility in New York City 1880–1915.* New York: Oxford University Press, 1977.

Knox, Sara L. "The Genealogy of Treason: Ethel Rosenberg and the Masculinist Discourse of Cold War." *Australasian Journal of American Studies* 12, no. 2 (December 1993): 32–49.

Koestler, Arthur. *The God That Failed: Six Studies in Communism.* London: Hamish Hamilton, 1950.

Kovel, Joel. *Red Hunting in the Promised Land: Anticommunism and the Making of America.* New York: Basic Books, 1994.

Lamphere, Robert J., and Tom Shachtman. *The FBI–KGB War: A Special Agent's Story.* New York: Random House, 1986.

Margolick, David. *Strange Fruit: The Biography of a Song.* New York: Ecco Press, 2001.

McCarthy, Mary. *Intellectual Memoirs: New York 1936–1938.* New York: Harcourt Brace, 1992.

Meeropol, Ellen. *Her Sister's Tattoo.* Pasadena, CA: Red Hen Press, 2020.

Meeropol, Ivy, dir. *Heir to an Execution.* New York: HBO/Cinemax, 2004.

Meeropol, Michael, ed. *The Rosenberg Letters: A Complete Edition of the Prison Correspondence of Julius and Ethel Rosenberg.* New York: Routledge, 2013.

Meeropol, Michael, and Robert Meeropol. *We Are Your Sons: The Legacy of Ethel and Julius Rosenberg.* Boston: Houghton Mifflin, 1975.

Meeropol, Robert. "Angels in America." Rosenberg Fund for Children, December 15, 2010. https://www.rfc.org/blog/article/853.

———. *An Execution in the Family: One Son's Journey.* New York: St. Martin's Press, 2003.

———. "A First for Elli and Me." Rosenberg Fund for Children, April 21, 2011. https://www.rfc.org/blog/article/940.

———. "Rosenberg Realities." In *Secret Agents: The Rosenberg Case, McCarthyism and Fifties America*, ed. Marjorie Garber and and Rebecca L. Walkowitz. New York and London: Routledge, 1995.

"Memorandum for the Attorney General." June 5, 1953. https://www.eisenhowerlibrary.gov/sites/default/files/file/rosenbergs_Binder10.pdf.

Miller, Arthur. "The Crucible and the Execution: A Memoir." In *The Rosenbergs: Collected Visions*, ed. Robert A. Okun. New York: Universe, 1988.

Minsk Charitable Public Organization (GILF). *We Remember Lest the World Forget: Memories of the Minsk Ghetto.* New York: JewishGen, 2012.

"Minutes of Cabinet Meeting." February 12, 1953. https://www.eisenhowerlibrary .gov/sites/default/files/file/Rosenberg_4.pdf.

Monk, Ray. *Robert Oppenheimer: A Life Inside the Center.* New York: Anchor Books, 2012.

Morgan, Ted. "The Rosenberg Jury." *Esquire*, May 1, 1975. https://classic.esquire .com/article/1975/5/1/the-rosenberg-jury.

Moskowitz, Miriam. *Phantom Spies, Phantom Justice.* Seattle, WA: Justice Institute, 2012.

Nadell, Pamela S. *America's Jewish Women: A History from Colonial Times to Today.* New York: W. W. Norton, 2019.

Neville, John F. *The Press, the Rosenbergs, and the Cold War.* Westport, CT: Praeger, 1995.

Okun, Robert A. ed. *The Rosenbergs: Collected Visions of Artists and Writers.* New York: Universe, 1988.

"The Old Days of Sheriff Street: An Interview with Sidney Fermaglich." Knickerbocker Village, April 30, 2011. http://knickerbockervillage.blogspot.com /2011/04/old-days-of-sheriff-street-interview.html.

Olmsted, Kathryn. *The Red Spy Queen: A Biography of Elizabeth Bentley.* Chapel Hill: University of North Carolina Press, 2002.

Pembroke, Michael. *Korea: Where the American Century Began.* Melbourne: Hardie Grant, 2018.

"Personal and Confidential." June 10, 1953. https://www.eisenhowerlibrary.gov /sites/default/files/file/rosenbergs_Binder12.pdf.

Philipson, Ilene. *Ethel Rosenberg: Beyond the Myths.* New York: Franklin Watts, 1988.

Phillips, James. *The Rubenstein Kiss.* London: Methuen Drama, 2005.

Plath, Sylvia. *The Bell Jar.* London: Faber & Faber, 2005. First published 1963.

Radosh, Ron, and Joyce Milton. *The Rosenberg File.* New Haven, CT: Yale University Press, 1997.

Reeves, Thomas. *The Life and Times of Joe McCarthy: A Biography.* New York: Stein and Day, 1982.

Robb, Inez. "Terribly Average Atom Spy Suspects Dumpy Not Dashing." *Minneapolis Star*, March 12, 1951.

Roberts, Sam. *The Brother: The Untold Story of the Rosenberg Case.* New York: Simon & Schuster Paperbacks, 2014.

————. "Figure in Rosenberg Case Admits to Soviet Spying." *New York Times*, September 11, 2008. https://www.nytimes.com/2008/09/12/nyregion /12spy.html.

Roosevelt, Eleanor. "My Day, December 11, 1952." *The Eleanor Roosevelt Papers Digital Edition*, 2017. https://www2.gwu.edu/~erpapers/myday/displaydoc .cfm?_y=1952&_f=md002402.

Rosen, David. *Sin, Sex & Subversion: How What Was Taboo in 1950s New York Became America's New Normal*. New York: Carrel Books, 2016.

Rosenberg, Julius, and Ethel Rosenberg. *The Rosenberg Letters*. London: Dennis Dobson, 1953.

Saypol, Irving. "Obituary." *New York Times*, July 1, 1977.

Schneir, Walter. *Final Verdict: What Really Happened in the Rosenberg Case*. New York: Melville House, 2010.

Schneir, Walter, and Miriam Schneir. *Invitation to an Inquest*. London: W. H. Allen, 1966.

Schrecker, Ellen. *The Age of McCarthyism: A Brief History with Documents*. Boston: Bedford Books, 1994.

Schrecker, Ellen. *Many Are the Crimes: McCarthyism in America*. Princeton, NJ: Princeton University Press, 1999.

Sherwin, Martin, and Kai Bird. *American Prometheus: The Triumph and Tragedy of J. Robert Oppenheimer*. New York: Knopf, 2005.

Shrank, Bernice. "Reading the Rosenbergs After Venona." Labor/Le Travail 49 (Spring 2002): 189–210.

"60 Minutes II: The Traitor." CBS News, December 5, 2011. https://www .cbsnews.com/news/i60-minutes-ii-i-the-traitor/.

Smith, Glenn D., Jr. *Something on My Own: Gertrude Berg and American Broadcasting*. Syracuse, NY: Syracuse University Press, 2007.

Snyder, Brad. "Taking Great Cases: Lessons from the 'Rosenberg' Case." *Vanderbilt Law Review* 63 (2019): 885. https://scholarship.law.vanderbilt.edu/vlr/vol63/iss4/1.

Sobell, Morton. *On Doing Time*. San Francisco: Golden Gate National Parks Association, 2001.

Spock, Benjamin. *The Common Sense Book of Baby and Child Care*. New York: Duell, Sloan and Pearce, 1946.

Stevenson, Anne. *Bitter Fame: A Life of Sylvia Plath*. London: Penguin Books, 1989.

Stout, David. "Dorothy Whipple, 94, Doctor Who Advanced Women's Rights."
    New York Times, May 8, 1995. https://www.nytimes.com/1995/05/08
    /obituaries/dorothy-whipple.

———. "Meredith Gardner Obituary." *New York Times*, August 18, 2002.

Tanenhaus, Sam. *An Un-American Life: The Case of Whittaker Chambers.* London: Old
    Street Publishing, 2007.

"Testimony of Ethel Rosenberg." National Archives Catalog, August 11, 1950.
    https://catalog.archives.gov/id/2364090.

"Testimony of Helene Elitcher." National Archives Catalog, September 20, 1950.
    https://catalog.archives.gov/id/2364114.

"Testimony of Max Elitcher in the Rosenberg Trial." https://www.archives.gov
    /files/research/court-records/rosenberg-elitcher-1950-08.pdf.

"The Traitor." CBS News, July 14, 2003. https://www.cbsnews.com/news/the
    -traitor/.

von Hoffman, Nicholas. *Citizen Cohn.* New York: Bantam Books, 1988.

Walker, Stephen. *Shockwave: Countdown to Hiroshima.* New York: Harper Perennial,
    2006.

Weiner, Tim. *Enemies: A History of the FBI.* New York: Random House, 2013.

Weinstein, Allen, and Alexander Vassiliev. *The Haunted Wood: Soviet Espionage in
    America—The Stalin Era.* New York: Random House, 1999.

West, Nigel. *Venona: The Greatest Secret of the Cold War.* London: HarperCollins,
    1999.

Wexley, John. *The Judgment of Julius and Ethel Rosenberg.* New York: Cameron and
    Kahn, 1955.

Williams, Evelyn. *Inadmissible Evidence: The Story of the Black American Trial Lawyer
    Who Defended the Black Liberation Army.* Chicago: Lawrence Hill Books, 1994.

Yergin, Daniel H. "Victims of a Desperate Age." *New Times Magazine,* May 1975.

Zion, Sidney. *The Autobiography of Roy Cohn.* New York: Citadel Press, 1989.

Zipperstein, Stephen J. *Pogrom: Kishinev and the Tilt of History.* New York: Liveright,
    2018.

Zuckerman, William. *Jewish Advocate,* April 12, 1951.

Index

Note: First names and abbreviations are used for brevity. "Ethel" and "Julius" (or "E" and "J") refer to Ethel and Julius Rosenberg. "David," "Ruth," and "Tessie" refer to David, Ruth, and Tessie Greenglass.